P9-CJF-383

Designing for User Engagement on the Web

WITHDRAWN
UTSA LIBRARIES

Designing for User Engagement on the Web: 10 Basic Principles introduces and illustrates a set of principles developed to guide the design of user experiences rich in communication and interaction. It explores a variety of case studies and presents an overarching framework for designing for user engagement.

Designing for User Engagement on the Web: 10 Basic Principles delivers the results of this innovative work in a way that can be used by working practitioners interested in developing engaging user experiences, educators whose students are seeking to understand and develop these experiences, and managers and resource teams who need to create and design these experiences.

The book begins with the design principles, which can be used to evaluate a current interactive technology or to guide the development of a new website or other interactive technology. The principles can also be used as a guide in the analysis of interactive technologies and as a springboard for a more theoretical discussion of new directions in the development of interactive technologies.

In the second half of the volume, each chapter presents a case study of a single project, walking the reader through the original and redesigned user experience, and showing how the basic principles were used to drive the development of a more engaging user experience. These case studies include:

- an information system gallery
- wikis for collaboration
- cultural websites
- distance-learning platforms
- an interactive poster.

Each case study represents a distinctive type of technology, so taken together the cases illustrate the remarkable breadth of applicability of the basic principles.

For all readers, *Designing for User Engagement on the Web: 10 Basic Principles* brings together an articulate and practical vision of successfully addressing the expectations of users of the new generation of highly engaging technologies.

Cheryl Geisler is professor of interactive arts and technology at Simon Fraser University, where she is the inaugural dean of the Faculty of Communication, Art and Technology. Geisler received her PhD in rhetoric from Carnegie Mellon University and taught at Rensselaer Polytechnic Institute, where she played a leadership role in the development of programs in human-computer interaction, electronic media, arts, and communication and information technology. She has published more than 50 articles, book chapters, and conference proceedings as well as 5 books. She served as principal investigator on the major research grant that lead to this book.

WITHDRAWN
UTSA LIBRARIES

Designing for User Engagement on the Web

10 Basic Principles

Cheryl Geisler

with Contributors
Roger Grice
Audrey Bennett
Janice W. Fernheimer
Robert Krull
Patricia Search
James P. Zappen
Rachel Spilka
Bill Hart-Davidson

Routledge
Taylor & Francis Group

NEW YORK AND LONDON

First published 2014
by Routledge
711 Third Avenue, New York, NY 10017

Simultaneously published in the UK
by Routledge
2 Park Square, Milton Park, Abingdon, Oxon OX14 4RN

Routledge is an imprint of the Taylor & Francis Group, an informa business

© 2014 Taylor & Francis

The right of Cheryl Geisler to be identified as the author of the editorial material, and of the authors for their individual chapters, has been asserted in accordance with sections 77 and 78 of the Copyright, Designs and Patents Act 1988.

All rights reserved. No part of this book may be reprinted or reproduced or utilised in any form or by any electronic, mechanical, or other means, now known or hereafter invented, including photocopying and recording, or in any information storage or retrieval system, without permission in writing from the publishers.

Trademark notice: Product or corporate names may be trademarks or registered trademarks, and are used only for identification and explanation without intent to infringe.

Library of Congress Cataloging-in-Publication Data

Geisler, Cheryl.
Designing for user engagement on the Web : 10 basic principles / by Cheryl Geisler.
    pages cm
    Includes bibliographical references.
1. Web sites—Design.   2. Internet users.   3. Web site development.   I. Title.
    TK5105.888.G445 2013
    006.7—dc23
    2013000534

ISBN: 978-0-415-82347-0 (paperback)
ISBN: 978-0-415-82343-2 (hardback)
ISBN: 978-0-203-52622-4 (ebook)

Typeset in Sabon
by Apex CoVantage, LLC

Printed and bound in the United States of America by Edwards Brothers Malloy

Library
University of Texas
at San Antonio

Contents

The Case Studies

Foreword

Rachel Spilka

Designing for User Engagement on the Web is destined to have a profound impact on the way we understand and design products for users. This book presents a compelling argument, based on a solid body of research, that before we design and develop engaging web-based communications, we will need to update and revise some entrenched frameworks and notions about usability and users.

As we all know well by now, the social web—including forums, weblogs, blogs, microblogs, vlogs, wall postings, wikis, podcasts, instant messaging, social bookmarking, social networking, social news, social photo and video sharing, and so much more—has become the most significant personal and professional arena of communication of the early 21st century. New uses and types of social media emerge all the time, and more people are using the social web daily for an increasing number of reasons. The social web has become so popular that studies have emerged that focus on its possible dangers—for example, some fear that it has begun to replace face-to-face relationships or that some might even become "addicted" to it. In 2010, Facebook surpassed Google in the number of hits, which suggests that engaging web communities is becoming more important to users than conducting information searches.

The social web has infiltrated industry and academia. Businesses are adding Facebook and Twitter links to their websites in efforts to reach more potential customers, and academic programs (e.g., in communication, technical communication, information design) are developing new courses that focus exclusively on social media, creating new assignments that involve the use of social media, and incorporating social media into hybrid and distance-education course delivery.

This book is a timely response to all these developments. The authors, all situated professionally at Rensselaer Polytechnic Institute (RPI) at the time of the work, report findings from an impressive three-year, large-scale, collaborative research project in which they completed five case studies of user experiences rich in communication and interaction. What the authors discovered is that the goals, needs, preferences, capabilities, and habits of users of engaging web-based communications are quite different from those characterizing users of more traditional print and digital media. Implied throughout this book is that instead of reapplying to the design of user engagement the same guidelines that we have used in the past, the time has arrived for our design decisions to be based on a new set of guidelines that are informed by a new understanding of modern users of social media.

Because this book introduces all of the above—a new portrayal of users, a new understanding of how and why they use social media, and a new set of principles aimed at helping designers and developers create successful products for them—it has the potential to alter the work that we do. In this foreword, I will highlight three of the features that contribute to this impact: the empirical strengths of the study, the call for a new theoretical understanding of users, and the "gift to practice"—a set of user engagement guidelines that can inform and improve the design of social media.

The Research Design

One reason this book is quite unique is that the authors report the results of a well-designed collaborative, longitudinal study conducted over three years (approximately from 2005 to 2008) with the help of a large-grant award from the Society of Technical Communication (STC). For those of us who have become a bit concerned about the questionable design and integrity of some recent research related to information design and technical communication, the strength of this project's structure, design, and methodology is a welcome change.

In 2004–2005, STC's Research Grants Committee, which I managed at the time, was charged by STC leadership to write and issue a request for proposal for a large grant competition. STC's goal was to fund a single, large-scale, longitudinal study with the potential to add new knowledge that could lead to significant improvements in practice in the field of technical communication. Joining the Research Grants Committee during different stages of the large-grant award competition were well-respected leaders from industry and academia, including Philippa Benson, Patricia Goubril-Gambrell, Jonathan Price, and Chauncey Wilson from industry and Ann Blakeslee, Davida Charney, Carolyn Rude, and Mark Zachry from academia.

After two rounds in this competition, the committee recommended to STC that it fund the proposal submitted by the authors of this book, faculty researchers from RPI who proposed to study the users of different types of web-based communications. In addition to their project goals, what we especially liked about the RPI project were the following features of the research design:

- The RPI team proposed a three-year study (most recent studies have been completed in less than one year).
- They planned to conduct five case studies of different types of web-based communication, a design that would enable them to detect and track patterns of user behavior and features across all five cases over time.
- These five cases were diverse. They included two that were situated at RPI (one examining the use of wikis to support collaborative coursework and the other analyzing distance-learning environments) and three that focused on both local and international social and cultural goals (one case would focus on the development of a photo gallery interface for a local nonprofit agency information system on the web; a second on the analysis and revision of cultural websites created by aboriginal groups to sustain and communicate their cultural heritage; and a third on the transformation of a Kenyan print poster into an interactive web-based poster aimed at promoting HIV/AIDS awareness and capable of being modified by users in any cultural context).

- The entire RPI team adopted what they call "a deeply collaborative approach" to conduct three rounds of iterative usability testing of successive drafts of the 10 Basic Principles of User Engagement. They developed these principles during a three-year process of creating social media exemplars based on the five case studies.
- The team also planned to use Nielsen's heuristics (1994b) to perform seven task-based heuristic evaluations of each case study exemplar.
- The entire research team—consisting of the two study principal investigators (PIs), the five case study PIs, and assisting students from PhD, master's, and bachelor's degree programs—would meet regularly during a repeated Usable Content Seminar, a process that would encourage regular interaction and collaboration across all teams.

During this three-year process, based on their research results, the RPI team emerged with at least two major contributions for information design and development: a shift conceptually from the focus on usability to a focus on user engagement and community, and a set of 10 Basic Principles for User Engagement that designers and developers could apply, easily and right away, to their work.

The Concepts of User Engagement and Community

User engagement, a process of maximizing and optimizing the experiences of those who use web-based communication, is the heart and soul of this book. To achieve user engagement, the authors explain, we need, first, to question long-held assumptions about who will be using the products that we create and how best to make their experience meaningful. In particular, as Geisler and Grice, the directors of the study that gave rise to this book, explain in their introduction, From Usability to User Engagement, we need to shift from our traditional focus on functionality (and what Mirel (2003) calls "usefulness") toward a new focus on the user's experience on the web. According to the authors, this process will involve the following framework trade-offs, on the part of designers:

- A shift from designer control to user control: This involves a ceding of control from designers to users.
- A shift from high design to amateur design: The new reality is that with a new user control of social media and a new priority on accommodating local cultures (contextualizing), a more likely outcome will be a decline in design standards.
- A shift from a canonical path to a narrative path: Instead of the conventional usability focus on helping users get information or complete tasks and on warning them against pitfalls and encouraging them to stay on task, designers would benefit, instead, from using digital storytelling or narration as a way to engage users and guide them toward choices that enable them to achieve goals that matter to them: exploring their own identities and building new communities.

As the authors acknowledge, their conceptual development of these framework shifts and their focus on a new goal of user engagement are based on recent trends in scholarship that have emerged from the new possibilities of active user participation, input, and sharing in web-based communication (think in terms of users being able to post or revise Wikipedia entries and, by doing so, assuming the role and status of writers). In their introductory chapter, for example, Geisler and Grice mention that the research team has been influenced by the arguments that we need to do more to facilitate reader interaction with documents or systems (e.g., Sless, 2004) and to acknowledge and design for the fact that users have grown in control and power in web-based communication (e.g., Spinuzzi, 2003).

As the book authors make clear, power and control have moved back and forth between designers/writers and users/readers since the late 1970s. Their main argument is that, although in the 1990s, usability theories advanced the concept of designers and developers guiding or warning users, a more accurate theoretical perspective for new social media reveals just the opposite: The needs and goals of social media users now should guide the decisions and choices of designers and developers. As Zappen, one of the book's author-researchers, points out in his chapter on Principle 7: Share Control, "designers need to acknowledge user control and facilitate user freedom of choice and freedom of movement."

This book focuses mostly on the need to acknowledge this shift by enabling and encouraging user engagement—that is, by designing social media in ways that will maximize opportunities for users to interact and share with each other so that they can ultimately meet their goals of exploring their identities and building new communities. Of the authors' 10 Basic Principles for User Engagement, two of them ("Design for Usability," and "Test the Backbone") encourage designers to continue following basic usability and readability guidelines that can enable user engagement. The other eight principles focus on other ways that designers can enable user engagement to:

- Understand ("Design for Diverse Users") and welcome ("Extend a Welcome," "Set the Context") users;
- Enable and motivate users to use web-based environments for interactions and sharing ("Make a Connection," "Share Control," "Support Interactions Among Users," "Create a Sense of Place"); and
- Encourage a continuation of interactions, connections, and sharing beyond the current user experience ("Plan to Continue the Engagement"), which promotes the notion that discourse needs to be viewed as intertextual and ongoing instead of as a single, shared interaction that occurs just once.

At times, this book takes user engagement to a higher level of conceptualization than might be apparent initially. One author who does this is Zappen, who points out how focusing on just user control or designer control is not enough for achieving a full understanding of the complexities of the distributed system where design and writing take place. As he puts it, "user control is neither a designer nor a user option exclusively but the result of a complex interaction of all of the components of a distributed system." It is this vision of a shared social space—one in which users and designers have, perhaps, ever-changing degrees of control and power—that I find especially interesting in terms of how web-based communication promises to move information design and related fields forward, conceptually, toward an increasingly expansive, adequately complex vision of what takes place (relationships? partnerships? collaborations? power negotiations?) in the distributed system(s) of design/writing. Zappen's description of his vision of the future reflects the extraordinary optimistic and hopeful nature of this book. After describing how the roles of all participants in these environments (designers, users, others) are becoming increasingly blurred and less meaningful, he suggests that:

> In web-based environments meant to engage, this complex interaction becomes still more complex—an interaction not only between designers and users but also between users and systems and users and other users. As users become both consumers and producers of information—"prosumers" and "produsers" (Tapscott & Williams, 2006, pp. 124–150; Bruns, 2008, pp. 15–23)—the control issue becomes less an issue of who is in charge or who is in control and more an issue of quality control. In a distributed system in which anyone and everyone with access can contribute content and everyone—and no one—is in charge, who is to judge the quality of the result? The answer, of course, is everyone!

The ultimate goal identified by Zappen, achieving quality, works well within the authors' theoretical vision in this book: Because everyone has a stake in quality, everyone needs to participate in the type of identity work and the building of communities (which we can also perceive as collaborative ventures, partnerships, or alliances). In the context of this book, user engagement can be viewed as the first critical milestone toward those all-important goals.

A common theme throughout the book is that to engage users, designers need to allow users to explore their own social and cultural identities, make connections, join a community, and develop a sense of place—all concepts that are essential even if they might seem elusive in some types of web-based communication. According to the authors' research, users crave the discovery of their own social and cultural identities. Designers therefore need to move beyond a focus on usability toward the creation of new socially and culturally meaningful spaces where users can seek and find their own identities and then become empowered (for example, to build new communities) through more expansive rhetorical and social roles. To enable all of this to happen, the authors explain, designers need to contextualize social media in ways that users will find familiar and motivational.

The 10 Basic Principles

A major gift to practitioners and educators is the authors' development of 10 Basic Principles for User Engagement, the result of their iterative testing and detection of patterns across their case studies. The authors collaboratively distilled patterns they noticed in the study into a list of straightforward principles that designers and developers should be able to apply with ease as they attempt to achieve user engagement for their social media products.

As a former practitioner and current educator, I am grateful for this list of principles. It reminds me of how much my students and I, in the 1980s, came to value, and make frequent use of, Felker et al.'s (1981) list of document design guidelines. Those guidelines were also the major outcome of a large-scale collaborative study that was conducted by a consortium of researchers from industry (Siegel and Gale), government (American Institutes for Research), and academia (Carnegie Mellon University). Researchers from that consortium, from their study and testing of consumer forms, identified specific guidelines for document design or revision. In all technical communication and rhetoric courses I taught during the 1980s and 1990s, I included copies of these guidelines in every course pack and required students to apply the guidelines in at least one assignment per course that involved an analysis and subsequent revision of poorly designed documents.

Similar to Felker et al.'s (1981) document design principles, I believe that the 10 Basic Principles for User Engagement presented here are likely to influence information design/writing choices for decades to come. I can envision the 10 Basic Principles for User Engagement picking up where the document design guidelines left off in terms of providing specific principles for making texts more meaningful for users. By providing principles that we can apply easily and immediately to our goals, thinking, and design choices, the authors are helping us elevate the quality and value of our work as we strive to make an important, positive difference with our work, and in particular, as we attempt to elevate the status, power, and impact of the users of social media.

I urge all readers of this book to take their time with it. Devote some attention to the introductory chapter by Geisler and Grice, which explains the theory behind the authors' research project, introduces the five cases, and suggests ways to use this book. Read the descriptions of the principles slowly and carefully so that you can appreciate the purpose and value of each one. Then look through the final part of the book, where you will find a full and rich description of each of the five case studies, which will be useful for readers who want more details about what the author-researchers discovered during their study. I predict that once you have read this book, your perspectives on users and usability, and, subsequently, your approach to the design and development of engaging communication, will forever be changed.

From Usability to User Engagement

Cheryl Geisler
Roger Grice

In this chapter, Geisler and Grice introduce the 10 basic principles that characterize engaging user experience and place them in the context of user-centered traditions. With a focus on the user, on design, and on engagement, the principles provide the foundation for designing user experiences rich in communication and interaction. This chapter also introduces the research through which the basic principles were developed. Five projects were taken through an iterative design process, coordinated and communicated through a common seminar and a common methodology. The introduction closes with an overview of the organization of this book and some suggestions of how it could be used.

Designing for User Engagement on the Web introduces 10 basic principles that we believe characterize engaging user experience. These principles were developed though research funded by the Society for Technical Communication (2005), which gave us the mandate in 2005 to address the topic of making content usable. We proposed an iterative design process as a way to develop and test design principles for web-based communications whose main purpose is the engagement of users. And in work undertaken at Rensselaer Polytechnic Institute (RPI) over three years beginning in the fall of 2005, we undertook a set of case studies designing and redesigning five web-based exemplars.

Focus on the User

In developing principles for user engagement, we took as our foundations two traditions that have attempted to put the user squarely in the center. In the area of document design, the focus has been on making life easier for the reader, especially the reader of public documents. For this purpose, sets of guidelines have been developed over the years with changing focus. Guidelines in the early 1980s focused on characteristics of documents themselves, including such features as organization, writing, typography, and graphics (Felker et al., 1981). By the late 1990s, document design guidelines were extended to cover the techniques by which documents should be produced, including audience analysis and usability testing (Schriver, 1997). By the opening of the 21st century, the emphasis was on making readers' interactions with public documents easy, efficient, and productive (Sless, 2004).

Developing around the same time as document design and with many of the same people was the allied discipline of usability, with its focus on interactive computing applications (Butler, 1996, p. 73). In the mid-1980s, Gould and Lewis's key principles for designing usability included an "early and continuous focus on users" (1985, p. 300). At the beginning of the 1990s, Nielsen and Molich articulated a set of heuristics (Molich & Nielsen, 1990; Nielsen & Molich, 1990) that, with refinement (Nielsen, 1994b), became the basis for the most popular informal usability method: heuristic evaluation.

Our 10 basic principles for user engagement have strong connections to these traditions aimed at improving user experience. As Dumas and Redish (1993, p. vi) point out, "Anything that people use or read has an interface that can and should be developed with usability in mind." But, although our principles were built in the user-centered tradition, they are distinctive in two important ways.

Focus on Design

To begin with, we emphasize the role of our 10 principles in design rather than in testing. That is, while our 10 principles can effectively be used to test web-based communications, we believe that they will have more impact if they are incorporated early in the design process. This emphasis on design is in keeping with the original fundamentals of usability. In their first articulation of usability heuristics, Molich and Nielsen (1990, p. 338) acknowledged that "following such guidelines during the design phase imposes little extra effort." Admonitions to get to "know the user" were common in early usability engineering (Gould & Lewis, 1985; Nielsen, 1993). As Dumas (2007, p. 55) recalls, usability engineers "favored integration of usability teams into product design teams." And, as he and Redish pointed out in their guide to usability testing in 1993, "usability has to be thought about, planned for, and designed into the product from the beginning" (Dumas & Redish, 1993, p. 40).

Despite these intentions, however, usability principles—particularly usability heuristics—have come to be more closely identified with testing rather than design. The latest version of the usability.gov website, for example, introduces usability heuristics only as part of explaining heuristic evaluation, "a usability inspection method for computer software that helps identify usability problems in the user interface (UI) design" (U.S. Department of Health and Human Services, n.d.).

The scope of conventional usability work has also been narrower than we intend, frequently limited to interface issues rather than system functionality as a whole. In her 2003 book on developing useful and usable software for complex problem solving, Mirel critiques this conventional tendency. While her focus is on usefulness rather than engagement, Mirel makes the point that "usefulness—doing better work—is not the same as using an application more easily" (Mirel, 2003, p. xxxi).

Focus on Engagement

If we substitute the word *engagement* for Mirel's *usefulness*, her statement pretty much sums up the second way in which our approach is distinctive from many conventional approaches to user-centered practices: our focus on user engagement. The idea of engagement is often associated with the social web, a term coined by Hoschka in 1998 to describe the possibility of "turning the net into a social space" (Hoschka, 1988a, p. 6).

"How can we," Hoschka asked, "turn information environments into rich communication and interaction environments?" (Hoschka, 1998b). The cascade of social web applications that we are now familiar with—blogs, consumer reviews, wikis, and social networking—have provided an on-the-ground response to Hoschka's prescient question.

One way to understand our 10 basic principles is to consider them a principled rather than on-the-ground response to Hoschka's question. That is, what are the principles underlying the design of user experiences rich in communication and interaction? For the most part, conventional usability does not attempt to address this question. For Dumas and Redish (1993, p. 4), "usability means that the people who use the product can do so quickly and easily to accomplish their own tasks." As they go on to point out, this assumes that "people use products to be productive" and "users are busy people trying to accomplish tasks." Even when Nielsen and his colleagues updated usability to reflect web-specific issues, they characterized the web as a "tool" driven by "real-world needs" (Nielsen & Loranger, 2006, p. xx) and deliberately restricted their discussion of usability to "web sites that have a business goal and that aim to support users in getting something done" (Nielsen & Pernice, 2009, p. xvii). In considering sites such as Facebook, Nielsen and Loranger (2006, p. xxii) claim that, "when young people make personal web sites to express their personality, traditional usability simply doesn't apply."

Although traditional metrics of usability—efficiency, accuracy, and satisfaction—may no longer be an adequate yardstick with which to measure user experiences meant to engage, it is hardly the case that the design of such interactive experiences should be considered simply a matter of personal taste. Donald Norman's (2010) work on sociable design points in the direction we would like to go. According to Norman, sociable design is more than product design; it is the design of services, the design of a set of interactions. And web design, Norman suggests, is a species of service design, requiring the same kind of sociable design to be successful.

> Design of both machines and services should be thought of as a social activity, one where there is as much concern paid to the social nature of the interaction as to the successful completion of the activity. That is sociable design. (Norman, 2010, p. 141)

The impact of the social web need hardly be argued for. In one of the earliest books on the subject, Joshua Porter described a usage life cycle characteristic of social web applications. In contrast to informational websites that seek to provide users with content quickly and efficiently, social web applications attempt to move users through a cycle of five stages of engagement: unaware, interested, first-time use, regular use, and passionate use (Porter, 2008, p. ix). Indeed, it is the fact that users in the final stage (passionate) can become recruiters for users in the opening stage (unaware) that can make a social web application go viral.

An Example

For us, the difference between usability in the convention sense and usability for user engagement became clearer through a comparison we explored early in our project, looking at three treatments of the same content: adding memory, in this case to the iMac G5. Our starting point for a good example of conventional usability came from Chapter 4 of the *iMac G5 User's Guide* (Apple Computer, 2005), winner in the category of Hardware/Software Combination Guides of the 2005 STC International Technical Publications Competition. For comparison, we looked at two web documents covering the same material: a *Legit Memory Review* (Kirsch, 2005), which in February 2006 was the number-one hit in a Google search for "iMac G5 adding memory," and *Moblog, The Mobile Log of Ryan Kawailani Ozawa* (Ozawa, 2005), which was the number-one hit in a Google image search for the same terms at the same time.

The first page of Chapter 4 of the G5 manual (p. 41; available at http://manuals. info.apple.com/en/iMac_G5_2005_Users_Manual.pdf) illustrates well the principles of usability laid out in the document design literature. Type size and color have been used to call out document functions. Warnings appear in clearly labeled boxes. Chapters open with information on what the chapter contains. The table of contents and index provide alternative routes to information. Procedures are laid out in numbered steps (i.e., p. 42). Graphics are beautifully done, with callouts, and integrated with the text (also p. 42). Overall, this document is an example of high design, one that makes full use of the apparatus of the book, the principles of typography, and technical illustration.

The two web documents we compared were less well designed. The *Legit Memory Review* is from a blog and opens with the amateurish picture of a cluttered desktop shown in Figure 0.1. Even more amateurish, *Moblog* is made up of a string of pictures taken with a mobile phone to document an attempt at memory upgrade of "my iMac," shown in Figure 0.2.

Figure 0.1 Cluttered desktop from *Legit Memory Review*. Photo used by permission of Nathan Kirsch, Legit Reviews.

Figure 0.2 Picture of iMac open for memory installation, posted to Moblog. Photo used by permission of Ryan Kawailani Ozawa.

In addition to lacking high design, the two web documents brought to the memory task two features missing in our informational document but characteristic of many social web documents. To begin with, they both make an effort to contextualize their content to a specific place and time using a *narrative*. For *Moblog*, the story is a pictorial account of the author's own upgrade, "my iMac G5." For the *Legit Memory Review*, the narrative is the story of the reviewer's visit to an old friend:

> On a recent trip to California we stopped by to visit an old time friend who is just starting to mix his own music and create his own tracks from his home. After purchasing an Apple G5, speakers, microphones, amplifiers, guitars, a computer desk, and Pro Tools with the Digi 002 rack he thought he was ready to lay down some music and make some songs. Now that over ten thousand dollars was spent he finally realized that he already needed to upgrade his system because his audio editing software took so much application memory that he was unable to run any other programs and was having slow system performance when using many different audio tracks." (Kirsch, 2005, p. 1)

In addition, both web documents pay a great deal of attention to *recruitment*, key to moving a user through Porter's usage life cycle from unaware to passionate. In the *Legit Memory Review*, the reader is repeatedly reassured that the process is not a difficult one: "While the system is sleek with no obvious handles or case doors it is very simple to take apart." In addition, the user is invited to join in appreciating Apple's design prowess:

Once the cover is removed one can see how tightly Apple crammed everything into the iMac G5 case. Much to our amazement the memory slots are located on the right hand side and nothing needs to be done to access them. (Kirsch, 2005, p. 2)

Though less attuned to users, *Moblog* also invokes appreciation for Apple with its caption to the photo shown in Figure 0.2: "Adding RAM to my iMac G5. The insides are almost as pretty as the outside."

This kind of encouragement and praise was absent from our informational document. In fact, the only emotional appeals are negative, coming in the form of warnings:

> *Warning*: The ambient light sensor is located to the left of the middle screw, as shown in the illustration. Don't mistake the ambient light sensor for a screw. Sticking a screwdriver or other sharp object in the ambient light sensor could damage your computer. (Apple Computer, 2005, p. 42)

Here we see a good illustration of the way conventional usability presumes a canonical path, attempting to control users' movement, steering them away from dangerous possibilities (damaging your computer) and toward the more appropriate path (the middle screw). At the same time, the document remains indifferent to the goal of recruiting users to add memory. Indeed, in the face of such a warning, a nervous reader might abandon the task of memory upgrade altogether.

A Framework for User Engagement

Although frequently accessed, neither the *Legit Memory Review* nor *Moblog* can be considered excellent documents. They do, however, suggest ways in which usability shifts as one moves from the conventional usability of document design and computing applications to the user engagement of the social web. In fact, we have found that three critical trade-offs characterize user experiences that are engaging.

The first and most obvious trade-off concerns the locus of control, as shown in Figure 0.3. In conventional documents such as user documentation (Weiss, 1991), the document designer is expected to be in control. In the social web exemplars we worked with, by contrast, control had been shared with the user in some way.

Not surprisingly, control has been a much-discussed aspect of the new web documents. Kress (2004), for example, discusses the way the screen privileges the will of users, whereas the book privileges the will of authors. Gurak (2001) notes that interactivity, where the user shares control, is one of the critical new dimensions of online content. The social web, of course, is by definition interactive.

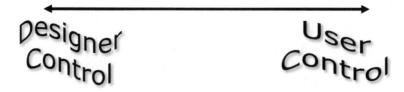

Figure 0.3 Trade-off between designer control in conventional documents and user control in the social web.

Figure 0.4 Trade-off between high design in conventional documents and amateur design in the social web.

Figure 0.5 Trade-off between a single canonical path in conventional documents and personalized narrative path in the social web.

The second trade-off emerging from our work is that between high design and amateur design, as shown in Figure 0.4. In our comparison, we saw that conventional documents prized high design, but the emergence of user control was often associated with a decline in design standards. Obviously, both the *Legit Review* and the *Moblog* fall far short of the design quality exhibited by the *iMac G5 User's Guide*. But we found that even in projects where designers were heavily involved, standards of good design needed to be modified in the face of local culture. We have found that the social web requires not so much a lowering of design standards as a shift in the locus of design work. In sites that invite user collaboration, many of the traditional areas of high design—text and graphics—are left to the user, and the work of the designer moves under the covers to the functionality that will allow that user input and to the orchestration of an increasingly complex set of media. Although it may appear that the results are simply personal, we suggest with our 10 basic principles that user engagement does not eliminate the need for design so much as require a new set of guiding principles.

The third trade-off, as shown in Figure 0.5, we encountered in our work was that between having a universal canonical path and providing a contextualized, often personal, narrative. As our comparison suggested, guiding users along a canonical path, warning them against pitfalls, and encouraging them to stay on task is typical of conventional usability. By contrast, digital storytelling is an emerging motif in the social web; technology reviews may open, as we saw, with a story of a friend's need to upgrade.

Underlying this use of contextualized narrative is the growing prominence of identity and community in the social web. If the underlying user process in conventional usability is to help the user avoid error and get tasks done, the process in the social web might be conceptualized as moving users from control through identity and toward community. As shown in Figure 0.6, we can begin by asking ourselves: Why do users want control? What do they do with it? The answer seems clearly to involve the exploration of identity. The users of the social web are not so much engaged in getting information or completing a task as in using system-offered choices to explore their own identities.

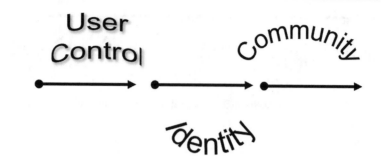

Figure 0.6 Underlying movement in the social web from control to identity to community.

And, we can ask ourselves, for what purpose is such identity work supported? Why do social web designers create environments in which such identity work is afforded? The answer to this second question also seemed clear: to build community. Motives for community building are various, of course. As we shall see in our case studies, designers may aim to build community to support education, connect kids to community resources, introduce users to other cultures, foster collaboration, or encourage activism. For whatever motive, the designer who aims to create social web applications, moving users from control through identity and toward community, clearly faces a different task than that addressed by conventional usability principles.

Our Projects

To develop new principles for designing for user engagement, we took a deeply collaborative approach, coordinating five projects through an iterative design process aimed at generating and testing general principles for user engagement. Each project grew out of an existing research program led by a member of RPI's Program in Communication and Rhetoric, which was then developed over the course of the STC project through coordinated communication and a common methodology. Each project focused on one or more exemplars of web-based communications that were designed and redesigned over the course of the project to better reflect our emerging principles. By using five projects, we ensured that our 10 basic principles had legs beyond any specific application.

The first project, led by James P. Zappen, aimed at the development of a photo gallery interface for the Connected Kids information system. Connected Kids is a social web application (http://connectedkids.rpi.edu/index.php/) that had been developed with support from the National Science Foundation Digital Government Research Program to serve families and children in Rensselaer County and the capital region of upstate New York (Harrison, Zappen, & Adali, 2005; Zappen, Adali, & Harrison, 2006). During our work, Web Galleries were developed and refined as kid-friendly interfaces to the children's services in Connected Kids. Figure 0.7 shows an early example of one of these interfaces, inviting young users to explore the services available at Knickerbacker Park, a local skating rink. Over the course of our work, the Web Galleries evolved in significant ways that are described in two of our chapters on basic principles: *Principle 1: Design for Diverse Users* and *Principle 7: Share Control.*

Figure 0.7 Early example of the Connected Kids interface.

A complete report on the project can be found in the section on case studies as *Case Study 1: Information Galleries for Young People.*

Our next project, lead by Jan Fernheimer, explored the use of wikis to support collaborative work. At the start of this project, no such wiki existed. The first version, shown in Figure 0.8, was developed to support interaction in the Usable Content Seminar, the university course that served as our hub for communication and collaboration. Over the course of our work, this very basic wiki evolved in significant ways, changing platforms and extending to other contexts for use. It serves as the example in two of our chapters on basic principles: *Principle 2: Design for Usability* and *Principle 5: Set the Context.* A complete report of the project can be found in *Case Study 2: Wikis for Collaboration.*

Work on cultural websites in our next project, led by Patricia Search, involved analyzing websites created by aboriginal groups for the purpose of sustaining and communicating cultural heritage. By deliberately situating themselves at the intersection of indigenous and nonindigenous cultures, these cultural websites purposefully straddle the line between cultural ideologies. In the first phase of our work, we collaborated on the Tshinanu Television Network (http://www.tshinanu.tv) (see Figure 4.1). Later, we added an analysis of video and photographic materials from an online course produced at Emily Carr University of Art + Design on aboriginal crafts (see Figure 6.1). A comparison of user responses to these materials provides examples for two of our chapters on basic principles: *Principle 4: Extend a Welcome* and *Principle 6: Make a Connection. Case Study 3: Cultural Websites* provides a complete report on the project.

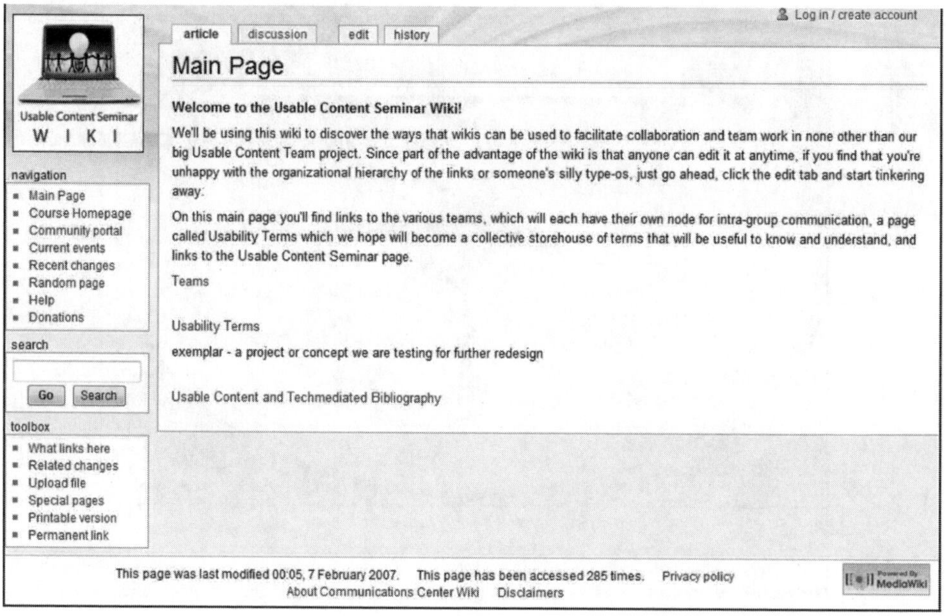

Figure 0.8 Original design of the wiki for collaboration used in the Usable Content Seminar.

A range of analyses of distance-learning environments made up our fourth project led by Robert Krull. Although a variety of technologies have been used in distance education at RPI over the years, we focus much of our discussion on user experience in two multiwindowed learning and conferencing systems—Elluminate (now Blackboard Collaborate, http://www.blackboard.com/Platforms/Collaborate/Overview.aspx) and Adobe® Connect (http://www.adobe.com/products/adobeconnect.html)—as they were used at RPI to support courses offered to students both on campus and at a distance. As shown in the Figure 0.9, these systems provide users with a number of tools for communication and interaction, including real-time chat, an electronic whiteboard, voice over Internet protocol (VoIP), and video streaming. Results from user surveys and user testing serve as the basis for our discussion in two of our chapters on basic principles: *Principle 3: Test the Backbone* and *Principle 8: Support Interactions Among Users.* A full discussion of this project can be found in *Case Study 4: Usability in Distance Education.*

Our final project, led by Audrey Bennett, was an exploration of cross-cultural graphics for HIV/AIDS awareness. Our starting point was a print poster (see Figure 10.2) that had been developed during a transnational, participatory workshop involving Third World laypeople situated in Kenya and First World educators situated in the United States (Bennett et al., 2006). During our work, this poster was made into an interactive web-based image (http://aninteractiveposter.info) that could be modified by users to communicate a more culturally appropriate message. This interactive poster provides examples for chapters on the remaining basic principles: *Principle 9: Create a Sense of Place* and *Principle 10: Plan to Continue the Engagement.* The project is also described in detail in our final case study, *Case Study 5: An Interactive Image.*

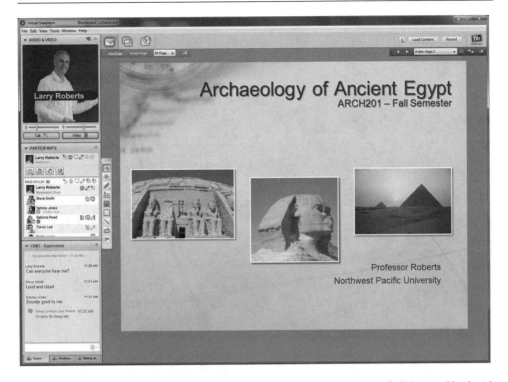

Figure 0.9 Tools for communication and interaction provided by Blackboard Collaborate. Used with permission of Blackboard.

Our Process

To facilitate the coordination and collaboration necessary to develop basic principles at the same time that we developed our five individual projects, we organized ourselves as the Usable Content Seminar, held three times, beginning under the STC Planning Grant in the spring of 2006 and concluding in the spring of 2008 with the completion of the STC Major Grant. The seminar recruited students from PhD, MS, and BS programs in human-computer interaction; communication and rhetoric; technical communication; electronic media, arts, and communication; and computer science. In spring 2007, the distance-learning seminar room shown in Figure 0.10 was brought online, allowing us to enroll students both on campus and at a distance.

The Usable Content Seminars linked parallel team efforts through a common seminar. The five project teams met weekly to carry out team-based activities in design, testing, and analysis on their own, but came together in occasional seminars like the one shown in Figure 0.10. Seminars met for several hours per week, using a combination of face-to-face interaction and chat, video conference, VoIP, conference call, shared applications, and a variety of distance courseware tools to allow the teams to work together.

The level of complexity in the interaction was high enough that we developed maps like the one shown in Figure 0.11 for the Usable Content Seminar II to help us remember who was who. The five projects are represented in triangles, with Roger

Figure 0.10 Usable Content Seminar, with distance students connected using VoIP and data sharing.

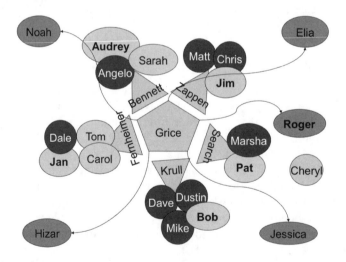

Figure 0.11 Schematic diagram of the Usable Content Seminar used to keep track of teams and speakers.

Grice as leader of the testing team in the center and Cheryl Geisler as the coordinator off to the side. On-campus team members are shown in black type with team leaders in bold. Distance team members are shown in white type. Every team had at least one distance member, and several teams were made up almost entirely of

Table 0.1 Summary of three-year effort.

Usable Content Seminar I	January 18 to February 15	Review the literature
Spring 2006	February 15 to March 29	Analyze exemplar
	March 29	Design charette
	March 29 to May 3	Final reports
Usable Content Seminar II	January 17 to February 7	Finalize exemplar
Spring 2007	February 7 to February 28	Task-based heuristic testing
	February 28 to March 28	Redesign of exemplar
	March 28 to April 18	Comparative user testing of original and redesigned exemplars
	April 18	Design charette
	April 18 to May 7	Final reports
Usable Content Seminar III	January 16 to January 30	Develop testing protocol
Spring 2008	January 30 to February 27	Pilot testing
	February 27 to March 19	Finalize testing protocol
	March 19 to April 16	Formal testing
	April 16	Design charette
	April 16 to May 21	Final reports

students working at a distance, all at different locations. Members of the testing team are shown on the periphery. As the map suggests, team members worked together to develop a common testing methodology but were assigned to work with specific project teams.

Seminar activities were designed to encourage generalization from the projects as well as to coordinate the development of a common methodology that would be applied in individual project work. At the culmination of each of the three courses, teams also came together for an extended design charette, an intense period of design activity, during which they shared their work and engaged in wide-ranging discussion. During the Usable Content Seminar I in spring 2006, teams produced a review of the literature relevant to their projects as well as an analysis of the exemplar selected for development. During the Usable Content Seminar II in spring 2007, teams conducted two rounds of testing on the selected exemplars, using the results of the first round of heuristic testing to produce a draft set of basic principles that were then used to redesign the exemplar for comparative user testing in the second round. During the final Usable Content Seminar III in spring 2008, testing methods were developed and used in a final round of formal testing of the exemplars, and a final version of the basic principles was produced. Table 0.1 summarizes our three-year effort.

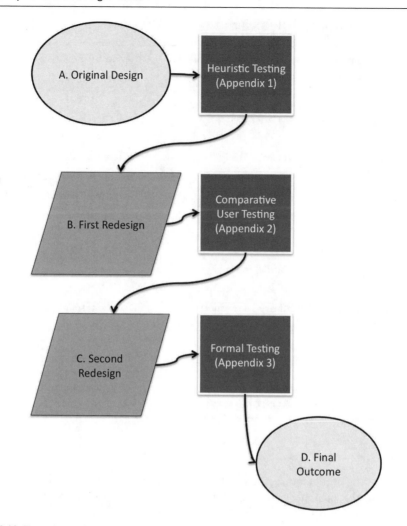

Figure 0.12 Flow chart of standard methods used, in adapted form, by all projects.

Our Methods

As shown in Figure 0.12, the generic project flow for our projects involved three rounds of usability testing that were used as a development tool as well as an evaluation tool. Our intention was to use the first two rounds of testing to conduct evaluations on our five web-based exemplars with the twin goals of improving their usability and developing an emerging set of basic principles for evaluating engaging web-based communication. We then used this set of principles in the third round of testing to evaluate the exemplars more closely.

The goals of our first round of testing were to determine ways to improve the original designs of the exemplars and to produce a set of principles. As a starting point, as shown in Figure 0.12, we performed heuristic testing using Jakob Nielsen's heuristics and methodology (1994b). RPI graduate students Elia Nelson, Mohamad Hizar Khuzaimah, Jessica Woods, Dale Bass, and Noah Schaffer worked as an evaluation team to ensure that each of the original designs was evaluated in a thorough and consistent way.

The major goal for heuristic testing was to establish some early ideas on principles. The test team took an informal approach to conducting the testing. Test users were selected from the members of each project team. On average, eight test sessions were conducted for each exemplar. Each session was moderated by a member from the testing team and accompanied by one observer from the exemplar team. Each member of the testing team tested at least one exemplar.

The protocol for the heuristic testing, found in Appendix 1, asked users to complete tasks, which, as shown in Table 0.2, were specific to each of the five exemplars. During the test session, a moderator and an observer monitored the users' performance and recorded time, number of clicks, and the task outcome (successful or not). After all the tests had been completed, the test team conducted individual meetings with the project

Table 0.2 User tasks used in each project for heuristic testing.

Information Gallery for Young People

Browse through the gallery and list all swimming images or media in the YMCA gallery.

Find and list all the figure-skating images.

You would like to find out more information about images that emphasize safety and making kids safe. Locate all images with the text name "Safe Kids ID Cards."

Go to the Connected Kids Web Gallery and find the youth-services organization description information.

Wikis for Collaboration

Log in.

Add definition to Usability Terms page.

Create a new page in the Community Portal.

Find time on testing schedule.

Find the external linking help document.

Cultural Websites

Explore a theme that you are interested in and comment on that experience.

Explore a theme that you are not interested in and comment on that experience.

Usability in Distance Education

Based on your experience with distance learning, make short lists of tools, etiquettes, and demands on users. For each item in the list, provide a phrase or two describing the item. Present your lists in Elluminate, in one or two pages. Use the Elluminate whiteboard and chat space to produce your materials. Limit yourself to about 15 minutes for the task.

An Interactive Poster

If you saw this poster on a wall, would you go over to it to read it?

What does this poster communicate to you?

If you were working in a health office and this image was given to you, what would you do?

Additional comments from evaluators

---

teams to discuss and analyze the findings. Based on the output from these meetings, the test team developed a draft of the basic principles.

Because our work group for heuristic testing consisted of students on campus as well as in our distance-education program, not all of the tests were conducted with evaluators and observers located in the same room. While this remote testing presented some challenges, it also heightened the awareness that the technology used in web-based communication allows for distributed participation and that the participation can be quite different for users depending on the technology available for use and their familiarity/ability with it.

Also shown in Figure 0.12, our second round of testing involved comparative user testing. Project teams used the results of the heuristic testing from the previous round of testing to produce first redesigns that could then be compared with their original designs. For this round of testing, we felt it was important to recruit users who hadn't been exposed to the exemplars previously and who represented the exemplars' targeted audiences. This produced results that were more useful to the project teams by providing data more representative of intended user interaction.

For comparative user testing, a more formal protocol was designed to capture quantitative data in addition to qualitative observational information (see Appendix 2). All first redesigns were web-based for this phase, making it easier to find methods for gathering comparative data. Based on the basic principles developed during heuristic testing, the test questions for this phase incorporated questions about the welcome, experience, connectedness, exploration, and sharing aspects of the exemplar as well as traditional task-based retrieval. A presurvey questionnaire was prepared to gather background information, and, at the end of the testing sessions, users were asked to complete a posttest survey that incorporated both open-ended questions and closed Likert-style questions to obtain both quantitative and qualitative user feedback.

During comparative user testing, a member of the testing team was assigned to each project team to help design and carry out the test. This provided a good opportunity for the test team and the project team to focus on developing the appropriate tasks. While this mode of testing distributed the members of the test team rather than having them work more collaboratively, as they had during the heuristic testing, it allowed them to work more closely with the members of the project team and focus more closely on how best to use the revised basic principles to improve the exemplars. This closer focus on exemplars allowed the members of the testing team to observe how particular basic principles came into play during use and evaluation and to get a better handle on how to measure the effects of the basic principles during a wider range of uses and by a wider range of evaluators.

The locations of the tests during comparative user testing were somewhat varied across teams: Some were done on campus, and some were conducted at the users' residences. As the protocol in Appendix 2 shows, at the beginning of each test, the moderator began the session by explaining some background information about the exemplar and informed the user about the purpose of the testing. After the user signed the consent form and answered the pretest survey questions, the moderator then guided the user through the test by asking questions on the user's feelings of welcome and appropriateness and initial impressions of the exemplar before use. The user was then given a few minutes to explore the exemplar. Next, the moderator asked the user to perform several retrieval tasks. Throughout the session, the moderator asked probing questions related to the user's level of engagement and interest, feelings of connectedness with the exemplar, and motivations for sharing.

The moderator, with the help of the observer, if present, recorded the user's feedback during the session in the form of success rate (whether the task was accomplished), number of clicks, and time taken to accomplish or give up on the task (quantitative data). The users' feedback and test's observations were recorded as testing session notes (qualitative data). On average, each session took one hour to complete.

To complete our work, as shown in Figure 0.12, following the comparative user testing, a second round of design work by the project teams produced the second redesigns that were the subject of the final round of formal testing. For formal testing, our protocol combined observational data with a posttest questionnaire. The protocol, given in generic form in Appendix 3, was adapted to fit each project and was designed to test each of the basic principles.

The results of this formal testing were used in different ways by each project. Some projects produced recommendations for the organizations for whom the designs were intended (Information Gallery for Young People; Cultural Websites; Usability in Distance Education). Other projects continued with further design work, producing new redesigns (Wikis for Collaboration; Interactive Image).

While the generic project flow provided the basic structure for all five projects, each project team had the freedom to modify the project flow as they saw fit: modifying the choice of original designs, the nature of the redesigns, and/or the testing protocols. To make these modifications clear to readers, the case study chapters provide a modified project flow chart specific to each project.

Using This Book

This book combines a handbook on the 10 Basic Principles of User Engagement with a more extended set of case studies that explore how the basic principles reflect and shape design projects in a range of engaging new media environments.

Each of the 10 basic principles is then explained in the chapters making up the first half of this book. Each of these chapters opens with the concept underlying the principle and then explains how to use the principle, drawing on examples from one of the five case studies. Each chapter ends with suggestions for further exploration of the basic principles using recent developments in the social web, such as the use of Twitter in natural disasters, the rise of the MOOC (massive open online course), the use of narrative in game design, and the implications of behavioral tracking for online privacy.

At the back of the book are the five case studies through which the basic principles were developed. Project flow charts at the beginning of each case study clarify the exact methodology used and a summary of relevant principles at the end of each case study summarizes the basic principles invoked during the project. Readers with a special interest in one of the social web technologies—web galleries, wikis, cultural websites, distance-education platforms, or interactive graphics—will want to consult the specific case study related to their interest. Those interested in an in-depth understanding of the basis for the 10 Basic Principles of User Engagement will want to work through all five case studies.

Who Should Use This Book

This book is aimed at all those concerned with making user experience engaging. This may include human-computer interaction specialists of all stripes: interface designers, usability specialists, interaction designers, web designers, and social application designers, just to name a few. Our particular staring point has been those interested in understanding what it means to move from a conventional user-centered focus to user experiences rich in communication and interaction. While these experiences certainly characterize social web applications, we also believe that aspects of the social web are becoming increasingly common in business and productivity applications, where the more ambitious goal of engagement is now being added to the conventional goal of efficiency.

Like all user-centered principles, the 10 Basic Principles for User Engagement presented here have a dual use. They can be used to guide the design and development of engaging user experiences, playing a role in establishing the original specifications of a project. They can also play a role in usability testing, providing principles that experts can use during heuristic evaluation to identify problems or missed opportunities in the interaction design.

Teachers and students interested in understanding social web phenomenon and applying principles to development will also find much of interest here. We hope the extended case studies at the back of the book can serve as starting point for the kind of lively discussion and absorbing work that they certainly provided to those of us in the Usable Content Seminars where they were developed.

Acknowledgements

Our acknowledgments need to begin with our acknowledgment of each other, the seven faculty members from Rensselaer Polytechnic Institute who, as part of the Usable Content Seminars from 2006 through 2008, set out on a collaboration that was for us unprecedented in scope, depth, and length. We committed to a process in which the multiple strands of our own research trajectories were to be woven together in the constant inquiry into underlying principles. Although some of us have scattered in the years since, none of us has been left without the influence of this work together.

Our second acknowledgment must go to the Society for Technical Communication and to Rachel Spilka, who, as the program officer for research grants, steered us through from our original planning grant through a major research grant. The STC challenged us to understand what makes content usable, and we responded by calling for a broader notion of usability, one that would encompass engagement as well as ease of use. To our delight, it accepted our call and provided the resources that would fuel our collaborative efforts. We are deeply grateful for its support.

Finally, we want to thank all of the students who, as part of the Usable Content Seminars, shared with us the intellectual exhilaration and the complex collaboration required to develop projects and articulate principles. For most of us, this was our first time working in teams that included all levels of the educational system, from students in undergraduate programs through master's and PhD students. For the students, it was also a first: Most were accustomed to having one professor in the classroom with an already developed knowledge base. In the Usable Content Seminars, they had seven of us around the table, none of us claiming to have the whole picture or already know the answer. It was quite a ride.

Cheryl Geisler, Simon Fraser University, Project Coordinator
Roger Grice, Rensselaer Polytechnic Institute, Usability Testing
James P. Zappen, Rensselaer Polytechnic Institute, Information Galleries for Young People
Jan W. Fernheimer, University of Kentucky, Wikis for Collaboration
Patricia Search, Rensselaer Polytechnic Institute, Cultural Websites
Robert Krull, Rensselaer Polytechnic Institute (retired), Usability for Distance Education
Audrey Bennett, Rensselaer Polytechnic Institute, Interactive Image

Design for Diverse Users

James P. Zappen

To design for diverse users is to recognize that nothing is intuitive to everybody. Once the designer gives up the impossible ideal of designing a match between diverse users' needs and system affordances, the design agenda moves toward developing a set of differential experiences. In designing and redesigning a photo gallery as part of a youth-services information system, Zappen and his team addressed the design challenges of creating differential user experiences.

The Concept of the User

Users of web-based communication systems are not like *audiences* or even *users* in the traditional sense of these terms (Brinck, Gergle, & Wood, 2002, pp. 1–11; Nielsen, 1993, pp. 26–37). Increasingly via the Internet and the World Wide Web, they are users who are also potential contributors or producers who modify systems to meet their own needs (Johnson, 1998, pp. 25–40, 43–67; Spinuzzi, 2003, pp. 1–23); contribute and retrieve content from systems (Bruns, 2008, pp. 9–36; Tapscott & Williams, 2006, pp. 124–150); and interact with systems and with other users (Potts, 2009; Warnick, 2005, 2007, pp. 69–90).

Users in this new and enlarged sense are not constant even for any one system but change and emerge in time and space and are subject to varying conditions of reception (Warnick, 2007, pp. 25–44). Unlike audiences of a speech or a performance, they often experience systems as individuals, in isolation from each other. Unlike readers of a book or a magazine, they interact with systems and sometimes also with each other. Moreover, given differences such as age, gender, ethnicity, literacy, and technical experience and expertise, a diversity of users is virtually inevitable. As a consequence, no system and no interaction will be intuitive for every user. Designers, therefore, need to provide a variety of system capabilities and user options, and perhaps even invite users to modify systems, to accommodate these differences. They also need to test systems with sensitivity to these differences in both users and the contexts of use.

Traditional approaches to usability emphasize functionality and efficiency in the performance of user tasks. These approaches advocate a fundamental shift from a system to a user orientation. Nielsen (1993, p. 26) emphasizes features such as system learnability, efficiency, memorability, and reliability ("a low error rate") and user satisfaction—all directed toward user performance and productivity. Brinck, Gergle, & Wood (2002, pp. 2–3) offer a virtually identical set of features for web-based systems, which should, they argue, be "functionally correct," "efficient to use," "easy to learn," "easy to remember," "error tolerant," and "subjectively pleasing."

More recent approaches to usability envision a more active role for users in system development both before and after implementation. Johnson (1998, pp. 31–33) urges not only a shift from systems to users but an expansion of user roles to respect the knowledge that users bring to systems and to embrace their activities of *"learning, doing,* and *producing."* Whereas traditional approaches to usability emphasize learning and doing—that is, learning a system and using it to perform a specific task—Johnson's expanded view emphasizes users' more active role in producing systems—that is, developing and maintaining systems and thus taking part *"in a negotiated process of technology design, development, and use"* (p. 32). To illustrate, Johnson recalls the University of Washington study of Seattle's traffic-flow problem, which suggested that *"the traffic problems might be best addressed by giving people daily information about traffic patterns so they could make choices about which route to take on a given trip"* (p. 65).

Spinuzzi (2003, pp. 1–5, 18–22) urges a still more active role for system users that recognizes users' creative adaptations both before and after system implementation. Unlike traditional approaches to user-centered design, which leave the designer in control and devalue the user as "victim," Spinuzzi recognizes users' creative contributions to system development: "Workers produce solutions that are devious, wily, and cunning, . . . solutions that work"—though he also recognizes that workers frequently need designers to promulgate their solutions "so that other workers can take advantage of them" (pp. 8–9, 19–20). This recognition of the more active role of users as producers seems prescient, given recent developments in web-based information systems.

The blurring or merging of the roles of user and producer has deep roots. Barthes (1977, p. 148) maintains that a text is not singular but multiple and that its locus of meaning is not the author but the reader:

> A text is made of multiple writings, drawn from many cultures and entering into mutual relations of dialogue, parody, contestation, but there is one place where this multiplicity is focused and that place is the reader, not, as was hitherto said, the author.

Drawing upon Barthes's insight, Warnick (2005, pp. 330–331) argues that a web-based text is similarly diffuse and dispersed—"a de-centered 'tissue of quotations drawn from innumerable centres of culture.'" Moreover, she argues, the entire context of information exchange fundamentally changes in a web-based environment: Authors are typically not singular and readily identifiable but corporate, multiple, or simply unknown to us; readers/users, in a sense, become authors by choosing their own paths through a hypertext; texts are not only texts but a complex mix of media forms; and readers/users are no longer mass audiences but individuals with attitudes, values, and beliefs largely unknown and unknowable, dispersed in time and space and subject to the constraints of widely varying systems of access (Warnick, 2007, pp. 28–41).

The advent of newer web-based information systems—the so-called Web 2.0, the new web, the social web—exacerbates these changes and further blurs the line between users and producers. Tapscott and Williams (2006, p. 37) explain that "the new Web is principally about participating rather than about passively receiving information." It is "a global infrastructure for creativity, participation, sharing, and self-organization." To illustrate, they describe the old web as a digital newspaper, the new web as a shared canvas: "Instead of a digital newspaper, think of a shared canvas where every splash of paint contributed by one user provides a richer tapestry for the next user to modify or build on" (p. 37). To extend the illustration, we might recall the Seattle traffic study referenced above: In a traditional communication model, traffic controllers would distribute traffic information to motorists, who would then be able to make informed decisions about their travel; in the new and complex digital communication environment, motorists themselves could communicate immediate (not daily) traffic updates to a central system for electronic posting or directly to each other via a variety of mobile devices.

Bruns (2008, pp. 15–23) captures these new users/producers in his description of "produsers" who both use and produce information. According to Bruns, produsers openly participate and communally share, examine, and evaluate information; operate in a fluid heterarchy in which anyone can contribute; engage in projects that are not holistic but granular, modular, and always unfinished, in "an openly accessible information commons"; and share information as common property even as they reap individual rewards from their participation (pp. 23–30). To illustrate this new communication environment and the new user as a user/producer of information, we might complicate the relatively simple traffic-flow situation by referencing the more complex instance of a disaster situation in which the normal routes of traffic and communication are disrupted.

Potts (2009) documents the uses of the new communication technologies in her case studies of several such disasters. She notes the limitations of the Hurricane Katrina CNN Safe List, for example, which posted valuable information but did not permit everyday users "to interact with the system to add important details, edit names, locate duplicates, or point out incorrect entries" (p. 283). She notes similar potentials and problems in the uses of Flickr during the aftermath of the London bombings, such as the instance of a user who was able to locate a loved one in a photo but was unable to post a comment (pp. 292–293). To address these problems, she concludes, we need enhanced social software tools "for coordinating and authenticating information, especially across multiple platforms and disparate systems" (p. 294).

Given this new and complex communication environment, designers need to recognize the inevitability of diverse users (and users/producers) and to design systems accordingly; to assume that no system is intuitive to everyone, either to users or to themselves; and to provide a variety of system options, including options that permit users to contribute and share information with each other. For diverse users, therefore, a system might be several systems, or several interfaces, not one; it might, and probably will, change dynamically over time; and it might be experienced differently by different users in different contexts of use. Testing of such complex systems, therefore, also needs to be sensitive to these differences.

Users of the Connected Kids Gallery

The Connected Kids information system (http://connectedkids.rpi.edu/index.php/) addresses these differences among kinds of system users. Designed as a youth-services information system for Troy and Rensselaer County, New York, Connected Kids initially included a single image gallery for children that seemed to be natural and intuitive for these users. However, when we tested this original design with older users—college students—we found that these users expected much more sophisticated system functionalities and user options. We therefore retained the image gallery for children and designed a new gallery as a photo and information gallery for teens and adults, with a range of options suited to the needs and expectations of these older users.

Recognizing That Nothing Is Intuitive for Everyone

In the process of testing, we recognized that what was natural and intuitive for younger users was not so intuitive for older users. We also recognized that we could not test a system designed for younger users with older users and expect to get meaningful results for younger users. Our intuitive hunch that we could test with average or typical users turned out to be counterintuitive. We cannot, therefore, conclude with confidence that the children's gallery either does or does not offer a quality experience for younger users, and we continue to make this gallery accessible to parents and children as a component of the larger system. We can, however, conclude that the children's image gallery is not suitable for teens and adults, so we designed a new gallery for these users.

Designing for the Inevitability of Diverse Users

Given our recognition of the diverse experiences of users of different age groups, we determined that we needed two distinct galleries, not one. Our original design of the image gallery for children included drawings and photos of children's activities representing several local youth-services organizations, including schools, after-school programs, and public libraries, plus a collection of images about local art, culture, and history, as shown in Figure 1.1. The images were arranged in three main groups: one for artwork, one for photos, and one for art and history. Within these groups, the images were arranged by organization, primarily to serve the organizations' publicity needs, and presented in simple slide shows, with a main page for navigation. We initially tested the children's gallery for functionality and efficiency in the execution of user tasks, such as retrieving an image of a particular type, and, largely as a convenience, we tested with college students, readily available in our classes. For these users, according to the results of the heuristic testing, the original gallery seemed "very casual and not task oriented," more like "slide shows rather than true 'galleries,'" "very linear" with "no hierarchy of information, no search functions, no category scheme or navigation system to assist users in finding images," no "library of types of images and thumbnail images," and "no help functions or contact information."

Given these results, and aware that our users would likely include teens of high school age as well as children of grade school and middle school age, we developed the first redesign of the gallery as a photo and information gallery for teens and adults, as shown in Figure 1.2. This new gallery deployed state-of-the-art open-source gallery software (http://galleryproject.org/), with search functions, breadcrumbs, thumbnails,

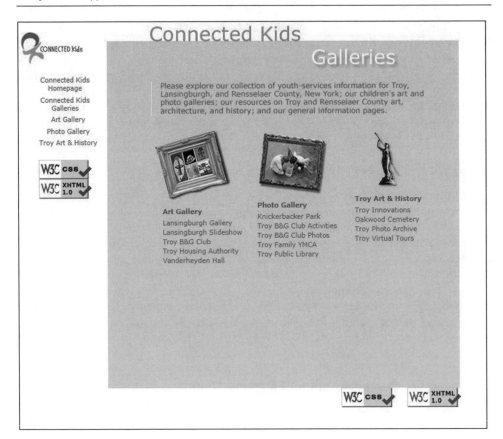

Figure 1.1 Original design of the image gallery for children. Used with permission of Sin-Hwa Kang.

a slide show, show-and-hide text, and caption and comment functions to permit at least minimal user-system and user-user interactions.

We then conducted comparative user testing, this time with a wider range of users, from children to adults, with the expectation that we would test the next iteration of the gallery with high school students. According to the test report, users found the first redesign to be "a significant improvement over the original exemplar." Not surprisingly, however, they also concluded that the gallery seemed to be designed for "adults, not children," and seemed to require "more interactive audio and video features," "more rich contrasting colors," and more "visual draw" to hold the attention of children. In addition, they identified a number of functionality/efficiency issues and a need for more dynamic content and more opportunities for collaboration in the form of user-generated content, including audio and video content, interactive components such as games, links to more information, mechanisms for sharing gallery content and other information resources, and opportunities for users to upload their own content.

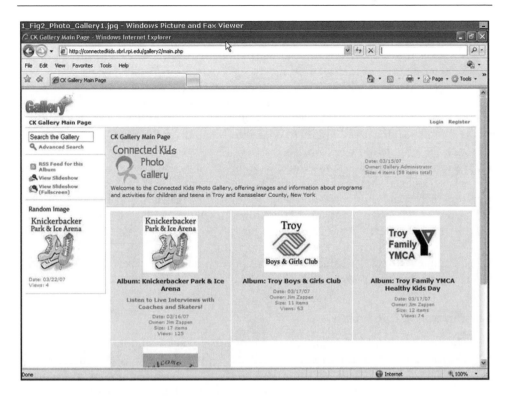

Figure 1.2 First redesign of the photo gallery for teens and adults.

Providing Options for Differential Experiences

These results emphasize the need to understand the different expectations of diverse users, to test with sensitivity to these differences, and to provide options suitable to each user group. In heuristic testing, college students seemed to bring to the children's image gallery their own experience with more sophisticated gallery software. In comparative user testing, a wider range of users seemed to bring to the photo gallery designed for teens and adults an awareness of the experiences and expectations of younger children. In the second redesign of the photo gallery, therefore, we decided to design for high school students, to test with this group specifically, and to provide options suitable to them. We return to this second redesign in Principle 7 and Case Study 1.

Designing for Diverse User Experiences

The changing concept of the user and the inevitability of diverse user experiences suggest that designers may need to develop multiple options to meet the needs of a variety of user groups. Recognizing that nothing is intuitive to everyone, they may also need to assess and reassess these options throughout the design process, from initial concept through testing to redesign. Specifically, designers need to:

- Recognize the need to design for diverse users and users/producers, not for a typical user or a mass audience.
- Anticipate the need to design several systems, or several interfaces, not just one.
- Design not only for system efficiency and functionality in the performance of user tasks but also for users' ability to contribute content and to engage in interactions with the system and with other users.
- Test each system, or each interface, with the specific users or user groups for which it was designed, not for an assumed average or typical user.
- Test each system, or each interface, not only for efficiency and functionality but also users' ability to contribute content and to engage with other users.
- Examine each test situation to determine the peculiarities of users, their prior experience, and their modes of system access and use.
- Examine their own assumptions as designers/testers and never assume that anything is intuitive to anyone, including themselves.

For Further Exploration

1. The newly released Caltrans QuickMap (http://quickmap.dot.ca.gov/) seems to be exactly the kind of user experience that Zappen cites Johnson calling for: one that provides users with real-time data on traffic patterns so they can make better choices in planning their own routes. According to the press release announcing its launch (Caltrans, 2012), "Visitors to the online interactive travel map can access nearly 1,000 freeway cameras and more than 700 electronic message signs on highways statewide. They can also monitor traffic congestion, California Highway Patrol incidents, travel time information, lane closures due to highway roadwork, and Amber Alerts. Other helpful features of the service include chain control information and color-coded traffic speed displays for freeways statewide." How does the QuickMap support active users? Can you imagine ways to make it more engaging? Do you see ways in which the map is designed for diverse users, as Zappen recommends?

2. Zappen mentions Potts's work on the use of communication technologies in natural disasters. Potts's more recent work explores the use of Twitter in natural disasters. In particular, Potts, Seitzinger, Jones, and Harrison (2011) have provided an analysis of hashtags during the New Zealand earthquake of 2010 and the earthquake in Japan in 2011. Consider their recommendation that folksonomies are key to supporting diverse users in the wake of natural disasters. Can you imagine how these flexible methods of categorization might be useful in engaging diverse users?

3. *National Geographic Kids* offers a photo gallery (http://kids-myshot.nationalgeographic.com/) where kids can view, upload, and comment on photographs. *National Geographic* offers adults a similar site (http://ngm.nationalgeographic.com/myshot/). On both sites, for instance, users can make and solve a jigsaw puzzle from a photo. How does National Geographic go about adapting to these diverse users?

Design for Usability

Janice W. Fernheimer

To design for usability is to follow general guidelines where available. Recognizing that users will draw on past experiences, the designer needs to build on familiar conventions for usability—orienting users, making things easy, and keeping things consistent. In the world of web-based communication, the traditional conventions for usability remain the starting point for design even when design goes beyond the familiar. In designing a wiki to support deep collaboration, Fernheimer and her team struggled to build a design that would capitalize on familiar conventions for editing while also encouraging users to engage in unfamiliar collaborative practices.

The Concept of Usability

The design for usability principle suggests that web-based communications function best when they:

- follow standard usability guidelines
- make things readable
- use professional-quality design components
- follow general conventions when available
- provide simple ways for users to do what they want or need to do.

Designing for usability encourages designers to create materials that allow users to build upon prior experiences and knowledge to learn, adapt, and assimilate new processes, applications, and interfaces more quickly. While these suggestions might seem easy enough to enact when creating traditional technical communication materials (public documents, press releases, instructions), which reflect and generate user expectations based on past interactions, what happens to usability when the system encourages users to engage in practices that are entirely new or unfamiliar?

The Wikis for Collaboration Team attempted to answer this question as it relates to wikis and the ways they might be successfully incorporated into classroom writing instruction to encourage collaborative writing. In the early stages of developing this exemplar, the team encountered a number of issues related to usability and wikis' confusing status as both web pages and writing platforms. While this status was what led our team to be interested in their capability for fostering collaboration, it was also the source of important usability issues during initial testing and implementation.

Wikis for Collaboration

At first glance, wikis appear to be like any other web page: A user accesses them with a web browser and a connection to the Internet, clicks on links to find related information, and relies upon web navigation tools to move through the space. But unlike other web pages, wikis allow users to create as well as access information. As such, they expand the range of possible authors by providing a tool that enables all users to contribute to web-based content rather than only those authors who initially created and published the site. As tools for collaborative authoring, they foster an environment for collaborative knowledge production where many individual users can make small changes in iterative, incremental steps.

The assumption behind this type of collective knowledge construction is that the sheer volume of user contributions becomes larger and more valuable than the sum of the individual parts. This tendency is perhaps most recognizable in the well-known (albeit controversial for this very reason), Wikipedia, a collaboratively authored on-line encyclopedia written in a wiki using the MediaWiki software. Since Wikipedia has been dubbed largely successful, with millions of articles authored in a variety of languages, wikis are often touted as the key to successful group writing in business, science, and educational environments (Moxley & Meehan, 2007; Carr et al., 2007; Garza & Hern, 2006; Chen et al., 2005; Hamilton, 2000; Kussmaul, Howe, & Priest, 2006).

But most users access Wikipedia as readers, not as contributors. Although users may be familiar with the term *wiki* and they may loosely associate collaborative writing with it, they may not fully understand how this web genre works, much less how they might be able to contribute to it. In this type of situation, the concept of usability takes on a slightly different imperative, as designers must educate users not only about the applications they design but also the epistemological assumptions they enact and facilitate. Moreover, designers are tasked with accomplishing these goals in a way that seems intuitive.

Designing a Usable Wiki

When we began the project in fall 2006, wikis were rapidly becoming a familiar web genre, but they had not yet been broadly adopted in educational contexts generally or in university writing classrooms more specifically. We wondered how best to design a wiki that would encourage students to willingly share and participate in this medium for class writing purposes. The following questions guided our initial investigation:

- What might motivate students to write collectively when traditionally they are evaluated in terms of individual contributions?
- What kinds of privacy concerns might they have, since the wiki enables them to share work in progress with other classmates and the broader audience the Internet provides?
- How would they establish group authoring procedures to encourage shared editing without the fear of deleting text or ideas another group member deemed valuable?

To solicit information that would help to address these concerns, our team designed and implemented a wiki to be tested by a group of student users in spring 2007. Over the course of several rounds of testing and implementation, we refined our goals to focus on the ways context affects the degree to which wikis are successful, a topic elaborated upon in a later chapter.

Initially our efforts focused on choosing and modifying open-source freeware to meet the needs of the writing classroom. We began our work in MediaWiki, the same software used to power Wikipedia, because we hoped users' familiarity with the interface (navigation and search on the left, discussion, edit, and history tabs at the top) from reading the online encyclopedia would translate into their ease of use in editing pages. We hoped users would be both motivated and able to add new pages, update other pages, contribute information they deemed relevant to other participants, and feel welcomed by the site.

We encountered early difficulties in customizing the page, because the MediaWiki platform provided few affordances for modifying the layout and design of the site. The logo area in the upper left-hand corner of the screen was the only graphical element that we could change, and the size was constrained to a predetermined dimension (see Figure 0.8).

The original design we created included a main page welcoming the user to the wiki and offering a brief explanation of the site's purpose ("to discover the ways that wikis can be used to facilitate collaboration and team work"), links for each team to communicate with one another, and an extensive help page that could be accessed from the left navigation bar. Not surprisingly, several of our testers later described the site as "utilitarian" and "stark."

We quickly discovered that users interacted with the site in ways similar to how they approached and interacted with traditional web pages. In the initial design, some users had difficulty discerning page elements that were links, because the links blended in with the overall body copy of the content. Since the links did not follow traditional web page conventions, where links are designated by underline and blue color, some users failed to recognize links as links. Users were, however, able to follow the appropriate links when they appeared in more traditional navigation schemes such as the left bar and the tabs at the top of the page. Additionally, users did not like reading large blocks of text. When we redesigned the page for the next stage of testing, we took this feedback into account and made an effort to format in-page links in a more visible way and to break up large blocks of text into smaller chunks by using more headings, bullet points, and lists. One strategy for making wikis more usable is to follow traditional conventions for web texts.

Aside from these simple changes, we also learned that part of the usability difficulties our exemplar encountered were due to the unique syntax required to edit content on the wiki. While some of the editing tools were familiar, such as formatting bold and italic text, MediaWiki's editing markup differs significantly from standard HTML, with which some of the users were familiar. Most of the other functions on the editing toolbar were nonstandard and caused confusion because they did not correspond with traditional desktop word-processing metaphors, which new users expected to accompany the text tools and display window. During the first-round testing process, users found it difficult to understand how to edit the pages—a fundamental task in achieving the goals of collaborative knowledge construction—because of the difficulties with wiki syntax. When faced with these challenges, users were more likely to give up in frustration than consult the help page of documentation we had constructed to aid them in this process. We learned that rather than creating a separate help section for users, it is best to provide help information or specific directions in context. In other words, another strategy for making wikis more usable is to provide explanatory information in smaller chunks embedded within the pages or areas where they would be most useful to the user.

To address some of these usability concerns, we opted to change wiki platforms for the prototype's first redesign. We redesigned the wiki in Twiki because it offered our team greater control over the general look and feel of the wiki and a more usable WYSI-WYG editing tool, which allowed users to create headings, change text styles, and create links without having to learn wiki markup syntax. The redesign paid close attention to traditional web usability standards using color and underlines to differentiate links from the rest of the content, bulleted lists where appropriate, and headings to break up large chunks of text. Additionally, we made a concerted effort to make the home page welcoming by including more images and providing more context-sensitive help in easy-to-read chunks on it as well as other appropriate pages, as can be seen in Figure 2.1.

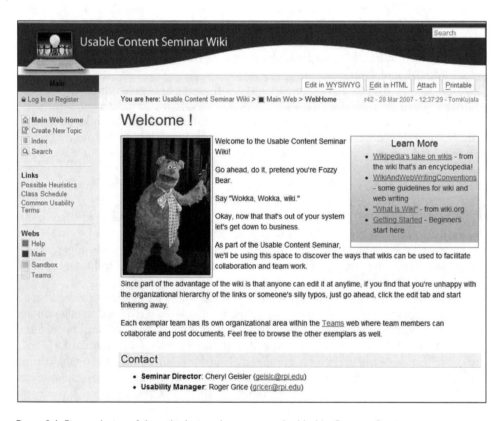

Figure 2.1 First redesign of the wiki designed to support the Usable Content Seminar.

These attempts to better meet traditional expectations for websites were met with moderate success. During second round of testing, all users were able to contribute something to a page through the editing process on the Twiki prototype, something that had not happened with the old MediaWiki prototype. Twiki users had no problem easily locating the "Create New Topic" link that we provided, while users of the MediaWiki prototype were confused by the various ways that a page could be created. Nevertheless, while our attempts to respond to the initial concerns were somewhat successful, new problems emerged. Users were unable to distinguish important from nonessential links both within and across pages. They were confused by the naming conventions associated with Twiki topics, especially the "Wikiwords" and the specially formatted strings that Twiki used to indentify internal pages and links. They did not understand the full meaning of selecting a parent topic, and at times randomly chose topics that were not the best contextual choices. Finally, while Twiki users who were familiar with WYSIWYG terminology appreciated the ability to edit using this tool, there was still some confusion since many users unfamiliar with the term WYSI-WYG chose to edit in HTML simply because the term was more familiar to them. In other words, they wanted WYSIWYG functionality but were unable to recognize or use it when it was presented to them because they lacked a shared vocabulary to identify it.

Even more important than these usability issues concerning navigation, link identification, and editing were users' complaints focused on the wikis' actual content. In both prototypes users expressed difficulty connecting with the information on the site, and they reported low motivation to complete the various tasks. From this observation our team learned the most important thing of all, which is that wikis, no matter how usable they might appear, are entirely dependent on the communities who populate them. Our users had no real motivation to participate in these wiki spaces without a real collaborative task. In other words, we learned that an important part of making a web-based communication usable is community context, a topic to which we will turn in a later chapter

Designing for Usability

Designing for usability in engaging web-based communication asks designers to build on what users know and to help them learn new genres and the epistemological assumptions that gird them by building on familiar frameworks. For example, when working in a web environment, designers should employ traditional web writing conventions by chunking text and using visual cues (fonts, headings, bulleted lists, spacing) to make text more readable and help users determine what is important. And when encouraging users to learn to contribute to and not simply read a web page, editing functions should be based upon and reflect common word-processing metaphors and capabilities. Many web-based communication environments like the wiki for collaboration, call on users to engage in new and challenging practices, but users will nevertheless rely on a base of familiar conventions and practices as they make their ways in these new environments. The designer's challenge is to identify and build on the old while imagining the new.

For Further Exploration

1. Although Wikipedia's comparison of wiki software suggests that most software now provides a WYSIWYG option (Comparison of wiki software, n.d.), many wiki developers still struggle with the issue of how to support editing in a way that users will accept. Marc Laporte and colleagues (2012) discuss the pros and cons of wiki markup and WYSIWYG at http://tiki.org/Why%20Wiki%20Syntax%20 Is%20Important. Can you think of other instances where functionality and user expectations are at odds with each other? What principles might you invoke to resolve these kinds of conflicts?

2. The U.S. government has an extensive set of usability guidelines at http://guide lines.usability.gov/. Chapter 10 of that document, dealing with links, cautions, "Provide sufficient clues to clearly indicate to users that an item is clickable." As described in this chapter, Fernheimer's first wiki interface clearly had problems stemming from violating this guideline. Make a list of the other issues that Fernheimer's team encountered. Which ones are addressed in the government guidelines? Which ones are not addressed? In general, how might we expect guidelines to change over time?

Test the Backbone

Robert Krull

The usability of web-based communications meant to engage is affected by the supporting hardware and software backbone. Using distance learning as a demonstration case, this chapter describes the importance of ensuring that appropriate backbone components are available to users, that the set-up time for those components is reasonable, and that the experience users have with the system is a positive one.

The Concept of Technological Backbones

When we discover that we are out of milk or beer, we can jump in the car, turn the key, and drive off. When starting our computers, we can push the power button and wait for the operating system to load itself and to enable our mouse, video monitor, and printer to do our bidding.

By comparison, getting ready to take a distance-learning course often demands a considerably more extended and complex process. After booting up our computers, learners may then have to spend another half hour loading a web browser, navigating past a security gateway, and launching one or two more specialized software programs. In addition, they may have to manipulate a microphone, change audio volume, and tell software about their web cameras. As the session continues, the brittleness of this backbone may require learners to shut down and relaunch hardware and software that have frozen up.

Hmm. Why is it simpler to boot up our cars than to start taking a distance-learning course?

Of course, cars and education weren't always in these comparative positions. In the early 20th century, getting ready to drive was more complex than it is now. Drivers needed to start the engine by cranking it with a lever, and then had to adjust the spark-plug timing and the ratio of gas to air passing through the carburetor. At the same time period, distance learning through correspondence courses involved exchanging information via the mail.

As this comparison illustrates, technological backbones change over time, and as they change, so do our expectations about what is possible. When we design and test the backbones for web-based communications such as distance education, we need to take into account both the state of technology and of our users' expectations. Doing so requires looking at usability in three areas: the components making up the backbone, the time required for users to set up the backbone, and users' experience using the backbone.

Selecting Backbone Components

The first step in designing a usable backbone is to specify the needed components. In providing education to working professionals at Rensselaer Polytechnic Institute (RPI), we had a 50-year history to draw on. In fact, in just the past 10 years, we have used four different technology platforms, as shown in Table 3.1.

To illustrate the implications of testing for the backbone, let's look at three examples: satellite, videoconferencing, and the Internet-based multiwindow platform.

The main advantage of a satellite backbone is its ability to deliver high-fidelity video and audio downstream from instructors to learners. Learners can clearly see instructors and learners in a face-to-face classroom, images of computer interfaces, and full-motion video recordings. If there is a budget for the specialized facilities required to send and receive satellite signals and a technical support staff to operate the equipment, then learners are not involved in running hardware, downloading software, or making any equipment work.

Aside from cost and complexity of the equipment, RPI found that the satellite backbone had a more fundamental problem: It failed to supply an upstream flow of information from learners to instructors. A satellite link generally does not provide for an upstream flow of information. To compensate, learners used telephones to talk

Table 3.1 Distance-learning platforms used over time at Rensselaer Polytechnic Institute.

Technology	Advantages	Disadvantages
Videotapes and CDs	• High-fidelity video and audio downstream • Cheaper delivery than for satellite • Much lower reception cost than satellite or videoconferencing • Comparatively inexpensive to produce if the content is just recording of live classes	• No upstream media • Time delay for delivery • Just watching live classes without being able to participate is demotivating for learners
Satellite	• High-fidelity video and audio downstream • Synchronous delivery	• No upstream media available • Very high cost
Videoconferencing	• Moderate fidelity video and audio both downstream and upstream • Cheaper delivery than satellite • Lower reception cost than satellite • Shorter time delay than mailed media	• Less downstream fidelity than satellite and video recordings • Several-second delay in conversational exchanges • Expensive reception facilities
Internet	• Multiple windows and media (instant messaging text, slide presenter, classroom audio downstream, application sharing to demo software, VoIP for live audio) for downstream delivery • Cheaper than satellite and videoconferencing	• Complex for instructors to learn • Content must be compressed for Internet bandwidth • Upstream communication pushes the limits of the platform and makes it brittle • Learners need to provide their own technical support

VoIP is Voice over Internet Protocol, a means of distributing compressed audio over the Internet.

to instructors. Unfortunately, not all satellite receiving facilities make available telephones at a reasonable cost for student use.

Compared to satellites, videoconferencing is an improvement by providing bidirectional communication. Instructors and learners can see and hear each other, thereby supporting interaction to face-to-face communication. The technical disadvantage of videoconferencing is that images and sound tend to be low in fidelity and slightly delayed in time. This means that faces can't be seen as clearly or voices heard as distinctly as over satellites; and conversations with seven-second transmission delays feel awkward. Finally, videoconferencing may not be as expensive as satellites, but it demands more expensive technical staffs and facilities than does Internet delivery.

Upper-end Internet-based learning platforms can provide bidirectional communication for audio and, to a limited extent, for video. Multiwindowed learning platforms such as Elluminate (now incorporated into Blackboard Collaborate; see http://www.blackboard.com/Platforms/Collaborate/Overview.aspx) and Adobe Connect (see http://www.adobe.com/products/adobeconnect.html) provide downstream signals for text-based chat, presentation slides, images from application software, and live video and audio. They also can send information upstream from learners, though with lower fidelity. The more complex forms of these systems may require institutions to supply expensive downstream facilities, such as classrooms, cameras, and the support staff to run them, but the costs to learners of receiving instructional material are modest. On the other hand, if many instructional sessions operate simultaneously, institutions may need to upgrade their broadband Internet trunks.

For learners, web-based instructional systems provide a mixture of advantages and disadvantages. For example, as mentioned, one prime educational advantage is that learners can send information upstream to instructors and other learners. But these systems also embody several disadvantages. First, the low fidelity of web-based media makes it difficult to see and hear content clearly. Images of instructors are small, fuzzy, and delayed up to a minute behind action in the live classroom. This can render important instructional information unreadable, inaudible, and unwatchable. Second, because learners must provide and maintain their own network connections, computers, and software, the overhead of learning greatly increases. Learners may need 20 minutes in advance of class sessions just to get the backbone running and may need to fiddle with the backbone during sessions as well. Particularly when the capacity of the backbone is pushed to its limits, learners' connections to the system are likely to break. As a result, learners may miss important instructional content.

In summary, downstream satellite distribution may produce high fidelity, but it is very expensive to buy and maintain and does not provide upstream communication. Videoconferencing provides adequate fidelity downstream and upstream, but also is expensive. Web-based distribution is less expensive than other systems, but it does allow downstream and upstream communication. Internet distribution also may shift expenses and psychological overhead to learners.

Of course, even once a backbone framework has been selected, other detailed decisions must be made. For example, a large organization such as the Society for Technical Communication and an individual subject matter expert (SME) may both decide to use the Internet to deliver training. But the large organization and the SME may have different aims and resources. The large organization may want to support a large number of training sessions, with many participants, and with minimal support cost.

The SME may want to offer one kind of training course on a periodic basis to a small number of technically skilled learners.

If both the organization and the SME decide to offer Web video, what should they decide about whether to use the video to show instructors' faces? Should the camera be capable of producing five-megabyte images or would one-megabyte images suffice? Will learners have the equipment necessary to view the images? Would learners think that seeing the instructors' faces would be necessary, optional, or detrimental to learning? Would they prefer hearing high-fidelity audio to hearing low-fidelity audio accompanied by video images?

Setting up the Backbone

Once we have chosen the components of the backbone of a web-based communication, we should move on to considering how much effort it takes to set up. Set-up time can include time for users to connect, time to download, and time to troubleshoot. In an ideal situation, users should set up their backbone just once. For example, users of Microsoft Word would not be very happy if they had to reinstall Word every time they used it.

Generally, users of complex distance-learning systems don't need to reconnect hardware each time they use it, and they don't need to download software except for periodic updates. In many current Internet-distributed platforms, however, we found that learners may need 20 minutes in advance of class sessions just to get the backbone running. So, when choosing a hardware and software platform, a professional association or an individual instructor probably should weigh the educational benefits of the complex technology versus the overhead that technology places on learners. How many minutes should learners be expected to spend getting set up for a seminar?

Making Sure the Backbone Works

Although careful analysis can guide the choice of a backbone for a web-based communication system, how such a system actually works in practice depends on the interaction among many variables. Sometimes it's possible to guess how the backbone will perform based on the experience of other users. For example, when the target users are professional associations and SMEs in technical communication, the backbone may be stressed in different ways than if the users are less technically inclined. To get informal information about that target audience, one could do some low-level market analysis (such as casual interviews with technical writers at a local meeting), which could provide hints about the kind of delivery system learners would prefer. To get more detailed information about instructional design, one could scan the research literature in that area (for example, Alessi & Trollip, 2000; Clark & Mayer, 2008; Gagné, Briggs, & Wager, 1992; Horton, 2000; Horton & Horton, 2003). After all this reading, one may find some useful tips, but also may find that research findings aren't consistent about technology and that even the instructional design theories need to be updated to the current state of technology and training practices (e.g., Carliner, 2008).

Because RPI was moving several hundred graduate students through its electronically supported distance-education program, it was worthwhile going beyond the existing research literature to conducting additional studies of its own. Case Study 4 describes this research in greater detail. This chapter will discuss only a couple of illustrative findings related specifically to the hardware and software backbone.

William Wetmore and Louis Ruggiero, two distance students enrolled in the RPI program, produced an extensive questionnaire at the time that RPI was switching to Internet-based delivery. Their data show that the backbone makes a significant difference in students' educational experience.

For example, distance students had access to text chat during class sessions, but students in the on-campus classroom did not. The result was that distance students had more peer-to-peer interaction during classes than did face-to-face students. On-campus students found their opportunities for collaborative learning limited.

This difference in backbone components led, in fact, to the development of separate communication networks for the on-campus and distance students. For example, on-campus students reported feeling more comfortable asking other on-campus students for information about classes; distance students reported doing the same thing with other distance students. We called this segmentation the "parallel universe" of distance education. Once reliable WiFi service became available in the on-campus classroom, however, on-campus students added text chat to their classroom backbone so that they could join in the real-time interactions with distance students. In fact, some on-campus students so preferred the distance environment that they started taking courses from home.

As indicated earlier, questionnaire data provided important information about differences in backbone use between on-campus students and those at a distance. Once the combination of media used by distance classes became more complex, however, we were no longer able to get enough information about student performance from survey questionnaires alone.

When RPI moved from the Elluminate platform to Adobe Connect, we took advantage of the opportunity to compare backbones by observing how instructors and learners responded to platform brittleness. To do so, we observed on-campus classes in person and watched distance students both in person and via the Internet-based learning platform. We found that distance students in particular spent so much time fiddling with the backbone that they had somewhat less time and energy left for the actual course content.

Crankiness of the audio component in particular often affected the manner in which participants conversed with each other and with instructors. For example, at different times the audio system had small or large time delays, no echoes or feedback or obnoxious echoes or feedback, and reliable connections or frail connections. This meant that speakers would stop to ask if other people could hear them, and it meant that listeners would not toss in small confirmations that they heard speakers because confirmations would overlap subsequent comments made by speakers. Some participants tried out several audio technologies in search of a system that was reliable. Since audio has been a part of computer functionality for 15 to 20 years, shouldn't it have become a reliable component of the backbone by now?

Another backbone component we explored was the use of the electronic whiteboards. Instructional design research has shown that students learn best when they applying theory to concrete design decisions. For this reason, we often incorporated workshop time into our classes to give students time to work in small groups on small problems. Our classroom observations suggested that the electronic whiteboards provided with the distance classroom platforms did not work well because they did not conform to the common interface standards. We decided to dig more deeply into that problem by conducting virtual laboratory tests.

In our virtual laboratory tests, we asked students who were working in separate locations to collaborate on workshop problems using electronic whiteboards from two manufacturers. We provided them with the opportunity to use live audio provided by the platforms in addition the text chat they normally had available in classes. Our results confirmed the problems that nonstandard user interaction produced for students. But the testing also revealed that live audio was greatly preferred to text chat as a way for students to talk about what to put on the whiteboards. While audio could be brittle and the loss of audio often frustrated participants, they very much wanted live audio to be part of the distance backbone.

Testing the Backbone

This chapter has described the value of testing the backbone's contribution to the user experience in web-based communication. Such testing can reveal which components are perceived to be essential to the web-based communication meant to engage, how long they take to set up, and how well they worked in use. In the case of distance learning, our survey questionnaires, observations of user performance, and virtual laboratory tests of specific components revealed much more about the perceptions and behavior of learners than could be gleaned by instructors from interactions with students or even from course evaluations. Although the example used in this chapter was distance learning, testing the backbone of any web-based communication meant to engage is important. Such information can be used to set backbone specifications that match user desires, goals, and performance.

For Further Exploration

1. Massive open online courses like those from Coursera (https://www.coursera.org/) claim to represent the next wave of distance education. How do the backbone requirements of these courses compare to Internet-based courses that Krull analyzes in this chapter and those delivered through web-based platforms like Adobe Connect (http://www.adobe.com/products/adobeconnect.edu.html)?
2. Krull describes using virtual laboratory tests to analyze the backbone needs of students collaborating with each other at a distance. This is a version of the remote usability testing described by Gough and Phillips (2009; http://www.boxesandarrows.com/view/remote_online_usability_testing_why_how_and_when_to_use_it). These authors claim this method has the advantage of efficiency, but at the cost of insight. Do you agree or disagree? What other options might you consider for observing web-mediated interactions among users?

Extend a Welcome

Patricia Search

Interface design guidelines emphasize the importance of designing for a specific audience. However, users of today's web-based communications often include many people who are not part of a target audience. Users visit websites to get information about new products or to explore new artistic, social, and cultural ideas. As a result, interface designers must find ways to engage a broad audience. Search and her team explore how multisensory and personal experiences can be used to make the audience feel welcome in cultural websites.

The Concept of Cross-Cultural Communication

With global networking, designers of engaging web-based communication need to address a broad audience with diverse cultural perspectives. Interface designs can reflect specific social structures that define how individuals and organizations interact and communicate with each other. The research of Edward Hall, Geert Hofstede, and Aaron Marcus creates a foundation for understanding how cultural differences impact intercultural communication in interface design (Search, 2007). Hall (1959/1973), the "founder of intercultural communication," points out that nonverbal aspects of communication such as time and space vary in different cultures. Hofstede (1980) identifies five cultural dimensions that reflect diverse social structures:

- Power distance: the degree of equality or inequality that exists between people in a society
- Individualism: the extent to which society values individual achievement or group achievement (collectivism)
- Uncertainty avoidance: the extent to which people tolerate uncertainty or ambiguity
- Long-term orientation: the extent to which a society focuses on long-term goals and tradition
- Masculinity: the extent to which a culture adheres to traditional masculine models of achievement, control, and power (a high masculinity ranking indicates a culture with significant gender differentiation).

Graphic designer Aaron Marcus (2005) shows how computer interface designs reflect Hofstede's cultural dimensions. For example, web-based communications that reflect an individualistic society like the United States might include customizable interface designs and language, stories, and content that focus on the individual needs of each user. A design that reflects a specific culture can also address a broader audience by including context and audiovisual elements that engage users and welcome them to the new cultural experience. Designers do not always recognize the power of multisensory environments in making the user feel comfortable in a new information space. This chapter shows how diverse media and storytelling can create multisensory experiences to extend a welcome to users of web-based communications.

Cultural Websites

Our research project focused on the role of web-based communications in conveying aboriginal cultures. The goal was to explore how users respond to information about these cultures. Aboriginal peoples have a history of incorporating technical innovations into their cultures as a means of survival (Leuthold, 1998). They began using the Internet to form collective communities in the late 1990s (Niezen, 2005).

The first exemplar we examined in this research project was the Tshinanu, All of Us website, the companion website for the *Tshinanu (Us Together)* television series, which began broadcasting in 2005. The website uses interactive multimedia to depict the social, economic, and cultural life of aboriginal communities in Quebec, Canada. The site received the Best Website Award from the Academy of Canadian Cinema and Television. The website also garnered top awards at the U.S. Horizon Interactive Awards Competition and the VIDFEST Interactive Design Festival in Vancouver, where the site was honored in the education division. The VIDFEST website provides the following description:

> The site Tshinanu.tv is the largest-scale production of digital (music, videos, animated presentations) and interactive content (blogs, interactive panoramas, games…) depicting all facets of the lives of Aboriginal communities in Quebec. Tshinanu means "us together" and this production aims to promote communication across cultures. This site emphasizes user communication and provides lots of easily accessed activities and resources for further learning about aboriginal culture in Canada. (Vancouver International Digital Festival, 2006)

The Tshinanu website presents 26 topics that cover various aspects of aboriginal cultures such as healing, cooking, music, dance, and song. Each section includes an overview about the topic, videos with people telling stories and engaging in various activities, and interactive games to test the user's knowledge. Since the objective of the Tshinanu website is to promote cross-cultural communication, the site was a good case study for our research.

The second exemplar we chose to work with allowed us to focus on the importance of storytelling in cross-cultural communication. This communication was not a website per se, but photographs and videos that were part of an online course about First Nations crafts at Emily Carr University of Art + Design in Vancouver, Canada. Our research project focused on the audiovisual materials for one particular craft, birch bark baskets. In particular, several videos and still images provided information about basket designs and the process of making baskets. The videos also highlighted the importance of baskets as social, cultural, and personal artifacts in the lives of the First Nations peoples.

Using Multisensory Experience

Both of these communications use diverse media to engage the user by creating sensory environments that help the user feel welcome and comfortable with new cultural experiences. Audio and visual media create affective domains that enable users to connect with new ideas and experiences on an emotional level. Once they are engaged and feel comfortable on this level, they are more likely to be receptive to the cognitive information that follows (Gazda & Flemister, 1999).

The home page on the Tshinanu website uses visual design to stimulate the senses (Figure 4.1). The background for this page incorporates warm colors (yellow, red, and brown) that glow like the sun or a warm hearth. In our tests, we found that users liked the graphics and noted that they were "warm and inviting."

The visual design of this page also includes curved, abstract figures that float in a suspended circle. Abstract symbols are engaging because they encourage the viewer to layer personal associations and experiences onto the visuals. For this reason abstract designs work well for diverse cultural audiences (Horton, 2005). The visual design of the Tshinanu home page tells users they are entering a new experience and sets the scene for the information they will encounter on the site.

The use of visual design to communicate this particular cultural experience continues on the rest of the screens on the website. Curved lines and forms reflect aboriginal designs and consciousness by communicating continuity and fluid relationships. Users become aware of this unique cultural consciousness on a perceptual level, which prepares them for the other information on the website.

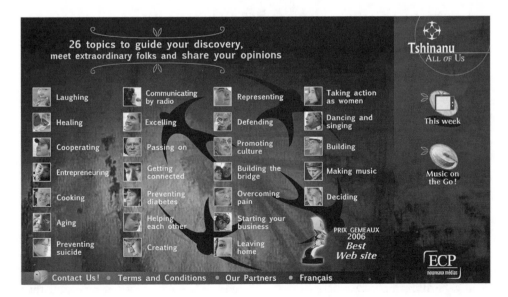

Figure 4.1 Home page of the Tshinanu Television Series. ©TSHINANU Inc. (www.tshinanu.tv/www.ecp television.com).

On the home page, the content and words also help users feel comfortable with familiar topics, so they will want to explore the new ideas and perspectives on the site. The title, "26 topics to guide your discovery, meet extraordinary folks and share your opinions," invites the user to explore the information space. Topics such as cooking, music, and dance use audiovisual content to engage the user's senses and communicate aboriginal traditions. Our test subjects felt comfortable with the site because they enjoyed learning new information and making comparisons with their own cultures.

Other topics deal with universal human emotions and experiences that involve humor, success and failure, aging, and death. These topics are engaging themes because they provide opportunities for users to relate to the information on personal and emotional levels. The universal nature of these themes helps users feel comfortable in the information space and encourages them to investigate ideas that present different cultural perspectives.

However, there were some weaknesses with the interface design. Some topic titles do not accurately describe the content for their sections, resulting in uncertainty and confusion for the users. For example, the title "Defending" is ambiguous and does not reflect the information in that section, which deals with the political representation of native peoples.

Users also needed more background information to feel welcome in the new information space. It is important to explain unfamiliar terminology and traditions. In cross-cultural communication, foreign words and languages can create uncertainty and make users feel uneasy if they don't know the meaning or pronunciation of words. For example the word *tshinanu* is a Cree word that means "all of us together." Providing this definition in the opening pages of the website would help users understand the objective of the site and create a conceptual bridge to this new cultural experience. It would also be helpful to include audio that shows users how to pronounce foreign words. These design elements would reduce language barriers and enhance users' understanding of the information.

The photographs from the course at Emily Carr University welcome the user to a new cultural experience by stimulating the senses and engaging the user in the process of basket making. The close-ups of the baskets highlight the texture of the bark and create a sensory awareness of the tactile and spatial dimensions of the basket. In Figure 4.2 the basket maker's hands enable the user to "feel" the materials and "know" the craft through the sense of touch. Some photos show the delicate designs on the baskets and highlight the aesthetic qualities of the baskets (Figure 4.3). This heightened sensory awareness creates an appreciation for the baskets that helps users feel more comfortable with the new information.

Camera distance and angle play an important role in engaging users in the process of basket making so they feel comfortable with the information. The close-up view and high camera angle in Figure 4.2 put users in the same space as the basket maker and helps them understand the process demonstrated in the photograph.

Using Personal Experience

Finally, both examples use people and narratives to present information about their cultures. The audience has the opportunity to meet aboriginal peoples and learn about

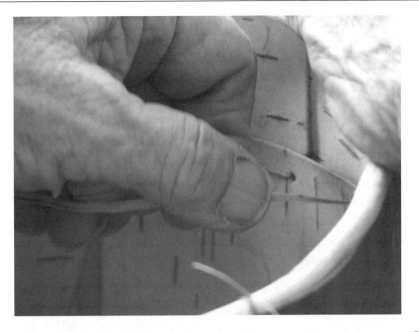

Figure 4.2 Close-up shots of the steps in basket making help users understand the process. ©Emily Carr University of Art + Design.

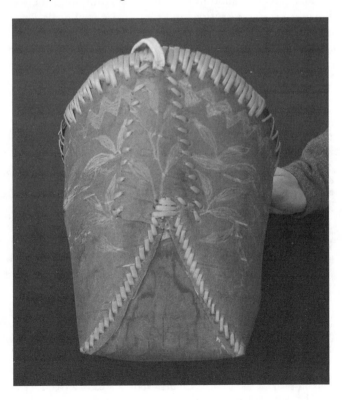

Figure 4.3 Delicate designs illustrate the tactile and aesthetic qualities of the baskets. ©Emily Carr University of Art + Design.

the cultures through the stories they tell. On the Tshinanu website numerous videos show people talking about their cultural traditions. This conversational approach to introducing the audience to a different culture is one of the strengths of the website. The personal interpretations help users relate to the new cultural perspectives.

In the Emily Carr photographs and videos, individuals share personal experiences with the audience as well. The user has "personal instructors" who teach the process of making baskets and the importance of this tradition in their cultures. Like the photographs, the videos also evoke sensory responses, especially the sense of touch. The woman making the baskets describes the feel and pliability of the fresh bark and roots used in the baskets. There is an emphasis on touch as she pats down the soil and moss to restore the ground to its original condition after harvesting the roots for the baskets. As she demonstrates the First Nations tradition of rubbing tobacco on the exposed area of the tree where the bark was removed (Figure 4.4), she says, "I hope I didn't hurt you too much." She shares her sensory connection with the natural environment with the viewer. Her sensitive actions and words help the viewer appreciate and respect the cultural traditions they are witnessing.

The power of the images in the videos in both these cases could be enhanced by additional visual editing. Native filmmakers use digital editing to engage the viewer and communicate their cultural traditions. In *Itam Hakim, Hopiit* (1984) Victor Masayesva carefully edits the sequences to communicate the meaning of Hopi designs and traditions. For example, he cuts directly from designs and forms visible in the ceremonial dances to similar images found in the natural surroundings. In one sequence, the viewer sees a flower in the countryside, and then sees a similar flower in a traditional ceremonial garment. To help the viewer understand the movements in the ceremonial dances and how they derive from the natural and the spiritual worlds, Masayesva cuts from the fluid movement of the dancers to waving stalks of corn in a field.

Figure 4.4 First Nations peoples rub tobacco on the exposed area of a tree after removing bark for baskets. ©Emily Carr University of Art + Design.

The similarity between these movements is evident, and viewers can understand the ceremonial dance by comparing it with events they have experienced.

Extending a Welcome

Digital technology enables designers to integrate different media into a multisensory environment that incorporates a holistic approach to describing cultures. Designers of engaging web-based communications can use multimedia information to weave audio-visual mosaics that reflect social and cultural traditions, thereby extending a welcome to users.

Images and sounds are powerful symbols for cross-cultural communication because their meanings are defined by stylistic forms as well as context and sequence. Kellner (2002) describes the polysemiotic nature of visual images and media texts as follows: "Visual images and media texts are often polymorphous, containing a wealth of meanings; images function in contexts and their meanings evolve in terms of narratives, sequences, and resolutions" (p. 85). Visual anthropologist Roderick Coover (2001) believes an audience should experience a culture through different forms of sensory input. A montage of images, text, sound, rhythm, action, light, and color creates a holistic, multisensory environment that *suggests* a particular cultural experience and encourages the viewer to become an integral part of an interactive, cultural space.

Creating interactive websites that use animations, video, and sound recordings may be too time-consuming and expensive for some projects. However, both of the examples in this research project demonstrate how two-dimensional design and photographs can create a multisensory environment that welcomes the user. Limited development budgets do not have to restrict the use of sensory experiences that engage the user.

For Further Exploration

1. The Tshinanu website (www.tshinanu.tv) analyzed by Search is an early example of a cross-media extra, an experience developed in one media (the web) to enrich users' experience in another media (television). Cross-media experiences are generally intended to provide a bridge from one media to another, increasing engagement (Crossmedia, n.d.). Can you think of other cross-media experiences intended to extend a welcome and provide a bridge?
2. Reconciliation Australia was established in 2000 as a nongovernment, not-for-profit foundation aimed at promoting reconciliation between Aboriginal and Torres Strait Islander peoples and the broader Australian community. Examine its website (http://www.reconciliation.org.au/). How would you account for the similarities and differences in approach between it and the Tshinanu website (www.tshinanu.tv)? To what extent does it use the multisensory and personal experience recommended by Search?

Set the Context

Janice W. Fernheimer and Samantha Good

In proposing that designers need to set the context, we suggest that making web-based communication engaging requires designers to prepare users for the experience and motivate them to participate by identifying an appropriate context for use, making changes to embed the communication in the context and acknowledging the inherent contextual dynamics. Fernheimer and her team moved through multiple iterations of a wiki for collaboration in pursuit of these goals.

The Concept of Collaboration

While most casual web surfers use a wiki to read rather than to write, edit, or contribute to the entries stored on Wikipedia (Warren, Airoldi, & Bank, 2008), the wiki-based encyclopedia's great success seemed to suggest that wikis ushered in a new way of thinking about collaborative knowledge production using web-based communication. Consequently, universities and boardrooms reverberated with questions about how to best harness the wisdom of crowds and use peer-to-peer production to stimulate collaboration. In *Wikinomics: How Mass Collaboration Changes Everything,* Tapscott and Williams (2006) argue, "Collaboration, publication, peer review, and exchange of precompetitive information are now becoming keys to success in the knowledge-based economy" (153). While these collaborative elements are often seen as keys to success, establishing a web-based environment in which they can flourish is a significant challenge for designers and usability engineers. We believe that part of what makes wikis so attractive is the collaborative capabilities they make possible. In fact, we argue that wikis provide an environment conducive to enabling what we term "deep collaboration," an iterative, recursive collaborative writing process where writers can engage one another in the writing process, from idea generation (invention) to turning in the final product (delivery) (Fernheimer et al., 2009).

In our original work on wikis for collaboration, we aimed to make a usable tool that would encourage users to populate a wiki and work collaboratively with others. Following traditional usability principles such as Jakob Nielsen's original design heuristics (1994b) and Steve Krug's (2005) more recent "don't make me think" approach to web design, we worked to address some of the interface issues encountered by users who are both consumers and producers of web texts. We found, however, that to encourage users to engage in more interactive practices such as deep collaboration, we needed a new framework for usability that extended beyond the technology itself.

In particular, we found that in focusing too closely on the usability of the tool itself, we had overlooked the design of the context for which our web-based communication was intended. In this chapter, then, we use our experience with wikis for collaboration to illustrate how setting the context for an engaging web-based communication requires designers to do the following:

- Identify a context for use
- Embed the specific prototype within the contextual practices that frame it
- Acknowledge contextual dynamics.

While characteristics of context are explored in some recent scholarship (Gurak, 2001; Warnick, 2005), we hope our hands-on learning with the collaborative wiki will help design professionals better understand the importance of setting the context with their designs.

Identifying Context for Use

The Wikis for Collaboration Team initially aimed to determine what factors might encourage students to post to or engage with class materials on a wiki. We began with questions that were motivated by the success of Wikipedia. Since wikis were still relatively new to the everyday user, we wondered how users might be encouraged to populate them. Ultimately we hoped to encourage student collaboration within a classroom context, but in this early development phase, we were thinking primarily about the tool itself. As a result, we initially designed a prototype in MediaWiki independent of any particular context. After two rounds of relatively unsuccessful traditional usability testing, we realized that we had not done the requisite work to set the context for users and that, as a consequence, our users lacked motivation to participate.

As any teacher who uses technology in the classroom has learned the hard way, the classroom context is a complex of multiple, interconnected factors including but not limited to other students, software, classroom community, and instructional materials. When our team failed to properly identify a context that integrated all of these elements, our users fell short of the deep collaboration that we hoped the wiki would facilitate.

To remedy this situation, we worked through two stages of development and implementation in classroom contexts at RPI. In the first stage, in fall 2007, we worked with a lower-level engineering course, Introduction to Air Quality, taught by Lupita Montoya. In the second stage, we continued to work with Montoya, this time in her course Introduction to Engineering Design, while also working with Dean Nieusma in his course Product Design and Innovation. All three of these courses included collaborative writing assignments that we believed would benefit from deep collaboration facilitated by a wiki.

Embedding in Context

After identifying an appropriate context for use, an engaging web-based communication must be appropriately embedded in that context. Such embedding requires adjustments to both the technological design and the design of the context. With our wiki for collaboration, embedding in the classroom context affected our choice of wiki platform as we sought features appropriate to the classroom context. It also required us to make changes to the classroom situation as well, in terms of both the collaborative writing assignment prompt and the assessment methods used to evaluate students.

Our move into the classroom affected our choice of technology. Moving away from Wikimedia, we opted to use Clearspace, a commercial wikiware with many features that responded to usability problems we encountered in our earlier testing. Clearspace also had a few features we thought particularly appropriate to the classroom context. It allowed for simple WYSIWYG editing conventions that were similar to desktop publishing metaphors, provided a clear and intuitive hierarchy for team spaces, offered centralized document storage, and had personalizable dashboards and home pages. Perhaps the most valuable of all was the revision/history tool, which provided for the easy comparison of multiple versions as shown in Figure 5.1. We thought this feature would help make students' writing process more transparent, while also aiding instructors by making it easier for them to monitor students' contributions and examine and evaluate the processes that take place as group members negotiate roles and participate in the collaborative process.

To introduce these and other features of the wiki to students, we worked with Barbara Lewis of the RPI Center for Communicative Practices to develop hands-on workshops to prepare students to engage in a process-based approach to writing and collaboration. We also developed and implemented workshops dedicated specifically to the technical elements; these workshops aimed to focus on two different but interconnected elements necessary for students to engage in deep collaboration. First,

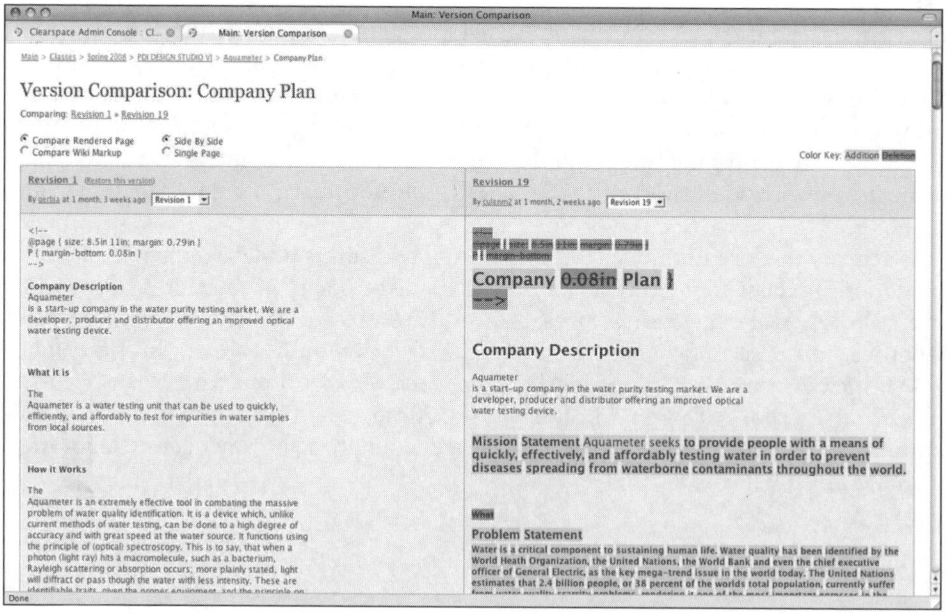

Figure 5.1 Version comparison in the Clearspace wiki, third redesign.

students needed to understand the difference between individual and collaborative writing processes, and, second, they needed to learn the technical details necessary to take advantage of the wiki and its editing features.

But we went further to make some important changes to the classroom context itself. First, although the courses all required collaborative writing, we still needed to make adjustments to the collaborative assignment. In the first stage of implementation, we made rather general adjustments: We simply asked students to use the wiki to collaboratively author a final project with their peers. They were required to use the wiki to facilitate and document the depth of their collaboration. Without a clear understanding of the collaboration required or the process for evaluating whether it took place, many students perceived the wiki as a "make work" step in between collaborative idea production and writing. In the second stage, we refined the assignment to better explain that the wiki was a tool to help make their required collaboration more transparent. We also tailored the assignment to the context of specific courses. Students were instructed to use the wiki for specific knowledge production purposes—to write the background section for a final group paper in Introduction to Engineering Design, for example, or to select and modify a template for writing the final paper in Product Design and Innovation. They were also told when to use the wiki—over the course of two weeks at the beginning of the project when they were initially generating ideas and discussing organization strategies for the assignment as a whole.

Our second major adjustment to classroom context involved a series of changes to the way the wiki assignment was graded. At first, we simply said that 5% percent of students' grade was to be determined by the depth of their collaboration. We hoped that counting collaboration as 5% of students' overall grade would provide strong motivation for students to overcome the cost of initiation. Eventually, we specified the number and type of contributions required by each participant.

We discovered that without explicit explanation of how collaboration would be recognized and evaluated, the grading aspect had an adverse effect on student motivation and participation. Since the criteria for how students' collaborations would be evaluated were initially unclear, students were quite concerned about their grades and about how their participation would be recognized. Students perceived the wiki as a tool for teacher surveillance rather than a tool to help them improve collaborative knowledge production. This reaction affected students' trust, commitment to the project, and the overall quality of the user experience. As a result, many students used the wiki *only* to receive their participation grade. Even after we further refined the assignment to explain the wiki as a tool to make collaboration more transparent, we found that students, although contributing more, did not fully engage in the deep collaboration we hoped the wiki might foster.

In the second stage of implementation, in spring 2008, we used the wiki in two separate courses. We also incorporated changes to the way the wiki assignment was graded that were more successful in embedding deep collaboration into the classroom context. Rather than providing nonspecific explanations of how collaboration would be evaluated, each class received a tailored assignment prompt that specified that the final group assignment would be graded both for the quality of the group essay produced and the quality of collaboration. We explained that collaboration would be measured and evaluated based on the revision history for each group and that, once again, it would account for 5% of each individual student's overall grade.

In this final iteration of the assignment, then, we tried to make motivation for participating on the wiki transparent, and we elaborated the grading criteria and process. Consequently, students were better prepared for the experience. They were also better able to control their grade by adjusting their behavior according to project guidelines. This knowledge enabled group members to determine their level of participation and their level of involvement in the group project community. By understanding the context of the site, they were no longer passive, and most students did make contributions to the wiki.

Acknowledging Contextual Dynamics

Although designers can do a great deal in identifying an appropriate context and embedding their web-based communications within a specific situation, the dynamics of context will never be within our total control. Sometimes the dynamics of context can have an unexpectedly positive impact, such as when an application goes viral in unanticipated ways. Often, however, contextual dynamics can limit the scope of the potential benefits a designer hopes the prototype will enable.

In the case of the wikis for collaboration, the dynamics of the classroom context affected use in three important ways. First, in the context of the face-to-face discussions through which students were accustomed to accomplishing their collaboration, we were unable to successfully embed the wiki in their work flow. Students believed that their face-to-face meetings were more productive and deeply collaborative than the writing that took place on the wiki; consequently, they either opted not to interact through the wiki or limited their involvement to surface-level revisions. Rather than engaging group members by writing on the wiki, they chose to engage in person. As a result, the wiki revision history simply did not reflect the iterative, recursive, and reflective process of deep collaboration that we had hoped to foster.

These limitations might be best understood within the context of discontinuous technologies (Christensen, 1997), which allow users or customers to solve old problems in new ways. Our wikis were intended to supplement rather than displace the face-to-face group meeting as a forum for collaborative essay composition. However, many students were more comfortable communicating face to face, by e-mail, over the phone, or through instant messaging. Despite our best attempts to articulate our rationale within the assignment prompts, students didn't understand why they were being asked to communicate in a wiki with students who they saw regularly in class.

As happens with most technologies, but discontinuous ones in particular, users may be reluctant to change their traditional methods for accomplishing a task if they feel more comfortable with a means that is already established. While some people are innovators or early adopters, most people wait until later in the technology adoption cycle. For these users, the motivation to try a new technology is low. Because RPI students are well known for their use of computers and their affinity for technology, we assumed an intrinsic desire to try something new and a quick adaptation to this technology.

The classroom context limited the use of the wiki in another way as well. Although the changes we made did leave students better prepared to engage, they tended to interact in ways that reflected their role as students. Unlike Facebook or Myspace—media primarily concerned with personal identity and self-expression—the wiki for collaboration was seen by most students as a space to express their role as student. This role was not only evaluated by a grade, it was based on students' online interactions and how they participated in the community. As a result, while some personalized their wiki profiles, most chose not to. Those who did take advantage of the personalization features used them as an opportunity to further understand their peers, their feedback on the task at hand, and the community their group formed through its interactions. For them, feedback was often immediate and immediately gratifying. But because they were exposed to the wiki within a classroom context, most students were unwilling to play with the wiki and less likely to personalize their spaces on it or problem-solve to uncover its basic functionality.

Finally, although we attempted to make our goal for deep collaboration explicit, we were less successful at explaining or persuading students to buy in to the promise of the wiki. Our refined assignment prompts and revised grading rubric did do a better job of preparing the students for the experience, but they could never entirely overcome the coercive nature of the classroom situation. Students' participation was not voluntary, and though we hoped the graded element would provide high motivation to participate, we did not account for the way that it would underscore rather than alleviate student fears about group work, assessment, and grading. We hoped it would provide a more equitable means for student participation to become accessible and evaluated, but students were well aware that it was a class assignment. The motivation provided by the classroom context was inherently different from what users bring to participation in web-based communications outside the classroom.

Setting the Context

As we discovered in our work on wikis for collaboration, designers of engaging web-based communication must work to set an appropriate context for users. While wikis, blogs, podcasts, chat rooms, and other web-based communications can provide a quick and easy way to create content and communicate, they are no more than tools in and of themselves. Designers, especially those seeking to design for a transformative practice like deep collaboration, need to consider issues of context. In particular, designers need to identify an appropriate context for use. They must work through that context to discover ways in which the web-based communication can be appropriately embedded. And, finally, they must acknowledge the contextual dynamics—often beyond their control—that will significantly shape the users' experience.

For Further Exploration

1. This chapter's admonition to design the context as well as the technology suggests that designers of engaging user experiences can and should have a good understanding of their users. In his discussion of Principle 1, however, Zappen suggests that users are inevitably diverse and "no interaction will be intuitive for every user." Look at Arjana Blazic's award-winning wiki, Greetings from the World (http://greetingsfromtheworld.wikispaces.com/), a wiki where students and their teachers contribute content. Has Blazic embedded her wiki in a specific context,

as Fernheimer recommends, or has she designed for diverse users, as Zappen suggests? Are these two recommendations consistent with one another? If not, how can they be reconciled?

2. Fernheimer and Good suggest that one of the contextual dynamics at work in their case study was the unwillingness of students to add a wiki to their current face-to-face communications. In effect, Fernheimer and Good are recommending a blended engagement that includes both online and offline interactions. One of these blended engagements that has received a lot of attention recently is the flipped classroom. How does the flipped classroom pioneered by Salman Khan, founder of the Khan Academy, follow this chapter's recommendation to set the context (http://www.ted.com/talks/salman_khan_let_s_use_video_to_reinvent_education.html)?

Make a Connection

Patricia Search

Users of many web-based communications browse quickly for information. If they can't find something interesting, they move on. Consequently, it is important for designers to help users make a connection. This chapter focuses on narrative or storytelling as a powerful design element that helps users engage. Search and her team describe the use of narratives in two examples of cross-cultural communication, where making a connection can be difficult, and they suggest how to create effective narratives that engage the user.

The Concept of Storytelling

Narratives are used in a wide range of applications in education, business, marketing, and e-commerce (Search, 2007). On websites, narratives appear in testimonials, customer reviews, wikis, blogs, discussion boards, and other social messaging websites such as Facebook, Myspace, and Twitter. Narratives create a sense of community and identity for users who have similar experiences and interests. Stories help users relate general principles to specific contexts and personal experiences (Edelson, 1993). As a result, stories can help users understand diverse cultural perspectives by mapping new cultural traditions to their own personal experiences (Search, 2002).

The art of storytelling was perfected by the aboriginal peoples of the world, who still use storytelling to communicate ancestral stories and cultural traditions (Search, 2007). Researchers have shown that one of the best ways to expand cultural awareness is to study how people *within* individual cultures use communication techniques and images rather than using information created by people outside the culture (Worth & Adair, 1972).

As detailed earlier, our research looked at two cultural exemplars: the Tshinanu, All of Us website and multimedia course materials from an online course about First Nations crafts at Emily Carr University of Art + Design in Vancouver, Canada. Both include excellent examples of storytelling that help users make a connection with information that would be otherwise difficult to understand or relate to.

Using Narratives

The Tshinanu website includes videos of individuals telling personal stories that illustrate themes from the opening screen. The most effective stories are the ones that deal with human emotions that are familiar to a wide audience, such as humor, success, failure, and death. These stories cut across cultural boundaries and allow the user to connect with the information.

When we tested this website, users identified with these universal themes because they had experienced similar situations in their own lives. Sometimes very specific events reminded users of personal experiences. For example, one of our test subjects was a military veteran, and he identified with an aboriginal veteran from the Vietnam War who talked about the financial and marital problems he encountered when he returned home after the war. Our test subject noted that he had experienced the same problems when he returned from his tour of duty in Iraq.

Numerous examples of narratives that enable users to make a connection can also be found in the Emily Carr course materials. One of the videos is an interview with a First Nations woman who has made baskets all her life. In the video she describes how she used the baskets to collect berries, and she tells a wonderful story about her encounter with a bear while she was picking berries. Her grandmother had told her that if she ever ran into a bear, she should just talk to the bear, and it would leave her alone. Remembering her grandmother's advice, the woman did talk to the bear, and the bear turned around and walked away. Then she dropped her basket and ran away as quickly as possible.

Her story revealed her anxiety and fear—emotions that viewers connected with even if they could not relate to her ability to talk to a bear. This story engages viewers by tapping into a universal human emotion that everyone has experienced. These types of emotional connections create a bridge for cross-cultural communication. If users recognize that they share similar experiences or emotions with a person from a different culture, they may be more open to exploring new cultural traditions that are not familiar to them.

Another basket maker in the Emily Carr videos talks about her family and the tradition of basket making. She shows a photograph of her grandmother and points out that it was very important for her to learn to make baskets that had the same quality as her grandmother's baskets. She also shows the baskets she made for her children and notes that some were birthday gifts for them. Even if users are not familiar with the process of making baskets, they can relate to family and cultural traditions, ancestral history, and the idea of passing down customs from generation to generation. About one week after the initial testing for this exemplar, we sent users a follow-up survey to see what concepts they remembered. All the users commented on the importance of maintaining cultural values and traditions.

Some of the Emily Carr videos also remind users of activities or experiences in their own lives. For example, two of the videos show individuals in the woods harvesting birch bark and spruce roots to make the baskets. In our testing some users said these videos reminded them of family outings in the woods. They were very engaged in the videos because of this connection to their own personal experiences.

Our testing also revealed that some of the people in the videos were iconic figures that reminded users of family members. For example, the woman who told the story about the bear was an elderly woman who reminded users of their own grandmothers. In the video showing how to harvest the bark for the baskets, two women are gathering the bark (Figure 6.1). Some users identified these women as "mother and daughter." However, this relationship is never specified in any of the information. It is not

Figure 6.1 First Nations basket makers gather birch bark for baskets. ©Emily Carr University of Art + Design.

clear if the users assigned this mother-daughter relationship because of their apparent age difference, or because the woman in this video talks about her family in a different video and shows baskets she made for her children, including her daughter. In this exemplar, family references became iconic symbols that helped users identify with the people and activities in the videos.

The still photographs of the basket-making process also include layers of narrative. To begin, they show how the baskets take shape and evolve over time. They also include the hands of an elderly basket maker that symbolically represent a history of life experiences (Figure 6.2). As noted in our discussion of Principle 4, camera distance and angle play an important role in engaging the user. The close-up shot in this photo puts users in the same space as the woman making the baskets. This position, along with the high camera angle, gives users a feeling of control, which helps them understand the process shown in the photos. The camera distance and angle establish a connection between the user and the activity demonstrated in the images.

Providing Background

Both exemplars demonstrate the importance of providing background material to help users understand new information. The still photographs about basket making show technical and aesthetic details that complement the information in the videos. They provide additional context that helps the user fully understand the basket-making process and the significance of this aboriginal tradition.

On the Tshinanu website there are some video narratives that do not provide adequate background for the stories. For example, one person discusses failure and success when he describes a test he initially failed and later passed. However, there is no information about the type of test or the context for this experience. Lack of background is an important issue in other areas of the website as well. When we tested this website, users said they wanted to see the geographic location of the aboriginal peoples

Figure 6.2 Photographs help users understand and appreciate the process of basket making. ©Emily Carr University of Art + Design.

in Quebec. A map would enhance the user's understanding and appreciation of this culture by using a familiar symbol to establish context and a landmark for orientation.

The question of geographic location also came up with the basket-making videos from Emily Carr University. One user wanted to know the exact location of the woods where the individuals harvested the bark and roots. Another user wanted to know why that particular location was selected. Familiar symbols (in this case, maps) that establish orientation for users are important design elements in a new information space.

Another interesting issue regarding background information emerged from the testing of the Tshinanu website. The videos use multiple languages, including aboriginal languages, French, and English. Subtitles are in French or English. Users were not interested in reading the English subtitles, and they didn't seem to understand why French was included. In a revised prototype we included an introductory statement that explained the significance of languages in aboriginal cultures and why these cultural groups strive to preserve their native languages. We also pointed out that aboriginal peoples had to learn Western languages to survive in Western communities. This information provided the necessary background for users to understand and appreciate the multiple languages on the site. When we tested the revised prototype with this explanation, there were no negative comments about the use of multiple languages or subtitles.

Digital Editing

The videos in both exemplars would benefit from some audiovisual editing that highlights key points, provides additional context, and improves the quality of the audio.

Digital processing techniques could be used to weave images, sounds, and rhythms into multisensory environments that reflect sociocultural traditions (Coover, 2001). Gazda and Flemister (1999) point out that it is possible to use multimedia to create "a new reality for the viewer" rather than just simulating existing reality (p. 94). Digital techniques can create multisensory narratives that reflect the multiple dimensions of a culture through "transparent immediacy" and "hypermediacy" (Bolter & Grusin, 1999). The result is an intuitive experience that suspends the viewer in another cultural space (Search, 2007).

As suggested with Principle 4, aboriginal filmmakers use digital techniques to create immersive environments where viewers learn about cultural traditions through multisensory experiences that allow them to make a connection in a new cultural space. In the film *Pueblo Peoples: First Encounter* (1990) Georges Burdeau uses transparent transitions between scenes to layer visuals and audio into multidimensional collages that symbolize the connection between the Pueblo peoples, the land, and the spiritual world. Victor Masayesva's film *Itam Hakim, Hopiit* (1984) incorporates carefully selected frame shots and editing techniques that enable the viewer to make a connection with the cultural traditions of the Hopi.

Close-up shots encourage a connection between the viewer and the people in the film. In one section of the film, the speed of the ceremonial dance is enhanced to communicate the intensity of the experience that cannot be felt without actually being there and participating in the ritual. The enhanced speed of this section engages the viewer by transforming the passive state of simply viewing the dance into a sensory experience the viewer can feel. This use of visual information to stimulate the other senses is called kinesthetic empathy, and it is a technique that filmmakers often use to help viewers identify with a cinematic experience. Masayesva, like many other native filmmakers, also incorporates abstract images into his films to engage the viewer. He uses digital processing techniques to reduce the details in realistic images and create abstract silhouettes of individuals and their natural surroundings. These abstractions encourage the viewer to fill in the meaning and find a personal connection with the ideas presented in the film.

Other Design Considerations

It was evident from the testing of both cultural websites that the users found it easier to make connections when they were learning new skills. On the Tshinanu website, users were interested in learning about the aboriginal foods in the cooking section, such as porcupine, cattails, and milkweed pods. With the Emily Carr course materials, users preferred the videos that showed the process of basket making over the personal interviews with basket makers. In a follow-up survey, all the users said they enjoyed the video that showed the harvesting of bark for the baskets in the woods. They were interested in learning a new skill, and through this learning experience, they gained a respect and appreciation for the First Nations peoples and their traditions.

Finally, once users engage with the information and start to become familiar with a topic, they often want to continue the connection and the learning process and obtain more information. They may want to participate in a dialogue about the information on the website. The design for a web-based communication should provide ways to continue this engagement (see Principle 10).

Measuring how users connect or identify with people or information on a website requires different approaches to usability testing. It is important to give users an opportunity to explore a website and find areas of interest instead of assigning specific tasks for them to complete. Users may find a connection in different ways, and these connections may evolve along different time lines. In this research the testing methods for both cultural websites included surveys with Likert scales. However, the data from these surveys did not reveal helpful patterns. Interviews and open-ended questions on written surveys provided more insights, because they gave users the opportunity to describe their experiences in detail. The testing of the course materials from Emily Carr University included a follow-up survey that was distributed about a week after the initial testing session. This survey provided an opportunity to gather additional information and see what key points users remembered after they left the website. The testing results for both surveys are discussed in greater detail in Case Study 3.

Making a Connection

This research demonstrates the importance of defining new principles that help users make a connection with people, experiences, and/or products in a web-based communication whose main purpose is the engagement of users. Narratives can engage the user and cut across cultural boundaries. The following design guidelines can help users make a connection:

- Include stories that contain experiences that are similar to the experiences of the audience. It is important to present the culture accurately, but at the same time it is necessary to identify universal themes, emotions, and/or experiences to help users understand the culture.
- Identify themes in the stories that create community.
- Provide background information when a culture is different from that of the audience to provide context for the story or online experience.
- Reduce communication barriers by describing unusual languages and experiences, and provide links to additional information. In the case of multilingual websites, explain the use of different languages in the website.
- Include familiar symbols (e.g., maps) to orient the audience and provide context.
- Provide ways for the audience to obtain more information or engage in a dialogue with others.

For Further Exploration

1. The website for the Aboriginal Peoples Television Network (http://www.aptn.ca/) is an example of a website designed to let aboriginal peoples tell their own stories. Look at a sample of a recent news story (http://aptn.ca/pages/news/archive/). How are narratives being used to help those outside the community make a connection with aboriginal communities?
2. The role of narrative in game design has been hotly disputed. Read Henry Jenkins's take on this issue (http://web.mit.edu/cms/People/henry3/games&narrative.

html). How would you compare Jenkins's arguments in favor of using narrative in games to Search's recommendation to use narrative to make a connection?

3. Take a look at Time's list of the 50 best websites for this year (Hint: Search for "the 50 best websites of 20xx-Time" using the current year). Pick any one of the sites. Does the site use narrative to make a connection with its users?

Share Control

James P. Zappen

In engaging web-based communication, user control does not rest simply with the designer or with the user. Instead, it is a participatory and communal process that engages multiple users in rich and productive interactions. To share control with users, designers need to maximize user options, provide for a wide range of user choices and preferences, and permit rich and varied user-system and user-user interactions. Zappen and his team illustrate these strategies using their design revisions of a youth-services information system.

The Concept of User Control

User control has long been an ideal in user-centered design, assumed as a reasonable and realistic goal. Traditionally, user control has been seen as a challenge for the designer, who should be encouraged to *give* or relinquish control to users; to provide them with resources and options for producing outcomes, performing tasks, and acquiring information; and to ensure that they can perform these tasks efficiently and reliably, without unrecoverable consequences. According to Nielsen (1993, pp. 115–116), system objects and operations should be sequenced to permit users to complete tasks as effectively and productively as possible. These sequences can sometimes be built into and enforced by the user interface, but "it is normally better to allow the user to control the dialogue [i.e., the interaction with the system] as much as possible such that the sequence can be adjusted by the individual user to suit that user's task and preferences" (p. 116). Such control, Nielsen (p. 33) argues, correlates closely with a high degree of user satisfaction.

One way to achieve this control, according to Norman (1988, pp. 21–23, 208–209), is to map system functions as directly as possible to match user tasks. The automobile provides a good example of such a mapping: "What is good about the design of the car? Things are visible. There are good mappings, natural relationships, between the controls and the things controlled. Single controls often have single functions" (p. 22). Indeed such a mapping also serves as a guard against overly much user control: "How many controls does a device need? The fewer the controls, the easier it looks to use and the easier it is to find the relevant controls" (p. 209). In essence, by this principle, each function should have only one control.

In a web-based environment, however—even a traditional one—user control is not always and only a designer option. As Nielsen (2000, p. 214) bluntly suggests, "Get over it. The user holds the mouse, and there is nothing you can do about it."

The practical implication of this suggestion is that designers need to acknowledge user control and facilitate user freedom of choice and freedom of movement. In traditional applications, users invest relatively long periods of time with each application; on the Web, they move rapidly from page to page (p. 217). In such an environment, user control is no longer a designer option—the user holds the mouse! As Spinuzzi (2003, pp. 13–22) observes, moreover, users exercise not only freedom to choose and to act insofar as designers permit but exercise freedom to innovate, embellish, and modify systems to meet local needs. Against the traditional view, Spinuzzi (pp. 14–15, 20) argues that these user innovations elude the control of either designers or users and enter into a "dynamic, ever-shifting balance between designers' contributions and workers' innovations" (p. 20).

In this more recent view, therefore, user control is neither a designer nor a user option exclusively but the result of a complex interaction of all of the components of a distributed system. In the traditional view, according to Norman (2004, p. 202),

> It was common to assume that intelligence required a centralized coordinating and control mechanism with a hierarchical organizational structure beneath it. This is how armies have been organized for thousands of years: armies, governments, corporations, and other organizations. It was natural to assume that the same principle applied to all intelligent systems.

In contrast, many natural and human systems—the actions of ants and bees, for example, or the workings of the stock market—"occur as a natural result of the interaction of multiple bodies, not through some central, coordinated control structure" (Norman, 2004, p. 202). Such "distributed control"—a complex interaction of multiple bodies—"is the hallmark of today's systems" (p. 202).

In web-based environments meant to engage, this complex interaction becomes still more complex—an interaction not only between designers and users but between users and systems and users and other users. As users become both consumers and producers of information—"prosumers" and "produsers" (Tapscott & Williams, 2006, pp. 124–150; Bruns, 2008, pp. 15–23)—the control issue becomes less an issue of who is in charge or who is in control and more an issue of quality control. In a distributed system in which anyone and everyone with access can contribute content and everyone—and no one—is in charge, who is to judge the quality of the result? The answer, of course, is everyone!

Raymond (2001, pp. 19, 21–22, 30) captures the traditional hierarchical system and the horizontal open system to which anyone can contribute in images of a "cathedral" and a "bazaar," and he takes Linus Torvald's open-source concept—"Given enough eyeballs, all bugs are shallow"—as his primary example of the bazaar. Bruns (2008, p. 24) sees an extension of this basic principle in new social web communications such as blogs and wikis, which depend upon many eyes to ensure quality control:

> A produsage approach assumes that quality control and improvement are probabilistic rather than linear: the assumption within the produsage community is that the more participants are able to examine, evaluate, and add to the contributions of their predecessors, the more likely an outcome of strong and increasing quality will be.

As web-based communications of the present and the future become increasingly more sophisticated, however, users risk losing control, not to designers or to other users but to the technology itself. Norman (2007, pp. 10–25) maintains that computer chips are responsible for shifting the balance of control from the user to the technology. Returning to his example of the automobile, he recounts the experience of a driver whose smart cruise control caused his car to accelerate when it left heavy traffic and turned onto an exit ramp, sensing lighter traffic but not the need to slow down at the exit (p. 10). With the advent of computer technology, "we often found ourselves lost and confused, annoyed and angered. But still, we considered ourselves to be in control. No longer. Now, our machines are taking over" (pp. 10–11).

Looking to the future, Norman (2007 p. 18) aims toward a more "symbiotic relationship" between users and their technologies. In contrast to the problem with the car and driver, he cites the interaction between skilled horseback riders and their horses:

> Horses communicate with their riders through body language, gait, readiness to proceed, and their general behavior: wary, skittish, and edgy or eager, lively, and playful. In turn, riders communicate with horses through their body language, the way they sit, the pressures exerted by their knees, feet, and heels. (p. 19)

In a distributed web-based system, all of the components—designers, users, technologies—need to work together in a symbiotic relationship of this kind.

To achieve this goal, designers need to work toward shared control, with the recognition, however, that control is not entirely theirs to give or even to share. It is not so much a possession of either the designer or the user but an experience enacted in use. Thus, designers can create affordances that provide users with resources for performing tasks and acquiring information efficiently and effectively. They can also provide choices and options, including options for user-system and user-user interactions that might elude their own control or even their own knowledge and experience—in the case of user innovations, for example, or shared content for which users, not designers, exercise quality control.

Building User Options

In the Connected Kids information system (http://connectedkids.rpi.edu/index.php/.info/) and the second redesign of the teens' gallery (Figure 1.2). We attempted to maximize several dimensions of user control, to the extent that we were able, given the affordances of the open-source gallery software that we used for this application (http://galleryproject.org/). In particular, we deployed many of the functions built into the gallery software. For instance, on the main page shown in Figure 7.1, in response to the results of comparative user testing, we decided to include breadcrumbs to enhance navigation and give users a sense of place. To illustrate this function, if the user selects the Dyken Pond image in the upper left corner and then continues to navigate through this section of the gallery, the breadcrumbs might be as follows:

CK InfoGallery > Dyken Pond > Facilities > Information Center

Figure 7.1 Second redesign of teens' InfoGallery main page.

As the gallery grows in size and complexity, the breadcrumbs become increasingly helpful as navigation tools and as orientation to the user's specific place within the gallery's hierarchical structure.

Building in more user options, we also enabled and displayed in the left navigation bar a variety of functions for both guests or visitors and album owners. For guests, the gallery includes an RSS feed, thumbnails, and slide shows, among other options. The RSS feed permits users to subscribe and receive regular updates on additions to the gallery. The RSS feed was subject to some debate in the user tests as perhaps unsuitable to younger children, but we retained this function in the current gallery implementation.

Creating Opportunities for Ownership

Both the thumbnails and the slide shows are conventional in gallery software and are readily accessible and more or less intuitive to users of all ages and backgrounds. The thumbnails are shown in the album images on the main page, and one of the slide shows is shown in Figure 7.2. For album owners and individual users, the gallery includes additional options to permit adding, editing, and deleting albums, images, and captions; rearranging or reordering items within the albums; and adjusting the slide shows to reflect individual preferences. On the individual image pages, not shown in the figures, we included images, titles, and captions, but we hid the photo properties,

Figure 7.2 Second redesign of teens' InfoGallery slide show.

which seemed of interest to skilled photographers but perhaps overly detailed for or-
dinary users.

On the slide-show pages, we retained most of the functions but adjusted the defaults
on some of them. These functions include size and speed adjustments; stop, pause,
back, and direction (forward or backward) options; and, perhaps most elegantly, a
show-and-hide option that permits users to choose whether or not to view titles and
captions beneath the images. As always, every choice of a default reflects a trade-off:
the 640-x-640 image size, for example, is suitable for smaller screen resolutions but
leaves overly much white space at 1,024 × 768. But this option, like the others, rests
with the user. Throughout all of these pages, we also sought to introduce a wider and
richer array of content and multimedia objects, including more user-generated content,
sound and moving images, and narrative elements, to which we return in Case Study 1.

Sharing Control

The newer concept of shared control within a decentralized, distributed system and
our own experience suggests that designers need to maximize user options, including options to ensure efficient performance; provide for a wide range of user choices
and preferences; and permit rich and varied user-system and user-user interactions,
even when these interactions extend beyond the designer's knowledge and experience.

Specifically, designers need to:

- Understand that user control is an experience enacted in the use of technology, not a property or possession of either the designer or the user.
- Provide resources to permit users to produce outcomes, perform tasks, and acquire information.
- Ensure that users can perform their tasks efficiently and reliably, without risk of unrecoverable errors.
- Provide varied options to maximize user choices and preferences.
- Provide resources to permit users to engage in productive user-system and user-user interactions.
- Provide resources to permit user-user collaboration and quality control.
- Develop systems that support symbiotic relationships between and among designers, users, and technologies.

For Further Exploration

1. The Bleacher Report (http://bleacherreport.com) is a sports website that claims to have thousands of active contributors, including "a mix of professional sports writers, bloggers and passionate fans who want to share their analysis and opinions with a broad audience" (Bleacher Report, 2010b) When it launched in 2008, the Bleacher Report was committed to user contributions, allowing anyone to post sports stories. After receiving significant criticism (Bleacher Report, n.d.), it instituted new protocols in 2010, including an application process, standards on writing, and a training program for prospective writers (Bleacher Report, 2010a). How would you analyze this change in policy in terms of Zappen's principle of sharing control?

2. One of the more recent developments in control on the web involves using behavioral data banks that tap data, including online browsing records, to personalize a website by altering its content (Sorensen, 2012). This kind of personalization often results in reduced options for the user. Steele and Angwin (2010) found, for example, that Capital One was offering different credit card options to users based on profiles developed from user data. What implications does this kind of behavioral tracking have for Zappen's principle of sharing control?

Support Interactions Among Users

Robert Krull

Research on engaging web-based communication suggests that users value and seek out interactions with other users. To design engaging communication, then, we need to focus on supporting interactions among users, creating opportunities for them to interact with one another, share what they create, and develop protocols to support those interactions. This chapter reports on work that suggests that, even in the context of distance learning, students will go to great lengths to establish and maintain interactions with other students.

The Concept of User Interaction

In the days before Twitter, blogging, YouTube, Facebook, and the World of Warcraft, people thought about mediated communication in terms of one-way interactions between humans and machines. Children were portrayed as sitting in front of TV sets like slack-jawed zombies (e.g., Winn, 2002). Early computer users punched commands onto computer cards and awaited output from the hidden mainframe. Somewhat later, CRT terminals replaced punch cards, but the interaction still involved isolated dyads of person and machine. Even early computer-based education was seen as a one-way interaction. Learners were expected to be happy consuming text and images displayed by a computer and to have their knowledge tested by the computer.

Technological determinists argue that the characteristics of media dictate user behavior. For example, they might say that Facebook, LinkedIn, and YouTube became inevitable when data storage became cheap enough for users to access these services for free. But, while technology may be important, clearly it is not the whole story. One need go back only one generation of communication researchers to find social models of communication adoption that explained how people force technology to serve their own purposes. Everett Rogers's (1995) classic work on the diffusion of innovations showed that users adopt a technology only if they can clearly see its advantages and only if they feel it is compatible with their values and work processes.

Some of the more notable developments in web-based communication suggest how far users will go to adapt a technology that supports their interactions with each other. Computer-based communication technologies that were invented for business purposes now are used as least as much for social networking (Wikipedia). Text messaging was not invented so that teens could maintain close ties with their peers, but now that seems integral to their networks. As a case study of supporting interaction among users, this chapter looks at the specific case of distance education. It will consider how distance-learning platforms create opportunities for interaction and sharing, and the ways in which users need clear protocols for interaction in these new web-based communications.

Creating Opportunities for Interaction

While the popular conception of distance education may be that master teachers lecture to rapt audiences, our research at RPI has shown that learners actually seek out opportunities for interaction with their peers. Instead of assuming that instructors will play the "sage on the stage," designers of web-based communications for distance learning are more likely to increase motivation and learning if they support users' natural inclinations for interaction (Danchak & Huguet, 2004; Kolb, 1984; Lowry et al., 2004; Rice et al., 2007; Terenzini & Pascarella, 1994).

In our investigations of opportunities for interaction in distance education, our team used the following metrics as a point of departure for more detailed analyses:

- How many times did users utilize interactive portions of a site?
- How much time did users spend on interactive portions of a site?
- How many times did users share what they created?
- With how many people did users share what they created?
- How many "mistakes" did users make when interacting with others?
- How much frustration did users express with the portion of site that supports interaction with others?

Using quantitative questionnaires, observations of face-to-face and distance classes, and virtual laboratory tests of learners' interactions on a collaborative task, we examined the very different ways that learners use the widely available components in distance education platforms shown in Table 8.1. These components were present whether the platform was Elluminate (http://www.blackboard.com/Platforms/Collaborate/Over view.aspx) or Adobe Connect (www.adobe.com/products/acrobatconnectpro).

Some components of distance-education platforms are primarily intended to support one-way communication. For example, students often access live video streams to see instructors lecturing. They may prepare for these classes by downloading slide presentations in advance. They may review class material by viewing video archives or may use archives to catch up on classes they missed.

In our observations, students accessed at least some of these downstream components during every learning session, and they tended to let the robust downstream media such as video streaming and slide presentations run constantly. Despite the limited interaction supported by these components, learners saw their ability to choose the place and time for learning as one of the prime advantages of distance learning. It allowed them to play a less passive role than the downstream nature of the media might suggest.

Other components of distance education platforms support more active roles characteristic of engaging communications. Many components—Internet-based video, text chat, electronic whiteboards, and audio via telephone or voice over Internet protocol

Table 8.1 Usage of interaction components of the distance-learning platforms.

Component	Description	Usage
Bulletin board	Allows users to post and respond to messages asynchronously	Rarely used except when required by instructors
Archive of class video stream	Allows users to watch class lecturers after the class has taken place	Used by distance learners who have conflicts with class times; used by all learners for missed classes and for exam review
Live class video stream	Allows users to watch classroom interactions as they happen	Used by all students who watch class live; video window is perceived as small and of low legibility
Slide presentations	Allows users to view and click through lecture notes being presented during a lecture	Used by all learners as a link to instructional material; most learners download slides prior to class
Live video	Allows users to present information themselves by using synchronous audio and video in the classroom	Used rarely due to bandwidth and connection issues
Telephone	Allows users to present themselves using synchronous audio in the classroom	The most robust way for learners to speak to instructors and other learners, though awkward to set up. It was used primarily for workshop reports.
VoIP	Allows users to present themselves using synchronous audio in the classroom via their computers	Used to connect learners to instructors and other learners. Less robust than telephone, but easier to set up. Often used for workshop reports.
Text chat	Allows users to interact with one another and instructors synchronously via text-based messages	Used by distance learners to communicate with each other during class sessions and to send questions to instructors. Also use by on-campus students once WiFi became available in the campus classroom.
Electronic whiteboards	Allows users to contribute to the construction of a common space supporting some drawing and text capabilities	Used for workshop reports

(VoIP)—allow users to interact with one another and their instructors. Our observations suggest that learners access these media at very different rates depending, in part, on technical limitations and, in part, on characteristics of human communication processes. Technical limitations, primarily low bandwidth and fragile connections, precluded learners from sending their video into classrooms for all but very occasional use during the time of our observations. Yet interactions via media less demanding of Internet bandwidth such as text chat, whiteboard, and audio were used very frequently.

Supporting Interaction Through Text Chat

Text chat was the medium learners used most for collaborative interaction. Learners would let text chat run constantly, although the volume and frequency with which individual learners accessed chat varied considerably. Sometimes chat interactions dropped off to nearly nothing, even though many learners were signed in. Other times, the text chat window scrolled through message after message. If the class was large, students could have problems scrolling back and forth in the chat window, laboring to read comments and leave responses for one another. These problems left some students feeling socially isolated because they wanted to make themselves part of class discussion.

Messages often dealt directly with class material, whether being commentary about what instructors were saying or learners' asking each other for clarification about class administrative matters such as when papers were due. At other times messages wandered off to either topics that were tangentially related to instructional content, such as learners' comparing work processes at their respective companies, or learners' doing largely social networking. Some participants very regularly contributed to text chat; others signed in but just lurked rather than contributing content. Some participants ventured off with others to private chat sessions; others stuck to the main public chat space.

The role of chat was so important to learners that at one point it produced what we began to call the "parallel universes" of on-campus and distance students. At first, on-campus students did not have access to the chat due to the lack of a WiFi Internet connection in the classroom. As a result, on-campus students regarded themselves as part of one network and distance students saw themselves as part of another, more active network. As soon as WiFi service became available in the campus classroom, however, on-campus students eagerly adopted text chat.

The frequency with which learners choose to be active in chat indicates how important interaction with others is to their learning. A recent study of several of RPI's distance courses has shown that the social networks among learners affects the respect learners have for one another, the motivation they have to participate in class, their satisfaction with classes, and their grades (Sundararajan, 2009).

Supporting Interaction Through Electronic Whiteboards

Electronic whiteboards also are largely text based. In our observations, learners used electronic whiteboards to support small group interactions during the workshop sections of class sessions. Generally, they used electronic whiteboards to enter, edit, and display the results of workshops. Students generally spent about 20 to 30 minutes per 90-minute class session on workshops. This meant that, although they might just use an electronic whiteboard once, they would use it for a long time on that occasion. RPI courses analyzed by Danchak and Huguet (2004) had found even higher proportions of workshop activities to lecture by instructors.

Questionnaires, observation of learners' working during classes, and observations of learner performance in laboratory tests all revealed that learners were unhappy with user interfaces provided in whiteboards. Whiteboards did not follow user interface conventions commonly found in word processors or presentation programs. Whiteboards did allow drawing of simple graphics, but the drawing tools tend to be even less developed than their text entry systems. These problems distracted users from instructional content and left them frustrated.

Electronic whiteboards were not used in isolation. Learners needed at least one additional medium to conduct workshops. Most of the time, learners used text chat to accompany their work on whiteboards, looking back and forth between the text chat window and the whiteboard as they worked. Our observations during laboratory testing suggested, however, that users really prefer audio-based interactions to text-based interactions.

Supporting Interaction Through Audio

Fragility of connections initially limited students' use of the VoIP component built into distance-education platforms. As a result, they preferred telephone service or more robust Internet-based services such as Skype. Additional experience with upstream audio showed, however, that lost connections, echoes, and other spurious noises could be reduced by muting the microphones of silent participants and by using headsets to reduce audio feedback between microphones and speakers attached to the same computers. We anticipate that future improvements in upstream audio should make accessing this medium less frustrating.

In our observations, learners used audio for much less time than text-based or whiteboard-based interactions. Unless learners gave a presentation, they would not spend much time on an audio call.

Judging by learners' very positive responses to audio during workshops, however, the appeal of audio may vary by its application. Learners seemed to value audio interaction with other students and instructors enough to persist in trying to find ways to make it work for them. During laboratory testing, we made live audio available to test subjects. They immediately dropped text chat as the medium for discussion during workshops in favor of live audio. Subsequent breakdowns in live audio forced test subjects to again use text chat. Test subjects uniformly complained about these breakdowns, demonstrating the perceived advantage of live audio for workshop discussions.

Creating Opportunities for Sharing

The opportunities for sharing provided by distance-education components varied considerably. Text chat, live audio, and text on whiteboards generally were shared with all participants, but this didn't mean that the audiences paid equal attention to all these media.

Text chat, for instance, was easy to ignore. Instructors busy delivering lectures might look at text chat only occasionally; teaching assistants were needed to call attention to learner questions posted via chat. During workshops, text chat would be limited to the members of an individual workshop group. When the group brought the results of their work to the entire class, however, they would switch to audio to draw the attention of everyone in the class.

The kinds of products learners created to share varied considerably in scale: short notes, short questions, bulleted lists, prearranged presentations with slide shows, and even the rare full-motion video. The electronic whiteboard was the most frequent medium for sharing, and instructors tried to encourage participation by all learners, but not always successfully.

Providing Protocols for Interaction

Because distance-learning platforms include so many media, technologies, and participants, the possibilities for breakdown are manifold. For example, one instructor I know quite well, repeatedly forgot to turn on his microphone when returning from intermissions in class sessions despite his best intentions. A lot of breakdowns, however, involved communication protocols.

One kind of protocol relates to turn-taking in conversations during class sessions. For example, downstream video and upstream audio both entailed time delays. When an instructor talked to a learner, the conversation could be awkward and disjointed. Conversational facilitators such as "uh-huh" would often be heard simultaneously with the other participant's talk. To manage the breakdown, both parties would stop talking, correct what was said, and then start up again. If participants tried to avoid this problem by eliminating facilitators, another kind of breakdown would occur: their counterparts, not sure they were being heard, would stop what they were saying to ask for reassurance. The protocol that seemed to work best was to avoid facilitators after making sure that the audio link was working.

Another kind of protocol involved learners' trying to decide when and if to ask questions. Because of time delays, they might hear what an instructor was saying after the instructor had moved on to another topic. Should learners nevertheless go ahead and ask a question that was out of sync with an instructor's verbal flow? Instructors could deal with this issue by setting up a protocol in which such interruptions were expected, thereby removing the stigma from out-of-sync questions.

Protocols also needed to be developed to manage the negotiation among workshop participants over control of the electronic whiteboard. Who, for example, would control text entry and editing? Could more than one person enter text? Who would lead workshop discussion and in what medium? Technology itself does not provide answers to these questions of protocol. For instance, one of the distance education platforms allowed more than one person to enter text simultaneously on the whiteboard by giving each participant a screen cursor with his or her name attached. The intended effect was to let participants see who was entering what text. Unfortunately, as soon as more than two participants were entering text and moving the cursors, the actual effect was that learners felt attacked by "cursor bees." A communication protocol needed to be established that only one person would enter text on the whiteboard and others would enter discussion comments on the text chat.

Some of these breakdowns could be reduced with improvements in hardware, software, and bandwidth, but the need to develop appropriate communication protocols to support interactions will always remain. Even if a distance-learning platform could reliably support audio links for 20 to 30 students, some kind of protocol will always be necessary to manage access among them.

Supporting Interaction Among Users

This chapter has focused on supporting opportunities for interaction in engaging web-based communications, using current distance learning platforms as an extended exemplar. Our research suggests that users of such platforms will go to great lengths to take advantage of opportunities to interact. People want to be active participants in communication, not just passive receivers of information. As options in web-based communication increase, options for interactions among users grow as well. The role of the designer of engaging communication is to provide support for those interactions, provide ways that users can share what they create, and provide clear protocols for interactions with others.

For Further Exploration

1. The problems that Krull mentions students having with electronic whiteboards is reminiscent of the issues that students in Fernheimer's study (Principle 2: Design for Usability) had with wiki-markup language: failure to use user interface conventions commonly found in word processors or presentation programs. Working with a partner at a distance, try out the whiteboard on Adobe Connect (free trial at https://www.adobe.com/cfusion/adobeconnect/index.cfm?event=trial). Together create a diagram with labels. What problems with user interface conventions do you encounter? Discuss possible ways you might address them.
2. Krull's research points to the importance of supporting interaction among users in the classroom. What does Krull's analysis of distance-learning platforms suggest about the probable success of massive open online courses, or MOOCs? You might also want to take a look at the experience of one MOOC dropout, Audrey Watters (2012), at http://www.insidehighered.com/blogs/hack-higher-education/udacitys-cs101-partial-course-evaluation.

Create a Sense of Place

Audrey G. Bennett

Engaging web-based communication creates a sense of place in two ways. It provides consistency in look and feel to signal a sense of *physical* place. And it gives users a sense of *cultural* place, through cross-cultural and culturally specific aesthetic cues about who users are. In this chapter, Bennett and her team use their work on an interactive image for HIV/AIDS awareness and prevention to illustrate how a sense of place can meld global and local cues.

The Concept of Place

In the 1970s, the first graphic computing introduced the concept of a virtual desktop—a sense of physical place that has been so profoundly integrated into our computing interactions that we can now sit at almost any computer and feel at ease. It provides a comforting familiarity—like the American living abroad for several months who suddenly has an inexplicable urge to eat at McDonald's.

Traditional approaches to usability recognize the importance of this sense of physical place with the injunction to make context recognizable and navigation visible and provide users with timely feedback. Through navigational cues and routine updates, users can keep track of where they are. Sense of physical place can be achieved through the use of way-finding perceptual cues or digital signage that imitates in functionality the environmental signage we depend on daily in our physical environment. Intersensory perceptual cues, used consistently from page to page, can also confirm the user's sense of physical place.

Creating a Sense of Physical Place

In our work to design an interactive image to engage users with HIV/AIDS awareness and prevention information, we used two separate strands of visual cues to provide users with a sense of physical space. As shown in Figure 9.1, Figure 10.3, and Figure 10.4, users access different sets of navigational buttons in three stages of interaction with the interactive image. In the first stage, represented by the image in Figure 9.1, the navigational buttons, colored gray and placed under the title of the image, provide the user with access to all pages of the interactive image successively (for first-time users) or nonsequentially (for repeat users). The navigational button on

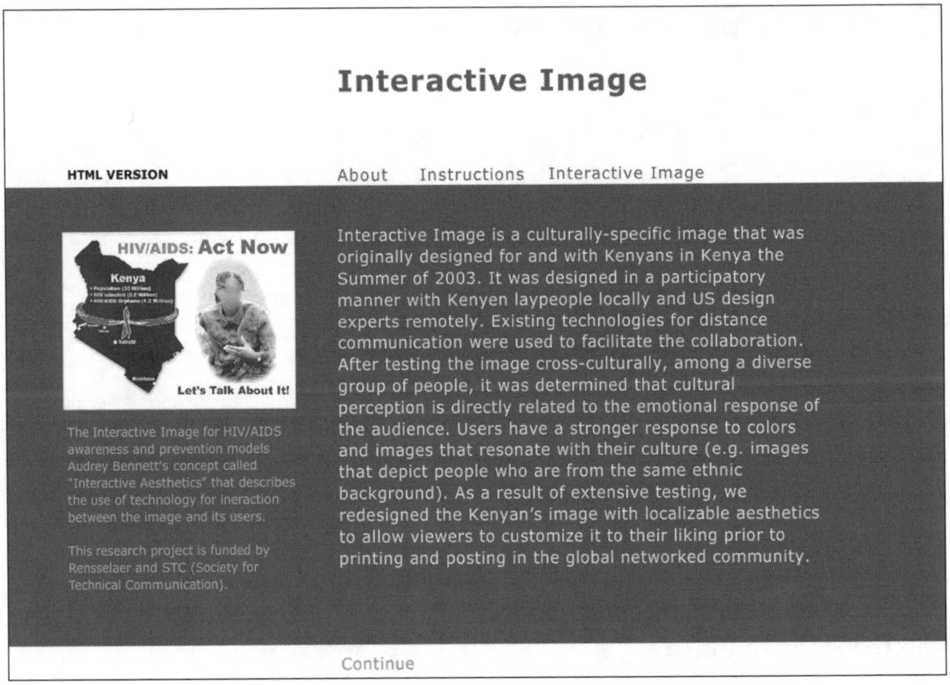

Figure 9.1 The first page of the final redesign of the interactive image.

the bottom of the first page, the welcome page, provides additional background information about the interactive image. After reading the instructions in the second phase of interacting with the interactive image, users become aware that they can modify it; and, through a link embedded in the verbal instructions, they learn how to go about doing so. When they finally get to the interactive image in stage 3 (see Figure 10.3), hidden buttons allow them to customize the interactive image, print it, or go behind the scenes to another navigational menu (see Figure 10.4), where they can go back to the interactive image experience or share their creation via Flickr. They can also connect with others via a Facebook group or obtain more information about HIV/AIDS via organizations such as the World Health Organization.

All of these navigation options communicate to users where they have been, where they are currently, and where they have left to explore. Both visual and verbal cues play a role here. Verbal cues communicate sense of place through spoken or typeset text, whereas visual cues communicate through typographic treatment, such as choice of font, typeface, point size, color, spatial or temporal positioning or grouping, shape, size, and style (i.e., illustrative, photographic, or digitally rendered). As this example indicates, sense of physical place in engaging web-based communication is often conveyed through cross-cultural and culturally specific aesthetic cues: a combination of global features like those in airplane emergency information graphics and local features like those on a stop sign in the United States.

Creating a Sense of Cultural Place

As the earlier example with McDonald's suggested, we are often reassured by cross-cultural associations. But, at another level, a sense of place can be at odds with our sense of cross-cultural association: My local coffeehouse has a character, history, and feel that the more global McDonald's will never supply. Computers have only recently become able to provide a local sense of cultural place through customization. We now take it for granted that we can customize our Google home page or Facebook site, but such flexibility was a slow achievement. As a result, we can now customize engaging web-based communications to convey cultural meaning and identity—that is, sense of cultural place.

With the advent of the World Wide Web and the increased interactivity of Web 2.0, giving users a local sense of cultural place becomes increasingly important. The World Wide Web provides content developers with access to global users from diverse cultural backgrounds, and Web 2.0, a relatively recent technological phenomenon, provides these global users with unprecedented opportunities to share control of the content's design and even its distribution. Access to diverse users creates a need for content to bridge cultural divides between the content developer and his or her target user.

Although Horton (2005), Coe (1996), and Pettersson (1982) explore the different ways images can be interpreted by different cultures, a lingering intellectual divide still exists between a cross-cultural approach to meaning and an approach that is more culture specific (Kostelnick, 1995). On the one hand, a modernist perspective claims that content that communicates cross-culturally comes from formally trained design professionals and represents high design. On the other hand, the postmodernist perspective purports that culturally specific content is socially constructed (Csikszentmihalyi, 1991) and represents low design.

The active user interaction of engaging web-based communication creates the need, however, for content to be usable in both cross-cultural and culturally specific ways. It is for this reason that we advocate a more collaborative and participatory design approach that gives users more control over the creative decisions that affect the final image outcome (Bennett et al., 2006). When professionals allow control over the design process to be shared with users and other stakeholders, the outcome has a better chance of reflecting sense of place in both a global and local sense.

Sense of Place in the Interactive Image

An inclusive approach is what generated the first redesign, the interactive poster shown in Figure 9.2. The original design, collaboratively designed in a participatory manner in Kenya with Kenyans for Kenyans, had reflected a culturally specific sense of place among the culture of people to whom it was targeted. As a two-dimensional, printed image, it was designed for distribution by way of community bulletin boards in Kenya.

When we tested the original design for cross-cultural communication with diverse users in the United States, however, it fell short from the perspective of the sense-of-place principle both culturally and physically. In terms of providing a sense of cultural place, the image incorporated primarily culturally specific images—a Kenyan

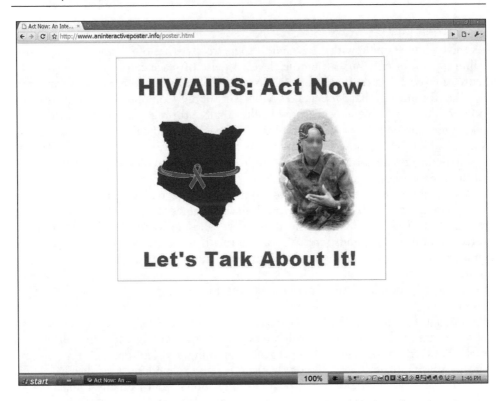

Figure 9.2 First redesign of the interactive image displayed via a website that provides interactive aesthetics for the user to customize the image. It includes a photographic image of a Kenyan woman.

woman and an illustration of Kenya. Although the woman could be interpreted as a woman of African American or Afro-Caribbean heritage, one would most likely deduce that, because her photograph is juxtaposed to an illustration of Kenya, she is Kenyan or has some relation to it. As a result, evaluators generally had a sense that the image was not for them since they are not Kenyans or even African American or Afro-Caribbean. In terms of providing a sense of physical place, evaluators understood the purpose of the image posted on a community board but could not retrieve the message. The image reads "Act Now" and "Let's Talk About It!" but does not give specific information about how to act or where to go to talk about it or with whom one would be talking.

When usability testing indicated that it failed to establish the same sense of place with culturally diverse users, the printed image evolved into the first redesign displayed in Figure 9.2. As an interactive image, it is more suitable for cross-cultural communication in that it incorporates the ideals of both global and local perspectives. The second redesign took reflecting cultural place one step further: On the third page, shown in Figure 9.3, the user is presented with four opportunities to customize the HIV/AIDS image to better reflect his or her cultural identity. Users may change the country to their own; change the graphic of the person to someone that reflects their cultural identity; or, edit the type—both the header and footer—to reflect the users' vernacular.

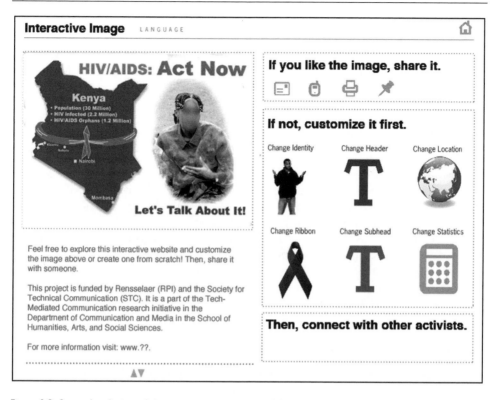

Figure 9.3 Second redesign of the interactive poster modified online via interactive visual aesthetics to reflect and communicate to a different culture by way of ethnicity and geographic location.

By allowing users to change the image's visual aesthetics to resonate with their own cultural identity and/or heritage, this engaging communication literally creates a sense of cultural place.

Thus, in the final design represented in Figure 9.1, cross-cultural and culturally specific resonance are reflected in the image's visual, verbal, and technical synergistic design. Situating the image in a web environment establishes sense of physical place— a comforting familiarity—since the World Wide Web has a common framework of interaction widely known globally. This framework includes two types of interactions: give and take. First, there is one-way interaction in which the user takes away information from what is presented on the website. Then, there is two-way interaction in which the user gives information that is added to the website. For instance, our ability to customize our Google, Facebook, or New York Times home pages exemplifies two-way interaction.

The interactive image reflects both one-way and two-way interaction for greater cultural resonance to achieve "communicative effectiveness" (Bennett, 2012). If there is cultural resonance upon initial perception, then the image communicates one way. The introductory and instructional pages give users background information about the image and instructions on how to interact with it. However, if there is cultural dissonance upon initial perception of the image, the user can engage in two-way interaction with it and customize the presentation of the poster's visual and verbal elements to achieve cultural resonance. All visual and verbal elements in the image are interactive—that is, modifiable—and the users know this if they read the background information and instructions that are presented in previous screens, prior to arriving at the page with the interactive image.

Creating a Sense of Place

As the example of the interactive image suggests, the goal to create a sense of place can be incorporated in all steps of the design process. In the original design process, sense of place was incorporated into the printed image through the use of a collaborative process that shared control of creativity with Kenyan users. As a result, the graphics were culturally appropriate for the targeted user. In the usability evaluation process, sense of place was also incorporated by employing heuristic evaluation with the intended users; this led to the development of the customization that allows users to localize their own content. And, finally, in the redesign, we incorporated a sense of place by analyzing the user experience and reflecting on user feedback to determine how best to aestheticize verbal and visual content for cross-cultural navigation.

For Further Exploration

1. Navigation is key to developing a sense of place on the web. Look at eBay's home page (http://www.ebay.com/). How many ways are available to planning your eBay journey? Click down on one of the offered links until you get to a specific auction offer. How can you get back to where you came from? How do you know where you are? How might you plan where to go next?

2. One of the problems with the social media application Twitter has been the potential to lose a sense of one's place in the Twitter stream (Potts & Jones, 2011). Twitter clients like TweetDeck and Janetter have been created to restore that sense of place. Analyze one of these interfaces to see how it provides users with a sense of place.

Plan to Continue the Engagement

Audrey G. Bennett

When you plan to continue the engagement in web-based communication, your design acknowledges an interaction beyond the initial one. With technical ease, you should clearly invite users to continue connections past the current encounter, to move outside of the formal interactions, to go behind the scenes. Users may be presented with opportunities to connect with other users, acquire more information, share a memorable experience, edit the current content, or even create new content. Bennett and her team explain how the goal to continue the engagement drove the development of an interactive image for HIV/AIDS awareness and prevention.

The Concept of Engagement

In *Wikinomics*, Tapscott and Williams (2006) note that mass collaboration has changed everything—from the way we conduct business to the way we interact with information. The facilitation of bottom-up, individually shared control over information development with collective, global users by way of open-source and other Web 2.0 technologies represents the next frontier for disciplines such as technical communication that produce verbal and visual rhetoric for public consumption on or by way of the web and other digital media. The existence of open source is just one piece of evidence that confirms that the new communication experience no longer needs to be confined to the initial experience. Users want to go behind (and beyond) the scenes to continue the engagement.

Extending Nielsen's heuristics (1994b), continuing the engagement requires the seamless synchronization of visual, verbal, and technical functionality, as shown in Figure 10.1. No longer are images solely enhancing the transmittance of verbal information. As we shall see, visual and verbal information are equally important in continuing the engagement.

The principle of planning to continue the engagement depends on what Benkler (2006) calls a networked infrastructure to reach broader, global users. This emerging networked communication infrastructure is important because it facilitates interaction between users around the world in the production, consumption, and distribution of user-generated information. Tidwell (2006) refers to these contexts as a key interface idiom that she calls social spaces that include Twitter, Facebook, Flickr, YouTube and, more generally, wikis, blogs, and podcasts.

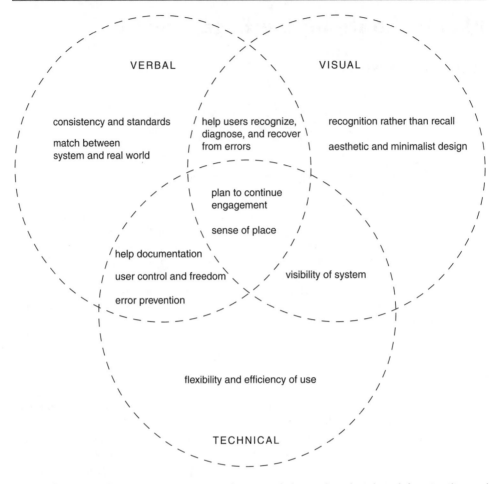

Figure 10.1 Nielsen's heuristics taxonomized into verbal, visual, and technical functionality and ex-tended to include the principle to plan to continue the engagement.

Extending Interaction

Continuing the engagement requires extending interaction beyond the static one-way communication of traditional print media. Michael Rush (1999, p. 216) posits that because of the emergence of new media, "interactivity is a new form of the visual experience." The new visual experience that Rush refers to is a deeper, more active interaction with images that includes interfaces. As we have seen with the HIV/AIDS project introduced in our discussion of Principle 9, the static printed poster of yester-day (Figure 10.2) is now the dynamic tech-based interface of today (Figure 10.3). New media technologies—such as Web 2.0; open source; algorithm-based, computational graphic manipulation; actionscript; and hypertext markup language—provide the digital backbone that facilitates more active interaction with images such as interfaces beyond simple "one-way, passive interaction" (Bennett, 2012, p. 66) of visual perception in which the user merely looks at an image to retrieve meaning.

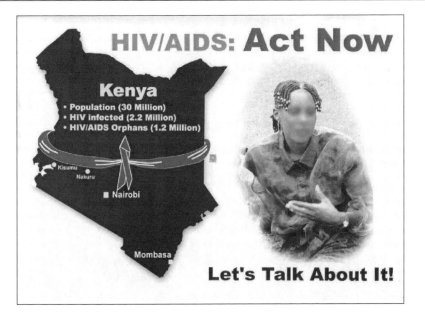

Figure 10.2 Original design of the printed image collaboratively designed with Kenyans for Kenyans.

These technologies provide "active interaction" (Bennett, 2012, p. 66) with interfaces that enable their consumption in unprecedented ways—including enabling, modifying, or completing their functionality. In Web 2.0 social spaces, users are like "smart mobs" (Rheingold, 2003) that expect to engage, sometimes synchronously, with content in immersive interactions which my previous work calls "two- and three-way active interactions" (Bennett, 2012, p. 66). These interactions go beyond the one-way communication transaction in which information is channeled from the encoder to the decoder. In two-way active interaction, as we have seen, users can talk back to the interface by customizing the way visual information is presented or by editing the verbal presentation of ideas (p. 66). Three-way active interaction moves one step further beyond the interaction between user and image to include all of those situations in which users can repurpose information for distribution to new users (p. 67). This is the heart of continuing the engagement.

But this enhanced interactive experience isn't limited to visual functionality. It is also inclusive of verbal and technical functionality. For instance, blogs, wikis, and the recent proliferation of social networking media (e.g., Flickr) epitomize the amalgamation of verbal, visual, and technical functionality to communicate effectively. They provide hearty opportunities for users to engage in two-way active interaction with each other to develop information. They also enable users to go behind (and beyond) the scene for content development or redesign purposes or simply to strengthen the rhetorical effect of the information being conveyed.

Married to communication technologies—like iPods, iPads, and smart phones—media innovation today enables users to engage in three-way active interactions, distributing information interpersonally with many others in a small amount of time and with minimal to no additional financial resources. New media have democratized information production in society (Benkler, 2006), giving users open access to the technical and human resources needed to be producers of their own content or facilitate a collaborative effort toward a common goal—such as engaging with other users in the production and distribution of information.

Engagement in the Interactive Image

To illustrate the change in the design process that is needed to plan to continue the engagement, we turn once again to the interactive image. Originally collaboratively designed with Kenyans as a printed image, as shown in Figure 10.2, it attempted to communicate HIV/AIDS awareness and prevention to Kenyans. As a pin-up image, targeted users engage in one-way interaction with its content. That is, they retrieve information and meaning from reading the image as they pass by it posted on community bulletin boards.

However, when we tested it with culturally diverse users in the United States, we found that, although one-way interaction was the intended goal, evaluators were unable to retrieve information from the image due to varying degrees of noise. For instance, due to cultural incongruences between the encoder and the decoders, passersby were not able to engage in one-way interaction with the image where they were able to quickly perceive and retrieve the encoder's message. The few who did culturally connect with the image and read it endured verbal and visual noise that prevented any plan to continue the engagement beyond the printed image.

Figure 10.3 The final redesign of the interactive image.

In particular, they all felt that more information was needed on how to "act now"—the main charge of the image. If they agreed that HIV/AIDS is a health threat for them, then how should they "act now" to help themselves and others? Many requested a URL to browse or telephone number to call for more information. Generally, they all wanted more information about what to do to prevent the further spread of HIV and information on HIV/AIDS in general.

The iterative process used to redesign the poster from a printed form to an interactive, digital one provided insight on the role of the plan to continue the engagement principle within the usability process. In fact, the decision to transform the poster from a print to digital format was made to provide the user with opportunities to continue the engagement. In the final redesign of the poster as an interactive poster, shown in Figure 10.3, users were given options to continue the engagement with the poster and its content.

- Through hidden buttons, intuitively accessed, users could navigate away from the image to get more information about its content, share it with others electronically, or print it for posting locally on a community bulletin board.
- Users were given the option to connect with others who are also HIV "affected" through a Facebook group.
- Users were also given the option to post their interactive image outcome on an image bank on the topic via Flickr. There they could also access other HIV/AIDS

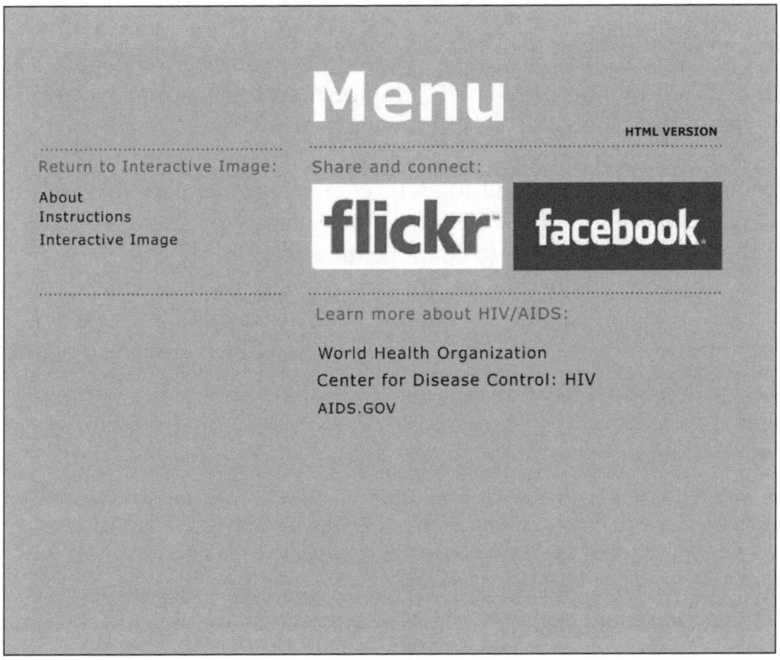

Figure 10.4 The final redesign of an interactive image menu with options for continuing the engagement.

awareness and prevention images or get motivated to design their own image from scratch and share it.

• Links to the World Health Organization, Centers for Disease Control, and AIDS. gov provide more fact-based information about HIV/AIDS.

These components, detailed in Figure 10.4, draw heavily on the existing social networking infrastructure and aim to meet the demand by users to continue the engagement beyond their initial contact with the poster. This page presents the user with clear options to continue the engagement beyond the interactive poster.

Planning to Continue the Engagement

This chapter has described how the evolution of a one-page, printed HIV/AIDS image into a tech-mediated, interactive image with multiple pages was driven by a plan to allow users to continue the engagement. Unlike traditional technical communications, engaging web-based communications often go beyond an efficient one-way passive interaction with content to invite users to go beyond the initial encounter. Through two-way interactions, users can customize visual and verbal content. Through three-way interactions, they can distribute this content to users beyond the original context of interaction.

For Further Exploration

1. Marketing agency Wieden + Kennedy made history in 2010 by offering to continue the engagement with viewers of Isaiah Mustafa's ad for Old Spice, "The Man Your Man Could Smell Like" (http://www.youtube.com/watch?v=owGykV bfgUE&list=PLB9F260CE56D04E73&index=1&feature=plpp_video). You can read about the campaign at http://www.readwriteweb.com/archives/how_old_ spice_won_the_internet.php (Kirkpatrick, 2010) and watch the Internet videos the company made to respond to users' comments at http://www.youtube.com/pl aylist?list=PL484F058C3EAF7FA6&feature=plcp. What lessons would you draw from the success of this plan to continue the engagement?
2. Zappos, the largest online shoe shop, uses a loyalty business model that generates high levels of repeat customers (Zappos, n.d.). Take a look at its web site (http://www.zappos.com/) and associated social media. How is Zappos designed to continue the engagement?

The Case Studies

Case Study 1

Information Galleries for Young People

James P. Zappen, RENSSELAER POLYTECHNIC INSTITUTE
Elia N. Desjardins, RENSSELAER POLYTECHNIC INSTITUTE
John Britton, PEER 2 PEER UNIVERSITY

The Connected Kids information system and galleries (http://connectedkids.rpi.edu/index.php/) afford opportunities for experiments in several aspects of designing engaging web-based communication, from traditional approaches to usability (Brinck, Gergle, & Wood, 2002, pp. 1–11; Nielsen, 1993, pp. 26–37) through newer concepts in experience design (Bolter & Gromala, 2003, pp. 2–7, 48–56, 62–69; Norman, 2004, pp. 35–60; Shedroff, 2001, pp. 2–11) to recent developments in user-generated content (Bruns, 2008, pp. 9–36, 69–258; Tapscott & Williams, 2006, pp. 34–64) and the special problems associated with the public sharing of creative content (Bruns, 2008, pp. 259–288; Lessig, 2006, pp. 169–232), especially content by and for children and teens. In addition, the galleries pose challenges for future experiments in media remix and convergence and digital storytelling across multiple platforms and multiple media forms (Friedlander, 2008; Jenkins, 2006, pp. 1–24; Lessig, 2008, pp. 23–83; Miller, 2008, pp. 41–68, 227–239; Nightingale, 2007).

In the course of development of the galleries, we sought to address specific design goals in web-based communication following the project flow shown in Figure 11.1. As explained in our chapter on Principle 1, we designed for diverse users, including children, teens, and adults, and we anticipated the new challenges in user-system and user-user interactions (Warnick, 2007, pp. 69–90), described in greater detail below. As explained in our chapter on Principle 7, we also sought to maximize user control (Nielsen, 2000, pp. 214–217), keeping in mind that control is not a property or possession of either the designer or the user but an experience enacted in the process of use. In addition, we sought to achieve a reasonable balance between designing for usability—with its traditional emphasis upon functionality and efficiency in the performance of user tasks—and supporting interactions between and among users and ensuring rich experiences that invite further engagement—consistent with the newer concept of experience design. Finally, we tested for both usability and the quality of the user experience and found that we needed to test not only with appropriate user groups but also with sensitivity to the specific contexts of use, which seem to affect the nature and quality of the user experience.

In this chapter, we provide some background on the Connected Kids galleries, sketch some recent developments in design theory and practice, describe our modest experiments with the galleries and some possible future directions for these experiments, and recount some of the challenges of testing with sensitivity to both appropriate user groups and the context of use.

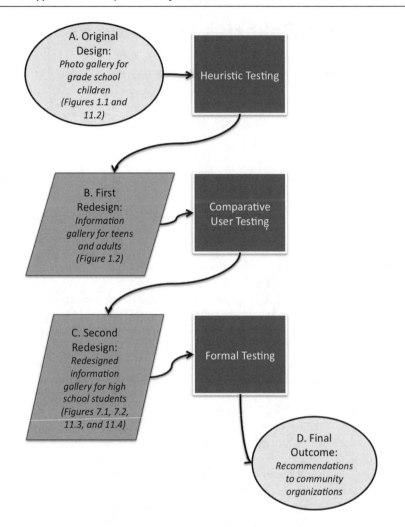

Figure 11.1 Project flow for the information galleries for young people project.

The Connected Kids Galleries

The Connected Kids information system was initially designed in partnership with Rensselaer County, New York, as a youth-services resource with listings of services and activities for children and teens in the area.[1] The system offers an easy-to-use copy-and-paste interface for data entry and separate interfaces for parents, teens, kids, and organizations—all accessible via the World Wide Web. The system also includes "About CK" and "Gallery" pages, with access to both parents/children and teens/adults galleries. The galleries provide opportunities for users to access information about youth services and activities in visual and audio rather than text-only displays, with artwork and photos for children and more diverse multimedia content for teens and adults. Studies of information and entertainment resources for children document the need to design with a diversity of approaches and media forms, to offer opportunities for both self-expression and social interaction, and to ensure a sense of ownership and control (Druin, 1996; Druin et al., 1999, pp. 65–70; Gilutz & Nielsen, n.d., pp. 14–103). Druin et al. (1999, pp. 65–67) report that children want highly visual and multisensory experiences; that they want these experience to be expressive and social; and that they want and need to feel in control, perhaps even more so than adults. As Druin et al. (p. 65) explain, "The nature of being a child is such that they are dependent on others. Children are empowered when they feel in control of their environment and when they feel they 'own' the environment." Gilutz and Nielsen (pp. 14–20) present 70 principles for the design of Web-based resources for children, emphasizing the need to offer rich multimedia content in intuitive and easy-to-use interfaces. They also emphasize the need to ensure user control.

Studies such as these highlight the special challenges of designing information resources for children, and their findings are not so different from our own. In our galleries project, however, we faced the additional challenge of designing for quite diverse audiences, including both children and teens, a challenge that we believe extends beyond our own work to the design of information resources generally. Recent developments in design theory and practice complicate this issue further by providing ever richer resources for creating a quality user experience and integrating user-generated content with multimedia forms. In addition, these developments present opportunities for media remix and convergence and digital storytelling across multiple platforms and media forms. Such new and enhanced resources challenge designers to create a wider array of user options and richer user experiences and at the same time to ensure optimum functionality and efficiency in the performance of user tasks and a reasonable balance of control between and among all of the elements of a user's experience.

Recent Developments in Design Theory and Practice

Usability principles might seem to be at odds with new and emerging resources for enhancing the user experience: efficiency in the performance of user tasks or a one-to-one match between functions and controls, for example, might seem to be at odds with opportunities for user interactions or users' sense of engagement in their experience. On the efficiency principle, users simply want to perform a task and move on; on the experience principle, they want to enjoy and perhaps repeat the experience. Recent developments in design theory and practice exacerbate this apparent tension, as the emphasis upon a quality user experience and the need to accommodate user-generated content stretch the performance capabilities of a system. In fact, however, these are not competing but rather complementary principles: if a user experiences a system as dysfunctional and inefficient, he or she will not have a quality user experience.

Recent debates suggest an either/or approach to the functionality/experience divide, but successful design in fact requires a both/and approach. Nielsen (2000, pp. 99–100) succinctly captures the traditional approach to World Wide Web usability when he compares the web experience to a theatrical performance:

> Ultimately, users visit your website for its content. Everything else is just the backdrop. The design is there to allow people access to the content. The old analogy

is somebody who goes to see a theater performance: When they leave the theater, you want them to be discussing how great the *play* was and not how great the costumes were.

Bolter and Gromala (2003, pp. 4–5) challenge this view, which seems to imply that "the most efficient design is one that becomes invisible and leaves the user alone with the information content," typically displayed in text rather than image. Against this view, they urge "the strategy of getting the user to look *at* the interface or object of design rather than *through* it" (p. 56). The traditional strategy operates on the principle of transparency, Bolter and Gromala's on the principle of reflectivity; one views the interface as a window, the other as a mirror (pp. 48–49, 55–56, 62–65). The strategy of transparency emphasizes information delivery, and the strategy of reflectivity emphasizes a compelling user experience (pp. 67–68). Shedroff (2001, p. 4) similarly argues that the essence of design in digital media is to capture the richness of the user's real-life experience: "Experiences are the foundation for all life events and form the core of what interactive media have to offer."

Norman (2004, pp. 35–45), however, urges a more balanced view that incorporates both perspectives—system functionality and user experience—and adds a third—emotion. Visceral design addresses the user's experience—its initial impact, appearance, touch, and feel; behavioral design addresses the system's function, performance, and usability; and reflective design addresses the user's feelings, emotions, and thoughts. On this view, both perspectives—indeed all three perspectives—are essential for successful design.

One way to enhance the user's engagement and experience is to create opportunities for users to contribute and share their own content. User-generated content helps to create a sense of ownership and control, enhance interactions with other users, and expand and enrich the resources accessible to other users. It also introduces special difficulties and challenges due to legal and ethical requirements to protect privacy and secure permissions, especially in a resource designed for children and teens.

This capability is especially prominent in Web 2.0 environments, which permit more dynamic user-system and user-user interactions. The underlying concept has deep roots in the open-source software movement: "Given enough eyeballs, all bugs are shallow" (Bruns, 2008, p. 24; Raymond, 2001, p. 30). In the newer web-based environments, however, the sharing of content extends well beyond the fixing of bugs or even the development of open-source software to sharing for the purposes of expressing oneself, exchanging information, and developing social relationships. Tapscott and Williams (2006, pp. 46–62) describe a new generation of digital collaborators who are inhabiting new social spaces such as Myspace and Facebook; engaging in global community-action projects; developing and sharing creative content; restructuring and revitalizing the workplace; and driving the development of a new global, collaborative economy. Bruns (2008, pp. 69–258) captures the range and diversity of this world of digital collaboration in his account of the emergence of citizen journalism in both mainstream and alternative media outlets such as blogs; the potential tension between folk knowledge and expert knowledge in information resources such as Wikipedia and Citizendium; the emergence of knowledge structures or folksonomies such as tagging, linking, and browsing to enhance access to these resources; and the explosion of distributed creativity in fan fiction and in photo, video, and music sharing spaces such as Flickr, ccMixter, and YouTube.

Such widespread information sharing raises challenging copyright, privacy, and protection issues (Bruns, 2008, pp. 259–288; Lessig, 2006, pp. 169–232). For users under age 18, the privacy and protection issues are especially challenging and require a careful balancing of the youngsters' right to self-expression and their parents' and guardians' obligation to protect their privacy, safety, and security. As Tapscott and Williams (2006, p. 47) observe, younger users—the digital generation—"tends to value individual rights, including the right to privacy and the right to have and express their own views" and has "a very strong sense of the common good and of collective social and civic responsibility." But the Internet is a dangerous place. Photo-, music-, and video-sharing resources have millions of potential viewers (Bruns, 2008, p. 259), and powerful search capabilities ensure ready access to these resources, by both innocent and not-so-innocent users (Lessig, 2006, pp. 204–205). Designers have a legal and ethical responsibility to guard against potential abuses.

Connected Kids Gallery Experiments

In the development of the Connected Kids galleries, we sought to provide rich and engaging experiences for children and for teens and adults, to develop content suited to each of these user groups, and to balance the need to develop rich content against the need to ensure the functionality and usability of the galleries. For the children's gallery, we sought to create a rich visual experience in a simple and intuitive interface. For the teen gallery (Figure 1.2), through several iterations, we sought to create both more sophisticated user options and an enhanced user experience. In the first iteration, we aimed primarily at increasing the range of user options, using the capabilities of the state-of-the-art gallery software (http://galleryproject.org/). In the second iteration, we sought to enhance the gallery content by including both youth services and activities and information of more general interest with visual, audio, and textual components produced by and for both organizations and, insofar as practicable, younger contributors, subject to privacy and protection constraints. As explained in our chapter on Principle 1, we were not able to assess the quality of children's experience with the children's gallery since we tested only with older users. We were, however, able to assess the functionality of many of the features of the teen gallery and also, to some extent, to assess the quality of the teens' experience since we tested with an appropriate group of students of high school age. We also conducted both preliminary and follow-up interviews with the teachers to ensure that we designed our tests and interpreted our test results with attention to the specific contexts of use.

For the original design of the children's gallery, we had created a simple navigation system and a set of slide shows depicting the services and activities of several youth-services organizations, as shown in Figure 11.2. With assistance from a student artist/photographer, we added photos from a Healthy Kids Day at the local YMCA and other events and created colorful photo collages for the main pages. The slide shows seemed simple and intuitive enough for younger users. In heuristic testing with college students, however, these older users noted the lack of standard gallery functions such as a category scheme, a search function, thumbnail images, breadcrumbs, a help function, and contact information. Given these limitations, we created a new information gallery for our first and second redesigns to meet the needs and expectations of older

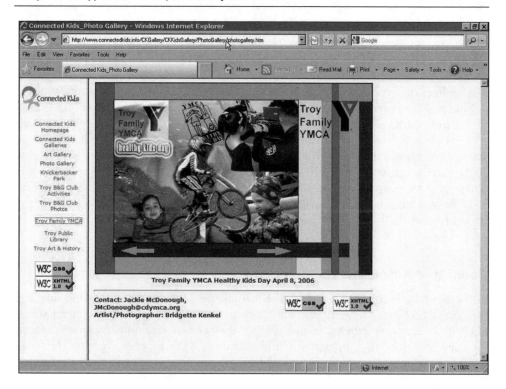

Figure 11.2 Original design of the Children's Gallery slide show.

users, from teens to adults. In the interest of serving each of our diverse user groups, however, we retained and continued to display the children's gallery for younger users.

For the new teen gallery, we sought to offer a wider range of user options to facilitate the performance of tasks such as navigation and information retrieval; to enhance the user experience by adding more rich and diverse content in several media forms; and to develop at least minimal opportunities for user-system and user-user interactions, including opportunities for user-generated content, using the capabilities of the gallery software and enhancing them as necessary. In the first redesign, as explained in our chapter on Principle 7, we streamlined the visual layout and added a range of user options. In the second redesign, we added more varied content, including images of teens' activities and basic information on topics such as ecology, history, and science of interest to a broader range of potential users, hence the change from a photo gallery only to a photo and information gallery or InfoGallery, as shown in Figure 11.3. We developed the information in several media forms—visual, audio, and textual—in cooperation with some of our organizational users, who, in some instances, created and uploaded the content themselves. To protect the privacy of younger users, we secured permission from parents or guardians for all images of children and teens displayed in the gallery. We also enabled the gallery's user comment function and added moderator oversight to permit use of this function by teens.

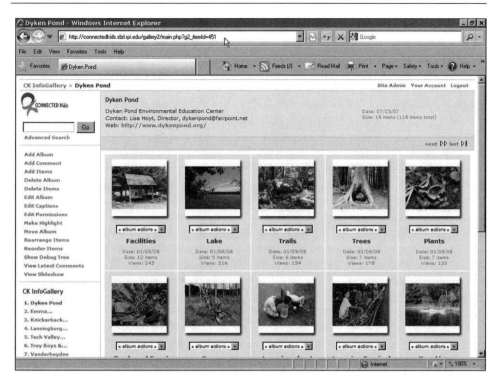

Figure 11.3 Second redesign of the Teens' InfoGallery thumbnails.

The thumbnail page shown in Figure 11.3 illustrates the wider range of user options and the more varied content. The breadcrumbs, search function, and navigation and performance options for guests and album owners appear on the top and left in the figure. The album images and titles appear in the center, in a five-by-three matrix display to accommodate as many images as possible at a 1,024-x-768 screen resolution. The development of the content presented both opportunities and challenges due to the missions and objectives of our organizational users and the problems of privacy and protection referenced above. Consistent with their varied missions, organizational users sought to both publicize their services and activities for teens and provide information resources for a broader range of users, including both teens and adults within the region and beyond. The album images illustrate this range of content, with thumbnails depicting both summer camp activities for teens and ecology information of more general interest. The summer camp activities include experiments with plants and wildlife and training in basic survival skills. The album titles show the addition of a category or classification scheme to facilitate navigation and retrieval of images of a specific type. Other gallery pages provide information about school and after-school activities, such as computer lessons at a local Boys and Girls Club and skating lessons at the local ice arena. Much of the content is user generated, posted by school officials and teachers who own and manage their own albums, sometimes with our assistance, sometimes on their own. The content includes artwork, photos, poetry, history and science reports with information about ancient cultures and vanishing bee colonies, web and video pages with information about conflicts in Africa—all produced by teens—plus some advertisements and brochures—posted by school officials.

These modest experiments in user-generated content illustrate some of the special challenges of privacy and protection for developers of systems for information sharing by younger users. The Children's Online Privacy Protection Act of 1998 (http://www.ftc.gov/ogc/coppa1.htm) protects children from information gathering by web service providers by requiring parental consent for children under age 13 (Clarke, 2005, p. 264). The act does not provide the same protection for teens ages 13 to 17, but numerous other sources urge Internet service providers to offer similar protection (Privacy Rights Clearinghouse, n.d.). We therefore require signed permission for all photos of children and teens and permit only school officials, teachers, and youth-services personnel to post content to the galleries. We also prohibit users from posting comments without moderator oversight. Since the gallery software initially had a comment function but no moderator function, we developed this function ourselves and shared it with the larger open-source community. These procedures delay response time and therefore serve as deterrents to usage by children and teens, who, even more than adults, expect that their actions will generate an immediate response (Clarke, 2005, p. 269).

These constraints compound the difficulty of finding the appropriate balance between creating an engaging user experience, with at least minimal user-system and user-user interactions, on the one hand, and accommodating diverse users and ensuring appropriate controls, on the other. Since we require signed permission for all photos of children and teens, we do not permit teens to post content directly to the gallery, and we also do not permit them to post comments directly, without moderator oversight. As a consequence, we need to monitor the permissions, and we also needed to develop the moderator function, submit the function for review by the open-source community, build it into the gallery software, and then install the updated version of the software—a lengthy but necessary process to ensure appropriate controls to protect younger users and, of course, also ourselves. The moderator oversight was not yet operational when we tested the second redesign of the gallery.

Other experiments presented control challenges of a different sort. In the album for the local ice arena, for example, we displayed photos of speed skaters, figure skaters, and hockey players, and we added brief audio clips of interviews with the speed- and figure-skating coaches, as shown in Figure 11.4. We expected that users would be able to view the images via the thumbnails or the slide shows and simultaneously listen to the interviews. The audio clips, however, presented both usability and control problems in the larger sense of control as an experience enacted in the process of use. In the first redesign of the teen gallery, we created simple links to the audio clips but no other cues to the purpose of the links. Not surprisingly, many users completely overlooked the interviews. In the second redesign, therefore, we added a large speaker image, which seemed to solve this relatively simple usability problem, on the principle of one control per function. The problem, however, proved to be more complex than it appeared at first notice. Upon repeated use and casual testing in a variety of computing environments, we observed that some users encountered technical difficulties with the interviews. Users with systems set to default to QuickTime were unable to listen to the interviews and view the images simultaneously because the QuickTime player

Figure 11.4 Teens' InfoGallery audio clip.

completely took over the browser window, thereby producing only an either/or choice. Users with systems lacking audio capability received only an error message. Many of our on-campus computers, for example, lack this capability, no doubt to avoid disruptions in the classrooms and computer labs. Of course, users ordinarily set these controls for themselves, but, in institutional environments, they do not always have this option. We do not have a simple, straightforward solution to the problem. But we observe, once again, that control is neither a designer nor user option exclusively but an experience enacted in use.

A few simple experiments hint at challenges for future development of a resource of this kind. In one experiment, we invited a summer camp participant to create an image collage using photos from the summer camp/ecology album. The collage, produced with photos, scissors, glue, and paper, as shown in Figure 11.5, illustrates the creative impulse that Bruns (2008, pp. 227–258) finds in the rapidly expanding photo-, video-, and music-sharing spaces. Our teen gallery does not have the capability to digitally manipulate images, however, and we could not develop this capability except at a prohibitively high cost. Of course, teens could create their own collages in software such as Photoshop, but, again, we do not permit them to post content directly to the gallery. In another experiment, we arranged some of the summer camp/ecology images in parallel sequences to show how two groups of teens—one group of boys, one of girls—constructed their shelters. But our gallery does not have the capability to permit

Figure 11.5 Paper collage made using images from the summer camp/ecology album by camp participant.

teens to select and rearrange images for themselves, and, again, we could not develop this capability, except at a very high cost. With the recent implementation of the moderator oversight, the gallery now permits teens to add comments on the stories and other images, but we suspect that the time lag to permit moderator approval might discourage use of even this function.

Future experiments will need to respond to a rapidly developing digital culture that permits the kind of creative expressiveness that we can only hint at here. Lessig (2008, p. 69) characterizes this digital culture as a remix culture that opens multiple media forms to masses of people, who mix and merge them to create new forms:

> Unlike text, where the quotes follow in a single line ... remixed media may quote sounds over images, or video over text, or text over sounds. The quotes thus get mixed together. The mix produces the new creative work—the "remix."

Jenkins (2006, pp. 2–3) explains this digital culture as a "convergence culture," a culture characterized by "the flow of content across multiple media platforms, the cooperation between multiple media industries, and the migratory behavior of media audiences who will go almost anywhere in search of the kinds of entertainment experiences they want." Such a remix and convergence culture fundamentally alters traditional author-reader, designer-user relationships and unsettles traditional notions of control, as Freidlander (2008, p. 179) suggests in his account of the creation of digital stories:

> In the digital realm, authorship is dispersed, collaborative, and unstable. Instead of issuing from the labor of a single author, the story emerges from the encounter between designer-writers, programmers, users, and the computer itself. The resulting collaboration is so many-sided and shifting that it is no longer clear who is telling the story, nor who is in control, nor where the story begins and ends.

If, as Barthes (1977, p. 148) observes, the author is dead, so also is the audience (Bruns, 2008, pp. 254–256).

In the formal testing of the second redesign of the teen gallery, we sought to assess both its usability and its experiential dimensions, and we engaged what we believe to be an appropriate user group of high school students. To assess usability, we might simply have tested users' ability to perform specific tasks. To assess the quality of user's experience, we needed a more comprehensive approach, and we also needed to ensure that our approach was viable—in effect, to test the test as well as the gallery. We therefore conducted a pilot test, on-site visits, and a follow-up interview with two of the teachers in an attempt to understand the specific contexts of use.

The pilot test was administered as a printed set of instructions with questions for the students to respond to in written form. The test physically resembled the students' typical classroom examinations and seemed to convey to the students that the test was akin to one of these examinations. Based upon this and other similar experiences, we determined that we needed to consider the total context of a user's experience with resources of this kind. That context includes, crucially, external factors such as users' perceptions of the appropriateness of socializing with other users or using multimedia elements in a classroom setting or even their perception of the formality of a set of test instructions, based upon its visual design. Drawing upon our observations of students' reactions to the pilot test, we revised and shortened the written portion of the test instrument so that it looked less like a school examination, and we added a period of group discussion similar to a focus-group session. The formal testing was nonetheless, necessarily, conducted in typical classroom setting, well equipped with state-of-the art computers, in the presence of the teacher, who did not, however, intervene in the test session. The group discussion was conducted as informally as possible and encouraged students to revisit elements of the gallery in pairs or small groups, to offer critical assessments of the design of the gallery, and even to brainstorm alternative approaches to the design. We believe that the group discussion was more typical of the kind of experience younger users might have since they often explore online galleries and other multimedia spaces in groups around a single display. We also believe that the group discussion generated more useful information than a written test alone. Test results showed that students had a mixed response to the gallery. From a usability perspective, the gallery seemed to perform well overall. From an experiential perspective, however, it seemed to lack clarity of purpose and opportunities for image and information sharing. The students had little difficulty navigating but generally preferred browsing to searching. They liked the organization logos on the main page but would have preferred larger fonts and larger images. Some commented that they did not play the audio clips because they did not want to disrupt the classroom setting. But the gallery seemed to convey a mixed sense of purpose since it was described as an information gallery but included photos and since it explicitly, in this iteration, included a welcome to both children (kids) and teens/adults. The term *information* suggested that the gallery would include locations, directions, maps, hours of operation, and the like. The reference to children suggested that the gallery should include activities or games and should have more color and visual appeal. As a consequence, the gallery seemed to be somewhat at odds with itself. Insofar as the gallery seemed to be directed toward teens, the students felt strongly that it should include more of their own content and should include opportunities for them to add their own descriptions and captions for their work. As one of them observed, "the people who made this know more about it than anyone else." In the summer camp/ecology and high school albums, in particular, they wanted to see more comments by people their own age, people more like themselves.

In the on-site visits and teacher interviews, we attempted to develop a better understanding of the specific contexts of the testing and use of the gallery. We observed, for example, that the students' laptops were set at a screen resolution of 1,680 × 1,050 pixels, which might help to explain why the fonts and images seemed small to them. We wondered whether the students had experience searching and, if so, why they seemed to prefer browsing to searching. The teachers told us that the students regularly used Google and Wikipedia, so we suspect that they had sufficient experience searching to be able to find and use the search function in the gallery. However, the teachers also told us that one of the students' favorite places to visit was Photobucket (http://photobucket.com/). So we also suspect that they have sufficient experience browsing and may prefer browsing a photo gallery to searching for information. These two experiences—searching via Google and browsing via Photobucket—might also help to explain why the concept of an *information gallery* seemed to be at odds with itself. Moreover, and significantly, the students' prior experience with a photo-sharing application such as Photobucket might help to explain their strong expectation of more opportunities to post their own content and add their own captions and comments to the gallery.

Implications

These expectations suggest that our high school test group is part of the larger digital culture described by Tapscott and Williams (2006, pp. 46–62), Bruns (2008, pp. 69–258), and others. If so, then we can anticipate that their expectations of image and information sharing will increase rather than diminish and that they will eagerly embrace the media remix and convergence culture that permits not only sharing but also a creative remaking of image and information resources (Jenkins, 2006, pp. 1–24; Lessig, 2008, pp. 23–83). These expectations are not unique to the digital generation. Bruns (2008, pp. 31–33) describes some of the impacts of "the rise of collaborative content creation" on both commercial and noncommercial cultures: the "crowdsourcing" by which organizations release public beta versions of their products as a means of gathering feedback from knowledgeable users and the various means by which organizations both contribute to and collect resources from "the information commons." In a commercial culture, our concern for the privacy and protection of younger users translates as a concern for the privacy and protection of product information, both before and after product release. As our high school student observed, "the people who made this know more about it than anyone else," and commercial organizations have a right to protect what they make. The flip side of this observation, however, is that the people who use a product might, from their own perspective and in their own way, know more about the product than the people who made it. In a commercial culture, what is the likelihood of information sharing by product users in open forums such as blogs and wikis? What is the likelihood that commercial organizations will sponsor such forums for their own products?

Our Connected Kids experiments in the development of user-generated content raise some traditional usability issues, which can be resolved, for the most part, through careful and thoughtful testing, especially testing with sensitivity to the specific contexts of use. They also raise larger questions about the quality of users' experience and their expectations of public exchanges and communal ownership of information, questions that will challenge designers of information systems to create an increasingly wide array of options and opportunities for users' self-expression, information sharing, and ownership and control of their own experience.

Summary of Relevant Principles

1. Design for Diverse Users	The Information Galleries were designed for diverse audiences, including children, teens, and adults.
2. Design for Usability	The original design of the children's gallery has a simple and intuitive interface to enhance its usability for children. The usability of the teen galleries was negatively affected by teens' familiarity with the conventions of photo sharing.
3. Test the Backbone	Characteristics of the students' technological backbone affected the usability of the second redesign in several ways. The audio function from the first redesign was enhanced for usability in the second redesign, but users still encountered backbone problems due to variability in QuickTime player installations. Screen resolution also affected performance, with the result that images appeared smaller to students than they were designed to appear.

5. Set the Context	The second redesign was tested informally to better fit teens' context of use and reduce their sense that they were being tested.
6. Make a Connection	By providing user-generated content around the activities of young people, all of the galleries created opportunities for connections with users.
7. Share Control	The Information Galleries were designed to maximize user control by allowing users to contribute content, subject to privacy and protection constraints.
8. Support Interaction Among Users	The second redesign provided for some user-to-user interactions, allowing users to make comments on the photos contributed by others.
9. Create a Sense of Place	The second redesign used breadcrumbs and search and navigation options to create a sense of place.

Note

1. This material is based upon work supported by the National Science Foundation under grant no. 0091505. Any opinions, findings, and conclusions or recommendations expressed in this material are those of the author(s) and do not necessarily reflect the views of the National Science Foundation.

Wikis for Collaboration

Janice W. Fernheimer, UNIVERSITY OF KENTUCKY

Thomas Kujala, FACTSET RESEARCH SYSTEMS

Samantha Good, ALBANY MEDICAL CENTER

Dale Bass, USABLESITE, INC.

Carol Sadowsky, RSA SECURITY

Dustin Kirk, NEUSTAR

The Collaborative Promise of Wikis

As shown in the flow chart in Figure 12.1, the wiki exemplar evolved over the course of three rounds of testing and four designs. The original design was first created for the Usable Content Seminar based on the increasing popularity of wikis as a form of web-based communication. This popularity was reflected in the growing numbers of users, editors, and articles on Wikipedia and the growing attention wikis received for their collaborative possibilities in both business and educational contexts.

Wikis allow any user to edit or contribute to a web page's content, and thus can be considered a collaborative subgenre of web pages that offer the potential to inspire or facilitate large-scale collaboration, irrespective of time or geography. Anyone with a functioning Internet connection and access to a wiki can begin to generate, edit, or modify content. Most wikis also include some sort of revision history tool that allows users to compare earlier and later versions while highlighting the changes that take place across them. Additionally, they provide a medium for contributors to discuss the rationale behind their content decisions, changes, and revisions with other users and content generators. When approached specifically as a writing platform, wikis are inherently collaborative spaces.

Not surprisingly, scholars in the sciences (Hamilton, 2000; Kussmaul, Howe, & Priest, 2006), engineering (Chen et al., 2005), as well as rhetoric and composition (Moxley & Meehan, 2007; Carr et al., 2007; Garza & Hern, 2006) have explored the potential of wikis to enhance or change the way that both students and researchers write. While many scholars discuss their attempts to use wikis to integrate writing into the science or engineering classroom, few address the specifically collaborative potential wikis might offer to college writing, which is traditionally seen, assigned, and assessed as an individual task. With their easy-to-edit functions and ability to track changes, multiple versions, and revision history, wikis would seem to be a natural fit for teachers, scholars, and students hoping to engage in a more collaborative writing process.

Since collaboration is often lauded as the key to success in business, science, and education, the Wikis for Collaboration Team aimed to determine how wikis might best be used to facilitate or deepen collaboration among groups. Specifically, we investigated how wikis might be used to foster collaboration and collaborative writing in higher education. This initial investigation was deliberately broad, because our

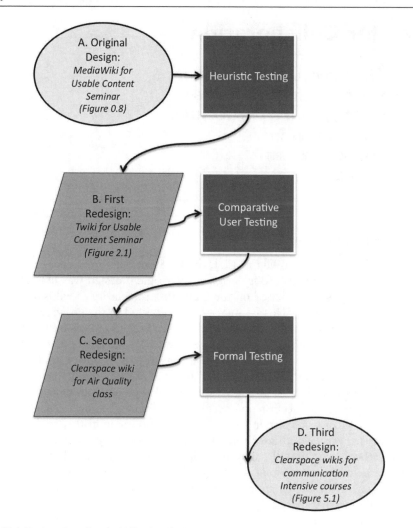

Figure 12.1 Project flow for the Wikis for Collaboration project.

explorations included learning just as much about wikis, who their audiences are, and how they work as they did about specific hypotheses for how best to harness their collaborative potential.

Although the exemplar eventually was designed and tested for an educational context, much of what we learned can be applied to any situation where designers ask their users to both engage in and understand the epistemological framework behind a new software, platform, or technology that allows users to perform familiar tasks in new and unfamiliar ways. In the case of the wiki, the technology facilitated three things: (1) collaborative knowledge production, (2) the iterative and recursive nature of writing, and (3) the way users can collaborate to achieve the first two tasks—both new knowledge production and polished writing through a web-based medium.

Because wikis facilitate knowledge production, collaboration, and writing, they share elements with other tools used to accomplish these tasks. For example, in educational and other contexts, people use a variety of tools to generate, share, and refine ideas: face-to-face meetings, telephone calls, computer-mediated phone calls using applications like Skype for video conferencing, e-mail, and electronic trading of word-processing documents using tracked comments, just to name a few. People also use a number of technologies and platforms to write: pen and paper, voice transcription software, word-processing tools, e-mail, instant messaging, blogs, microblogs, and social networking platforms. Like other web-based writing platforms such as blogs, microblogs, instant messaging, and social networking sites, wikis are accessed through the Internet; however, many individuals first encounter them and engage with them in ways similar to how they approach other web pages.

In fact, until a user begins to create or manipulate content through the wiki medium, a wiki page may appear no different from a typical, access-to-read web page. As such, the conventions for traditional web writing apply to wikis that are composed with the explicit purpose of being read by their intended audience. These read-only pages should follow traditional usability prescriptions for web pages. First of all, they should not be text heavy. If they do include blocks of text, they should be chunked, bulleted, or somehow visually cued to highlight the most important information (Nielson, 2000; Williams & Tollet, 2000; Krug, 2005). Additionally, they should have clear and easy-to-follow navigation, and they should display web-specific information in ways that follow the conventions of other web pages—for example, links should be indicated by underlining and color choice.

In addition to including some read-only pages, wikis also provide a web-based writing platform. Consequently, users not only expect wikis as web pages to be scannable and easy-to-read and navigate, they also expect wiki writing spaces to follow traditional desktop publishing interfaces familiar to them from word-processing applications such as Microsoft Word, Open Office, and others. Users expect the dialogue boxes for writing to offer formatting features such as italics, bold, underline, font color, type size, and so on. Moreover, since wikis are web-based, users also expect the ability to upload and link to media such as presentation software generated texts (PowerPoint, Keynote, or other slide-based media), other web pages outside the wiki, internal links to other documents within the wiki, as well as video, sound, and images.

Like other Web 2.0 applications, wikis are attractive to many users because they facilitate user contributions and participation. To succeed, they must garner their users' interest and willingness to generate and modify content. Blogs and social networking sites also thrive because of user-generated content, but these media tend to provide minimal opportunities for explicit and equal collaboration. With blogs, the main posts are author-generated, and outsiders' contributions are included only in the comments section, though others' work may also be highlighted in the blogroll, a list of other bloggers whom the main blogger values. In social networking sites, a profile is crafted by an individual, and others' contributions are relegated to peripheral comments in the form of wall comments or other messages. Unlike blogs or social networking applications, where the medium privileges an individual's contributions, wikis focus explicitly on the task of collaborative writing. While other web-based writing platforms may also invoke strong community elements, wikis are the only medium whose community focus begins with and expands out from users' desire to write together with others, across both space and time.

Our Project

To investigate the collaborative nature of wikis and the potential value of this tool for higher education courses that require multi-authored writing projects, the Wikis for Collaboration Team embarked on a three-year project that involved a wiki prototype that was transformed and developed across three wikiware platforms (MediaWiki, Twiki, and ultimately the commercially available Clearspace) and four designs (see Figure 12.1). With the original design, our team engaged in exploratory research. We created a wiki to better understand the issues at stake in asking students to write in and thus also populate a public writing platform such as a wiki. Because we weren't sure how best to incorporate the wiki, we tried to determine the relative salience and influence of issues such as users' perceptions of privacy, intellectual property, and general web usability. The questions that guided us in this initial stage included the following: What would motivate students to contribute? What would help them understand the tool as an aid for collaborative knowledge production? What would help them feel safe enough to be willing to create content?

After the comparative testing of the first redesign, we realized the importance of designing and developing the wiki portion of a collaborative writing assignment in conjunction with the other contextual classroom elements that influence and affect users' overall learning experiences. For the second redesign, then, we began working directly with professors to create an assignment that would both incorporate wiki writing and also fit seamlessly with the their overall course goals.

In the second redesign, we created and implemented a pilot assignment that was distributed in an engineering course, Introduction to Air Quality. Based on the results of formal testing, we modified and refined the assignment to implement the third redesign, a revised wiki-based group writing assignment, in two communication-intensive courses. We worked with two professors who agreed to use the wiki assignment in their communication-intensive courses. Lupita Montoya used it in Introduction to Engineering Design—a required first-year writing-intensive engineering course, and Dean Nieusma used it in Product Design and Innovation, Studio 6, the sixth in a series of design courses. By incorporating the assignment into two very different courses whose culminating final assignments included collaborative writing, we hoped to generate a broader range of contextualized responses and feedback.

Original Design

At the beginning of the project, our team wanted to determine how best to teach users who traditionally engage with most web pages as read-only interfaces to distinguish between these traditional web pages and wikis that facilitate the sharing of ideas and resources. For the original design (see Figure 0.8), we used the MediaWiki platform to create a collaborative space where we hoped members of the Usable Content Seminar would be able to share resources and ideas. Specifically, we created a page called "Usability Terms," where we hoped people would post and share information that would be relevant for all Usable Content Seminar participants. Although we had imagined this wiki as part of the Usable Content Seminar, since it was not included as part of the assigned work for students and since few members were independently motivated to populate it, the pages remained relatively sparse and unused until formal testing began.

Our protocol for the heuristic testing of the original design included several tasks: log in to the site, add a definition to the "Usability Terms" page, create a new page in the site's community portal, locate your time on the usability testing schedule, and find the help document that explains how to create an external link. After these task-based elements were completed, the moderator asked the tester the following questions:

- How do you feel about posting information that anyone can edit?
- What do you think about the layout and design of the wiki?
- Is the design of the wiki inviting or unwelcoming?
- Does the layout and design make you want to contribute to the wiki?
- Is there anything that would make you feel more comfortable when posting?
- Would you use the wiki in the future as a means of sharing information?

Testers were drawn from the Usable Content seminar and from the broader RPI student population.

From this first round of testing, we learned that users tended to interact with the wiki pages in ways similar to how they interact with other web pages. Although we provided directions for editing, they appeared as a lengthy block of text in a separate help page. Testers recommended that we follow traditional web writing conventions and use fonts, colors, alignment, and text size to cue which information was most important and thus guide their reading and interacting experience. They also suggested that the site should be made to appear more welcoming, as the limited visuals of the MediaWiki interface did not allow for significant customization. Finally, testers experienced difficulty performing the task we thought was most important—editing the actual wiki page, largely because they found it difficult to use the specific wiki syntax, and because their expectations for that syntax to follow HTML conventions and to find a what-you-see-is-what-you-get editor (WYSIWYG) were frustrated.

First Redesign

We carefully considered this valuable user feedback as we revised the prototype and switched wiki platforms from MediaWiki to Twiki in an attempt to better address user concerns for the first redesign (see Figure 2.1). Twiki offered our team more control over the site's look and feel; provided a WYSIWYG editing option, which lessened users' need to learn wiki markup syntax; and offered breadcrumb navigation at the top of all pages, which helped users better understand the site's organization. In addition to these added features, the Wikis for Collaboration Team worked hard to create a more welcoming home page, provide text that had been chunked and that followed visual cues for the web, and offer more contextual help rather than isolating explanations and how-to directions in a separate page.

We paid more attention to traditional web usability standards: In-page links were clearly defined by the use of color and underline, bulleted lists were used when appropriate, and headings broke up large blocks of text. We also created a specific "Learn More" box, located in the upper right-hand corner of the home page to chunk the text, visually cue important information, and offer users a way to learn more about wikis.

In comparative user testing, we asked some users to engage with the original design and some to engage with the first redesign. We asked all users to complete the following tasks: log in, add a definition, create a new page and link to it, find a date, share it with your team, find the last person to update a page, find a definition, and contribute to a discussion. Thus, we received responses in five areas we thought were important to consider for wiki usability: welcome, exploration, retrieval tasks, connectedness, and sharing.

Unfortunately, several factors made it hard for us to interpret our results as showing marked improvement. First, each prototype had different features that affected specific tasks. For example, Twiki users (first redesign) were required to register before they could log in, so naturally it took them longer to complete this initial task. Second, it was difficult to analyze and assess the relative success of open-ended tasks that were nonspecific in nature. It took users varying amounts of time to generate content, regardless of their experience level with technology more generally. For example, when users were asked to share something with the team, some users submitted anything simply to complete the task, whereas others took the time to read and consider what others had shared previously. After this process, they then carefully articulated their own content in response. While this process of careful consideration and then contextualized contribution was something we hoped to facilitate, not all users participated in this way. Generally, those who did go through this process took longer to complete this particular task.

Although both the original design and the first redesign were created with classroom use in mind, they were not incorporated into the overall assignment and assessment design for the course, and the testers were not always enrolled in the course for which they had been designed. Since we had come to realize the importance of the overall experience and context, we decided to work explicitly in our second and third redesigns with professors who intended to use the wiki for collaborative writing and to have that writing count toward the overall course goals and students' individual grades. We hoped this kind of seamless integration would increase students' commitment to the project and motivation to complete it.

Second Redesign

Interestingly, after these first two rounds of testing, we recognized that our testing process assessed individual use to understand group interactions with collaborative platforms rather than looking at how groups interacted using the medium. We decided our efforts would be better served by observing how actual groups used wikis to engage in real collaborative writing tasks. In the next phase of development, we worked directly with professors who already included multi-authored writing assignments in their courses to design and implement assignments that would help their students use the wiki. Moreover, once the wiki assignment became a built-in part of the course, an element that would be graded and used to assess an individual's performance in a collaborative task, we realized that the elements impacting the users' total experience were no longer limited to the wiki platform. Rather, the usability framework extended to include the actual assignment prompt, teacher instructions, interactions with the platform in class, and the particular interactions of individual groups. As Schneider (2005, p. 454) points out, "Distributed usability insists that we turn to the dynamic networks that constitute the entirety of the task environment if we want to understand what constitutes usability in a given instance." In the classroom context, all the various types of instructions—whether in class during a teacher's explanation or in the specific writing assignment prompt—must be treated as integrated technical documents that must also be usable for students to understand and excel at the tasks expected of them in the actual wiki. Rather than try to squeeze all the how-to directions in contextualized help sections on the wiki itself, we created a series of in-class workshops to help students understand what a wiki is and how they were supposed to use it in their writing process. Following Schneider (2005), we pushed our usability research to provide a "rhetorical framework that opens up the sociocultural terrain of technical communication to classroom inquiry" (p. 456).

Since users complained equally about the MediaWiki and Twiki interfaces in our earlier design, for the next stage of development we opted to use a proprietary wiki platform, Clearspace. We chose this platform because it offered several features that we hoped would better facilitate collaboration: e-mail notifications; customizable subspaces for individual teams; an RSS feed; improved search capabilities; blog capabilities; a discussion section with the ability to mark comments and questions; revisions history, which allowed users to compare multiple versions of a document; the ability to upload Word documents, PDFs, and presentations; and the ability to convert the final wiki document into a printable PDF. We also hoped that the commercial software would streamline the team's design tasks so we could focus our efforts on developing the appropriate context and framework to elicit the type of interaction we hoped the wiki would yield.

Within this next phase of development, we redesigned and implemented the new wiki prototype in two stages. For the second redesign, we worked directly with Montoya and with Barbara Lewis of the Center for Communication Practices to create a collaborative writing assignment that would encourage students to apply what they were learning in Introduction to Air Quality (a non-communication-intensive engineering course at RPI) to real-life problems. The assignment prompt asked students to research air-quality challenges facing society and write collaboratively to advocate for its solution or improvement. Students worked in groups to generate topics, conduct research, and ultimately produce a collaboratively authored final project. Students were told that 5% of their grade would be assessed on the extent of their collaboration, but beyond this instruction they were not given specific information about how their collaboration would be recognized or evaluated. Group projects included topics as diverse as reducing carbon emissions with fossil fuel alternatives (i.e., biofuels), using air-cleaning plants to reduce toxic fumes from Katrina relief mobile homes, assessing acid rain deposition in the Adirondacks, improving air quality in domestic dwellings in developing countries by changing cooking practices, and reducing car emissions by introducing more strict standards. We ran three workshops over the semester: The first introduced the students to the collaborative writing assignment, and the second provided a technical, hands-on workshop with the wiki software. Once students had selected topics, completed research, and begun drafting, a third workshop focused on organization and revision strategies for completing the final report.

While we had hoped the second redesign would encourage and document students interacting in ways we later termed "deeply collaborative" (an iterative and recursive process in which students interacted constructively at every step of the writing process, from idea generation or invention all the way through final delivery of the document), we found students were frustrated by some of the ways the task was both introduced and integrated into their overall grade. Because the assessment criteria were left undetermined, students were concerned about how they would be evaluated, and this concern affected their motivation to participate. Rather than requiring a specific number of required posts to or revisions on the wiki for students to earn their full 5% collaboration credit, the mode for determining how students would demonstrate collaboration was left unclear. In the end, the instructor used the track history function to see which students were contributing what and when. Since students did not know from the outset how their collaboration would be assessed for part of their grade, they felt insecure about being evaluated, even though at 5% the stakes were relatively low.

As Schneider (2005) has noted in his discussion of usability and course management software interfaces, "principles of user-centered design, catering to both teachers and students, replicate and intensify the power relations found in the classroom" (p. 460). In this case, the wiki was no exception. In fact during interviews, many students expressed the sentiment that they felt the wiki was used as a kind of surveillance tool rather than a medium for intense collaboration. Moreover, in this first implementation of the classroom-based prototype, students encountered platform-specific difficulties. Even though their final projects required the incorporation of significant graphs and figures, the Clearspace interface offered them few mechanisms to control how such images would be incorporated into the overall look of the final PDF document generated by the application. They also complained that they were not able to participate simultaneously on the wiki, a feature they would have liked and appreciated, especially during face-to-face meetings. From this round of implementation and testing, we realized we needed to explicitly define what we meant by deep collaboration and provide more specifics about how collaboration would be recognized and evaluated.

Third Redesign

Since we had multiple expectations of and hopes for what the wiki might be able to achieve in terms of collaborative writing in the classroom, in the final phase of implementation our team worked with two instructors to further refine and develop a third redesign to better respond to both instructor and student desires and needs. We also wanted to revise to make better allowances for the specific platform's shortcomings— that is, Clearspace's poor integration of visuals and limited ability to modify the final PDF document students would turn in for a grade. We worked again with Montoya and Nieusma and their respective courses: Introduction to Engineering Design (a required sophomore-level writing-intensive engineering course) and Product Design and Innovation Studio Six (the sixth in a series of workshops required of Product Design and Innovation students).

Our team worked with Montoya and Nieusma to modify both the assignment prompt to clearly specify what would count as collaboration and to provide a specific time frame for targeted interaction early in the students' collaborative writing process. We also revised the series of workshops used to introduce students to both the assignment and the wiki platform. The purpose of these revisions was multifold. First, since the interface seemed poorly equipped to handle the graphical content that students were expected to include in final reports, we decided to encourage and require student use early in their writing process—at the idea-generation stage and before they needed to include images. Second, we hoped this targeted traffic early in the writing process would also encourage students to begin the writing process earlier than they otherwise might. If students worked early and often, we thought there would be ample opportunities for both the instructor and other students to read, review, and respond to the collaborative text while it was still in process, thus deepening its development. Third, we specified not only what would count as collaboration, but also set a minimum number of contributions required of each student and articulated both clearly in the actual assignment prompt. Although the prompt was tailored to meet the specific collaborative writing needs of each course, in general it asked students to make two original contributions to the group writing project and offer two comments that provided feedback on other students' writing within a specified amount of time.

This commenting task required students to use the track history and revision tools (see Figure 5.1). Our team was particularly interested in better understanding these functions. We also hoped that getting the students to comment would create a written record of intrateam discussion of the final written assignment.

In Product Design and Innovation Studio, the students' final assignment was to generate a business plan of 10 to 30 pages based on a common template provided by the instructors but customized by each team. Students worked in two- to three-person teams to develop fully articulated business plans for original product concepts. Students were asked to use the wiki to modify and customize the template to provide both a working outline for teams' business plans as well as documentation of the collaboration behind their group customization.

In Introduction to Engineering Design, the students' final assignment was a 40- to 60-page final project report that was to include standardized sections: introduction, methods, results, and conclusions as well appendixes that included graphics, pictures, calculations, programming code, and results data tables. Students were asked to use the wiki to write the introduction, because the background information it required is typically gathered early in the project and thus requires no substantive graphics, images, or lab results. Montoya hoped the wiki would provide a place for discussion and document sharing, a vehicle for assessing individual and group participation, and an incentive for students to begin writing early. The wiki was introduced early in the semester, well before students had begun to compose any writing related to their final projects, and it was then reintroduced when students were expected to draft the introduction section of the project—the part that situated the problem within the scholarly literature and demonstrated how the students' approach would further the conversation. Students were given two weeks to complete this section.

Students in both courses used the wiki to varying degrees. Some completed the bare minimum of posts and responses, some went above and beyond using the tool after the initial idea-generation phase, and some immediately asked for permission to use other tools—namely Google Docs, with which they were more familiar and which they claimed had a better interface. Although students in both classes appreciated the fact that the wiki provided a central location to house and trade group materials, overall they were deeply dissatisfied with the wiki experience for two main reasons. First, they didn't like the interface and complained that it did not allow them enough control over the final appearance of their documents. Second, they were frustrated that the wiki didn't allow more than one team member to be working on the document at any time; thus, rather than providing a medium for collaboration by multiple users to take place in real time via the wiki, it forced them into asynchronous work flows. Since teams were already collocated and able to meet in person with relative ease, this second factor seemed to be the most significant one in causing user frustration.

Lessons Learned

The evolution of the Wikis for Collaboration exemplar provides a valuable case study for any designer wishing to design or create usable groupware applications or instructions. Through our work with several different classroom contexts we learned that, like other Web 2.0 applications such as blogs or social networking sites, wikis are highly dependent on a community of users. Within a classroom, some aspects of that community element are predetermined: students register for a specific course; they know their performance will be evaluated and assessed by the instructor; and, depending on the class context, they may or may not know whether their experience in the course will incorporate the use of technology.

Unlike other teams or groups, those working on wikis in a classroom context will be expected to perform their role as student in this space. Even though the platform may offer other opportunities for them to create a profile, or a more multidimensional online persona, the fact that their work is graded and will affect their overall assessment is not a trivial element that can be overlooked. We hoped such constraints would be positive and could be used to foster student motivation to participate, overcoming the hurdle posed by the cost of initiation.

The fact that instructors saw the tool as a means to facilitate assessment, however, impacted students' perception of the tool's utility for the completion of their own work. Rather than interpreting it as a useful feature that would benefit them by helping them to trace the changes and iterations of their group document, they came to understand that feature primarily as a tool for instructor surveillance. While this perception was not entirely misguided, instructors did hope the wiki would provide a mechanism to more equitably assess the degree and frequency of individual contributions to the group project. They saw this type of evaluation as providing an element of fairness in what might otherwise be a work burden carried by the most committed and diligent students rather than the team as a whole. As such, usability scholars need to pay greater attention to the ways in which power dynamics, such as those inherent to the teacher-student relationship, might bring unwanted or unanticipated effects to a particular situation involving groupware. Despite the students' complaints about the specifics of the interface we chose, our experiences testing the platform in context and in connection with actual groups suggest that designers may want to emulate this practice, especially if the tool they are developing is envisioned as one that will foster or facilitate group work or interactions. Moreover, we recommend that any wiki or groupware that is intended to aid in face-to-face collaboration should also include the ability to have multiple users working on the interface simultaneously without writing over one another's work. Any wiki that does not enable this kind of simultaneous editing may prove more useful for collaborators who are not collocated and who plan to work asynchronously.

Summary of Relevant Principles

2. Design for Usability	To enhance usability, the wiki team changed platforms several times to meet the expectations users had for WYSIWYG editing.
4. Extend a Welcome	The first redesign included a home page that created a more welcoming feel.
5. Set the Context	To appropriately set the context for use, the second and third redesign efforts extended their scope to include designing collaborative writing assignments and in-class workshops.
7. Share Control	Students' reservations about using the wiki stemmed in part from the difficulty they had in controlling the final look of their documents.
8. Support Interaction Among Users	The Wikis for Collaboration were designed to foster deep collaboration among users.
9. Create a Sense of Place	The first redesign included breadcrumb navigation to help users get a sense of their place in the wiki.
10. Plan to Continue the Engagement	Students' reservations about using the wiki also stemmed from their desire to continue engaging with each other outside of the wiki, in face-to-face interactions.

Cultural Websites

Patricia Search, RENSSELAER POLYTECHNIC INSTITUTE
Jennifer Ash, IBM
Marsha Harner, SEMATECH
Amanda Rotondo, ROTONDO CONSULTING, LLC

As shown in Figure 13.1, the cultural website project began by using the Tshinanu website, the companion website for the *Tshinanu (Us Together)* television series, as our first original design. We wanted to see if nonaboriginal users could identify with the aboriginal perspectives and traditions presented on the site. The cultural website project also evaluated a second original design, photographs and videos on birch basket making that are materials for an online course on First Nations crafts at Emily Carr University of Art + Design in Vancouver, Canada. This research focused on storytelling and how visual information creates narratives that bridge different cultures.

Although guidelines exist regarding internationalization and localization of websites, no guidelines are readily available regarding how to communicate, preserve, or promote cultural ideas through a website. A report by Vdrio-Baron, Townsend, and Shelley (2009) states, "We have identified from a recent literature review no unique set of scales, metrics, or instruments specifically tailored to include the cultural construct when assessing usability" (p. 332).

Research by Barber and Badre (1998) indicates that interface design elements and features may be more prevalent and possibly preferred within a particular cultural group. This idea of "cultural markers" extends to interface design elements such as color, typography, layout patterns, orientation, grouping, and organization (Sun, 2001). This literature specifically addresses the ability of these interface elements to close the distance between corporations and specific cultural groups through their faithful application. It seems this idea can easily be extended to include closing the gap between members and nonmembers of a cultural group, as would be the case with the Tshinanu and Emily Carr exemplars.

In the case of the Tshinanu website, communication and transmission of subjective aspects such as values, beliefs, patterns of thinking, and behavior were more important to the overall goals and success of the website and cannot be measured using traditional usability testing. This was also true for the Emily Carr materials, which aspired to the same goals of conveying the subjective feeling and nuances of a culture. The objective for this project was to measure the success of this effort to facilitate a human understanding (beyond the superficial) using the media of photographs and video.

Other studies have attempted to measure the success of this attempt at a deeper cultural connection and have come to mixed results. Komlodi et al. (2007) investigated interactions with a website promoting culture-bridging interchanges between Argentinean, Hungarian, and American children. From their research they were able to produce a helpful and pragmatic list of suggestions for the design of sites with similar goals. These are very useful for websites dealing with children but may not

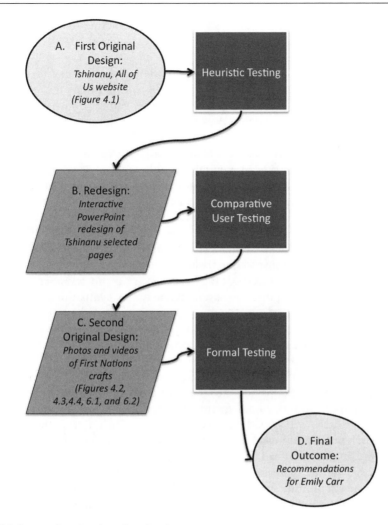

Figure 13.1 Project flow for the cultural website project.

apply directly to websites seeking to create this bridge between adult audiences. This is underscored by Neill (2008), who found significant differences between children's and teachers' reactions to an online museum with the mission to help Hungarians, recently admitted to the European Union, feel more culturally "European." Neither of these studies specifically outlines a set of heuristics for designers to use when creating sites intended to bridge a cultural divide for adults. Both studies shed valuable light on elements to consider when creating such guidelines.

Introducing the Websites

Our first original design, the Tshinanu website at www.tshinanu.tv (see Figure 4.1), is a companion website for a broadcast television series *Tshinanu (Us Together)*. The television series and its website have a shared goal of depicting the social, economic, and cultural life of aboriginal communities in Quebec, Canada. The website is primarily targeted to the viewers of the *Tshinanu (Us Together)* television series. Viewers of that series consist of both aboriginal and nonaboriginal peoples of Canada. It combines interactive media with noninteractive web content. It stimulates user participation through use of blogs, interactive panoramas, and games. It also presents digital media—music, videos, and animated presentations—in addition to traditional static text, graphics, and photographs.

The Tshinanu website was chosen as the first original design for the cultural website project after evaluating two other potential examples: gregorycolbert.com, a website showcasing the photographs of Gregory Colbert, and www.aptn.ca, the website for the Aboriginal Peoples Television Network. Each website was considered using three types of evaluation criteria: experience characteristics, experience qualities, and task comparison. Experience characteristics and experience qualities were based on Shedroff's (2001) work on experience design. These criteria are significant to cultural websites, because the goal is not just to impart information or aid simple task completion but to give the user an "experience" of the culture. Task comparison was made based on the tasks the websites supported for users. Based on the evaluation, www.tshinanu.tv was selected because it scored highly on all three types of evaluations.

The Tshinanu website provided a unique opportunity to look at the ways in which an aboriginal group embraced new media techniques to communicate rich cultural ideas. Through its use of new media, it opens the possibility of providing some of the experience of being a member of the culture to nonmembers. The importance of this cross-cultural communication is great. Many aboriginal cultures are at risk of becoming totally assimilated into the mainstream culture, their stories and values forgotten. The reach of the Internet to spread ideas is well known. The question that the cultural website research project addresses is whether ideas about culture, and even the experience of culture, might be spread through the Internet.

The Tshinanu website represents a unique class of web-based communications since it strives to impart cultural awareness and teachings to its viewers. Commonly, websites provide information or mediate routine tasks—such as banking or buying—but do not attempt to touch our emotions or bring meaning into our lives. Superficially the Tshinanu website operates as an adjunct to a television program. In that capacity, it only needs to entertain and provide additional information about the television series. But on a deeper level, it attempts to bridge communication between aboriginal and nonaboriginal viewers through the use of interactive technology.

For the second original design, we changed our focus to evaluate online course materials from Emily Carr University of Art + Design consisting of photographic and video materials for students learning about aboriginal crafts. First Nations birch bark basket making and the cultural elements of the craft comprise one part of the course. As part of various assignments or as further enrichment, students view videos and photographs of the process, people, and products and are afforded the opportunity to see and hear First Nations peoples talking about their craft. The materials are intended for students taking the aboriginal crafts course, which may include students who are not aboriginal. The materials include photographs and videos of baskets and the birch bark basket-making process. Several videos with audio show various elements regarding the role and importance of basket making in the First Nations culture.

The Emily Carr course materials were chosen because of their specific goals of sharing information about a culture and creating a connection with and deeper understanding of that culture. For this particular type of craft, it is important that the students not only learn the mechanics of how to assemble a First Nations–style birch bark basket but also come to understand the importance of these baskets to the First Nations peoples. The role the baskets play is far beyond that of a carrying tool. To meet the course objectives students needed to be able to understand and internalize this importance.

The video and photographic materials give the students at Emily Carr firsthand exposure to the First Nations peoples discussing and demonstrating their craft (see Figure 4.2) as well as telling stories related to birch bark basket making. For the students to truly connect with the people and the culture producing this craft, the course designer believed it would be helpful for them to see and hear the First Nations peoples speaking about the craft in their own homes and native geographical area. Beyond this pedagogical objective, the course designer also took the opportunity to document elders telling their own stories in their own words. As generations pass, these kinds of records may become extremely important in preserving the history of the craft and the culture.

Testing the connections users are able to make with the First Nations peoples helps us understand which aspects of this rich media approach foster a connection and which do not. Results may be helpful not just to the Emily Carr University of Art + Design course designers or designers of similar courses but also to a broader audience looking to create an online experience that promotes cultural awareness and appreciation.

The Emily Carr course materials on birch bark basketry consisted of photographs and video that provided a digital bridge between the users and the First Nations peoples and their cultural traditions. The videos include an interview with a woman speaking about her experiences with basket making (including her encounter with a bear in the woods as a young woman), a basket maker showing some of her baskets, and a trip into the woods to gather the bark and roots used to make the baskets. The photographs are primarily of the baskets themselves and of some of the steps involved in the process of making them.

Our Methods

In our first original design, the Tshinanu website offers 26 topics or themes for user discovery. Each theme relates to a specific area of aboriginal life. Within each theme, the user is encouraged to explore by viewing an overview, viewing a panorama, participating in an interactive activity, or contributing their opinion about the theme or topic. The panorama invites the user to click on specific areas to view a video or listen to narration about the topic.

Before attempting to redesign the website, we conducted initial heuristic testing with test participants. We felt that traditional task- and performance-based usability testing represented by the common protocol (Appendix 1) would not be adequate in providing answers regarding the success of the website. We felt the success of a website in providing a cultural experience to the user could be better described than measured. With this in mind, we designed test sessions where users were instructed to explore the site, and we recorded their actions and dialogue.

Each heuristic testing session was conducted by a team consisting of a tester, an observer, and a participant. During each session, a participant was asked to "explore a theme that you are interested in and make comments regarding that experience." The participant was also instructed to "explore a theme that you are *not* interested in and make comments regarding that experience." A talk-aloud protocol was used, and the test facilitator guided and encouraged the participant to make comments. We conducted five sessions for the heuristic testing.

At the conclusion of the sessions, we examined the responses and grouped them into the same characteristics that we used to determine which example to use. If an issue was reported that related to a particular characteristic, we noted it and prioritized the characteristic according to the test participant's response. The characteristics are as follows:

- High design/low design
- User control
- Navigation style/nonlinear style
- Participation
- Community
- Identity/authenticity
- Storytelling
- Sensorial design
- Immersion
- Symbols and icons
- Information and knowledge
- Meaning
- Information design

Once the test issues were characterized and prioritized, we explored possible design solutions for the issue. For example, many test participants reported that they were confused by the number of navigational choices on the home page. Our design recommendation was to reduce the number of choices, and we gave it a high priority in the redesign.

With our second original design, the Emily Carr course materials, we chose to investigate slightly different metrics than normally would be used in traditional website evaluation. The users were asked to evaluate their experiences based upon how connected they felt with the content of the site rather than their ability to traverse the material. Because of this focus, we decided for formal testing to give one questionnaire immediately after the participants watched the videos and viewed the photographs.

Prior to distributing the first survey, a single-participant pilot test was given to ensure the survey was effective and that the instructions were clear. After correcting minor wording and editing issues, the survey was then sent to the rest of the participants.

This questionnaire was followed approximately one week later by a shorter survey to discover what the participants had retained from the materials on the site. The follow-up survey also showed us whether the participants had discussed the materials with acquaintances. All of the surveys were conducted via e-mail, so testers did not observe participants viewing the materials or have an opportunity to conduct face-to-face interviews.

The first survey provided instructions for accessing the Emily Carr course materials. The survey asked for basic demographic information—such as age, occupation, and ethnic affiliation—as well as the participant's experience with online media, basket making, or other types of crafts. Then the participant was asked to answer 8 Likert-scale questions regarding their experience with the materials and their personal preferences for the media used to present the information. The next 13 open-ended questions asked the participants to reflect upon the content they had viewed. We changed from Likert-scale questions to open-ended questions to shift the participant's mind-set from comparison-based thinking to one of observation—forcing them to consider specific details they had observed. By obtaining information on the specific experiences the users had, it was possible to discern the effectiveness of the visual media in engaging and creating connections with the users as well as portraying a particular cultural narrative.

Testing the Original Designs

The Tshinanu website is well designed and has won a number of design awards. It looks professional and welcoming and is vibrant and interesting. On the surface, there didn't appear to be any design issues with the site. It seemed to serve its users well by providing an entertaining and rich experience for viewers of the television series.

After the heuristic testing, a number of issues were discovered that provided impetus to modify the site design and functionality. The characteristics for website evaluation (Table 13.1) provide a good way to describe the website at the beginning of the project.

The website offered the following experiences to users: exploring, feeling, learning, connecting, communicating, and knowing. Users could *explore* by creating their own path through the themes and then exploring selected elements within a theme. Users could *feel* by watching and listening to the personal narratives presented that might evoke an emotional response. Users could *learn* and *know* by viewing facts, participating in learning exercises and taking quizzes. Users could *connect* and *communicate* by posting comments on shared stories.

From a task-based perspective, the user of tshinanu.tv could perform the following tasks:

- View information about a theme.
- Search for information by keyword.
- Listen, watch, and interact with stories and story-related content.
- Post a comment.

The Emily Carr course materials consisted of photographs and videos designed for college-level learning. The course materials were neither created nor altered for this project. The first part of the formal testing simply evaluated the photos and videos with a survey. Out of the 15 surveys sent out, 8 individuals completed the first survey. Participants varied in age, occupation, and ethnic background as well as exposure to online media in general.

Identification with the course materials correlated primarily with participants' personal experiences with a similar activity to the ones presented in the videos or pictures or with memories triggered by their familiarity with the role a particular person represented. For example, the First Nations woman who told the story about the bear was an elderly woman, and participants regarded her as a grandmotherly-type person. Of all the materials the participants viewed, the story this woman told about the bear was one of the more memorable ones.

Participants also felt a strong connection to a video of First Nations peoples out in the woods collecting birch bark and roots for the baskets (see Figure 6.1). Participants in the first survey identified this experience with their own family outings in a natural

Table 13.1 Evaluating the Tshinanu website using characteristics for website evaluation.

Characteristic	Change
Design	Change color and size of font to improve readability.
Navigation	Reduce the number of navigational choices from the home page. Make labels more descriptive. Add a rollover on labels that provides a description of the link. Add descriptive labels to site sections. Reposition links to indicate their relative importance. Reposition home page button to a more visible location. Add a rollover that provides subsection content to section links.
Participation	Add a "Share Your Opinion" feature. Add instructive introductory text before displaying the first post.
Community	Add a prominent link and instructional text persuading the user to "get involved." Make the link viewable from each theme.
Identity and Authenticity	Provide an introduction that informs users on the importance of language in these cultures. Explain that the site uses both French and English. Explain use of native terms. Add audio translation of native terms in context of their use.
Storytelling	Clarify story topics by adding an introduction and description to each story. Incorporate good storytelling techniques.
Sensorial design	Provide a progress indicator on videos that indicates the duration of the video and its progress.
Immersion	Provide English audio version of narration.
Information and Knowledge	Provide links to more in-depth information. Include explanations of music and dances. Include maps and orienting information. Define special terms such as "First Nations." Include history and background information to put the stories and the site into the proper context. Provide follow-up information for high-interest stories where the outcome is not shown. For example, in a story about someone seeking a job, provide a follow-up that shows the outcome.

setting. Participants gained the most from the videos that included interesting stories rather than the videos that presented factual information. When a storyteller was involved with the video, the feedback on that video was more personal and enthusiastic. The photographs added a didactic value that enabled participants to gain insight into the information in the videos. The photographs seemed to supplement the video rather than work as a stand-alone feature.

Of the questions in the survey, the open-ended ones provided the most insight into the experience the users had with the course materials. The participants with an aboriginal background appeared to be more invested in the content of the site and wrote longer, more insightful answers to the open-ended questions.

The data from the Likert-scale questions and comparison/preference style questions had no outstanding patterns. The replies were very scattered and tended to reflect the answers provided in the open-ended questions.

Even though the participants were specifically asked to ignore the technology and quality of media, many of their observations regarding the material related to the production aspect of the information. Many participants complained of long load times or videos that were roughly edited. Some participants stated that the material took too long to complete and that the material lacked captions to quickly convey the gist of the story being portrayed. We were struck by the prevalence of these types of comments because the participants were clearly instructed to disregard the technical issues. This trend underscores the importance of the overall user experience in creating an environment where culturally based materials could be absorbed, enjoyed, and explored online.

Results of the Analyses

For the Tshinanu website, after the issues taken from the evaluation were characterized and prioritized, we made design changes by creating a prototype redesign. The prototype served as the basis for the comparative user testing. We wanted something we could create and quickly reevaluate to see if our design recommendations made any difference in the overall user response. The prototype was constructed using Photoshop and PowerPoint to allow us to produce it quickly and without having to do any application programming.

Since the issues from our first evaluation of the Tshinanu website had been characterized and prioritized, we used those priorities to decide which design changes to make. We also made some compromises on redesign work based on feasibility. For example, users had reported that having a foreign language on the interface and in the narrated stories was an issue, but we knew we could not translate the site, so we compromised and only translated an example phrase to test the concept.

Based on the issues reported by users, the Tshinanu website redesign addressed the issues that were feasible as outlined in Table 13.2. The redesigned Tshinanu prototype was evaluated through comparative user testing.

In our formal testing, the Emily Carr course materials were evaluated with a second survey. The second survey was distributed to the eight respondents of the first survey one week later. This second survey yielded interesting information around what the participants retained from the course materials. Only five of the eight participants completed the second survey, which contained no multiple-choice or Likert-type questions. We determined from the responses of the first survey that the Likert-scale questions were not as valuable to our research objective when compared to the open-answer format. The questions on the second survey focused on clarifying issues that surfaced in the first survey and in studying the retention of the materials. The results of the second survey provided fewer negative reactions to the materials than the first survey. This could be linked to the fact that the second survey was considerably shorter than the first and was not filled out directly after the participant had experienced frustration by the long load times.

The second survey results illustrated that, even though participants had intentions of sharing the information they had recently viewed (as documented in the first survey), overall they did not discuss the content with others. Participants also did not pursue the crafts or similar activities demonstrated in the videos after the survey, although they had initially expressed interest in doing so. Any initially expressed passion to pursue basket making dissipated as participants distanced themselves from the materials and returned to their everyday activities.

Nature was a main facet of the content that participants remembered. They also retained information about family traditions and the gathering of materials to make the

Table 13.2 Experience characteristics and recommended changes.

Characteristic	Tshinanu.tv
High design/low design	Site provides a feeling of participatory design and seems informal and playful.
User control	User can explore site in any order. Interactivity is supported at several levels.
Navigation style/nonlinear style	Narrative. Multiple-thread but preset choices.
Participation	Users can comment on themes.
Community	Strong community focus through stories, images, music.
Identity/authenticity	Stories told by real people.
Storytelling	Site organized around storytelling themes.
Sensorial design	Engages through tactile, visual, auditory, and time-based media.
Immersion	Immerses user with music, video, animation, and interactivity.
Symbols and icons	Uses cultural symbols and icons.
Information and knowledge	Users are urged to create personal content with a "what do you think?" link.
Meaning	Provides possibility of connection and meaning through stories.

baskets. There was a strong sense of connection to the people in the videos conducting these activities. The participants also retained the informational aspect of the videos and considered them enjoyable. This type of feedback may have been prevalent due to the fact that many of the participants surveyed had or were seeking higher education and enjoyed learning.

Most of the participants treated the course materials as a stand-alone experience and did not seek out further information regarding the location of the First Nations peoples or explore similar aboriginal cultures. The *doing* actions of bark gathering and the craft making held more meaning to the participants than the background culture of the activities.

Further exploration with participants with different backgrounds and cultural associations may yield different results. The method in which the information was provided to the users could also have significantly influenced the results. Displaying information in a friendlier manner (instead of a list of links to videos and pages of photographs) could have contributed to a more welcoming experience and cultivated a stronger desire to connect with the people portrayed in the materials.

Lessons from the Case Study

The test results from the Tshinanu website and prototype and the Emily Carr course materials indicated the following general guidelines for successful design of cultural websites:

Storytelling	Include stories that contain experiences that are similar to users' experiences and relevant to current affairs that are familiar to users from different

	cultures. Common knowledge helps users identify even if other information is new or foreign. Include stories that are unique to a culture within the context of something that is familiar to users.
Information and Knowledge	Include more background when the culture (or experience) is different from that of the audience. Background information (e.g., history) provides context for other information. Provide links to more in-depth or related information to tie threads of knowledge together. The Emily Carr example reflects aspects of this principle. Many participants enjoyed the finer details of basket making and appreciated the ability to see them up close in the photographs. Participants retained information that related to their own experience of learning a new craft or learning the how-to aspect of objects they had seen before.
Identity and Authenticity	Reduce language barriers by describing use of language on a site that uses more than one language. Reduce jargon or unfamiliar terms. Explain unfamiliar terms. This principle is also demonstrated by the Emily Carr example. Many participants stated that they could identify with the activities or the situation depicted in the materials. This identification helped participants to connect with the people in the video, even when their cultures were different.
Information Design	Include familiar symbols such as maps to help orient the audience when the information is new.
Participation	Make the user feel welcome and secure in a new environment. Provide ways for the audience to get involved in the topics.
Sensorial Design	Use warm colors and inviting graphics that are friendly and welcome the user (especially important when the user is dealing with new information.). In both the Tshinanu website and the Emily Carr example, presenting information in more than one media aided the sense of immersion.

The cultural website project contributes to the current body of literature involving culture as well as internationalization and localization of websites. It also contributes to the body of literature concerned with evaluating websites and online media. It highlights the need for new methods and techniques to assess the success or failure of websites whose goal is to engage and communicate subjective ideas such as values and beliefs or whose main goal is to evoke an emotional or sensory experience in the user.

Further, the project underscores the difficulty of measuring experience through traditional user evaluation techniques. The survey approach for measuring the experiences with the Emily Carr course materials produced some interesting insights into what users found memorable, or potentially even endearing, but fell short of truly capturing the extent to which the users connected.

The ability of a user to satisfactorily experience a cross-cultural example appears to depend on how prepared the user is to engage with a presentation that is different from his or her expectations. We can aid the user in preparing for and enjoying new experiences by providing the right context and by setting expectations within that context. By welcoming the user, the site can let the user know that the site is inclusive rather than exclusive. By bridging unfamiliar topics and territory with the familiar and looking for commonalities rather than differences, the website can promote connection.

By paying careful attention to cultural markers in design and using them in a friendly and welcoming way, we can make the path easier for users to accept differences. With the right amount of explanation, description, and supporting content, we might help users even take an interest in cultures other than their own.

By considering design for the senses, and not just usability or task performance, we can give users a taste of a culture and allow them to relate on an emotional as well as an intellectual level.

Videos are effective for storytelling. Illustrations and still photographs are effective for supplementing information contained in videos, providing the user the opportunity to study details.

When providing materials that demonstrate activities or cultures, choice of media and presentation is important. Avoid frustrating users with videos that take too long to load or are of poor quality. Using progress indicators and providing the duration of videos allows users to decide if they have the time to view or load a file. Providing professionally produced and edited videos also helps users stay engaged. Keep the user engaged and prevent downtime when presenting media online to avoid the user getting sidetracked or becoming disinterested.

Summary of Relevant Principles

3. Test the Backbone	Users complained about backbone issues resulting in long load times for the Emily Carr videos. When the content of an experience is unfamiliar, users may react even more strongly to backbone issues.
4. Extend a Welcome	The original design of the Tshinanu website provided users with a warm welcome, using warm colors and inviting graphics.
5. Set the Context	When users encounter unfamiliar content, it is important to provide context. The redesign of the Tshinanu website provided users with an explanation for videos not being in English, reducing users' earlier usability concerns.
6. Make a Connection	The design of the First Nations materials showed that users made a connection across cultures when the material connected with their personal experience. Users found materials related to nature and to family highly memorable, and they found meaning in the craft activities, the "doing."
9. Create a Sense of Place	The redesign of the Tshinanu website simplified the number of navigational options presented to users on the home page to provide users with a better sense of place.
10. Plan to Continue the Engagement	The designs for the Emily Carr materials were intended to foster interaction with the culture after the initial experience, but results of the formal testing suggest that this goal was not achieved.

Usability in Distance Education

Robert Krull, RENSSELAER POLYTECHNIC INSTITUTE
David Lumerman, NEW YORK LIFE
Michael J. Madaio, QVC
Michael F. Lynch, RENSSELAER POLYTECHNIC INSTITUTE

Shank (2008a) and Driscoll (2008) argue that, although the hype for e-learning promises that professional training can be made available for easy access by removing the time and cost needed for travel and by allowing learners to shift the schedule for learning at their convenience, the reality is that e-learning has not been very successful. Only a small percentage of corporate training has been moved to e-learning, and user satisfaction is not high. Why is there such a disjunction between the supposed value of professional training materials and their low rates of usage?

Using research conducted at RPI, we will describe features that make distance education—one kind of e-learning—effective. Though we will use RPI research as a point of focus, we will project our findings to other forms of distance education, particularly to the kinds of training and support that could be provided by professional associations. Our discussion is based on the pragmatic experiences of faculty and students with a wide range of technologies. And, as shown in Figure 14.1, we will also report on results from three kinds of research: three years of surveys distributed to on-campus and distance students, qualitative observations of classes and meetings, and comparative user testing of students using distance-education platforms.

What we will not do is analyze all forms of e-learning. E-learning and its subspecies (e.g., computer-based training) encompass a broad range of activities, each with its own technologies, usage patterns, cost structures, and effects. The form of distance education we will discuss involves instructors teaching live classes to students at distant locations via electronic media. Driscoll (2008) provides data showing that about 10% of professional training is of this type; computer-based training comprises about 15% of professional training; and face-to-face (F2F) classroom instruction constitutes about 70% of professional training.

At RPI most of our distance courses include an on-campus, F2F classroom plus distance students who generally are watching class at the same time. Over time RPI has used several technologies, which we will discuss, to connect distance students to the live classroom. Other universities have successfully used other distance-education systems supported by different classroom structures and technologies.

The Distance-Education Dream Deferred

Shank (2008a) and Driscoll (2008) note that good marketing can make e-learning sound wonderful. Shank (2008b) describes how Web 2.0 may bring an updated,

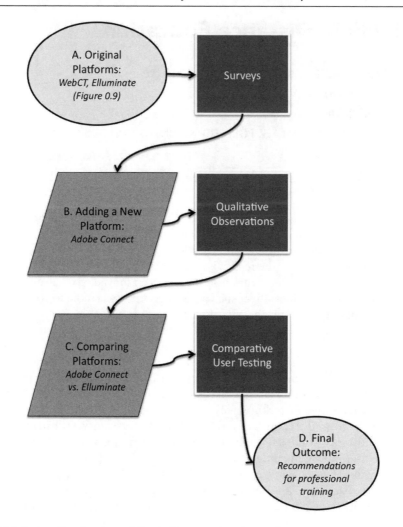

Figure 14.1 Project flow for the usability in distance-education project.

and potentially more successful, instructional model to fruition. But these research-ers also describe organizational, pedagogical, technical, and financial problems that prevent e-learning from living up to the vision. This chapter focuses more narrowly on pragmatic and technical reasons that distance courses cannot operate in the ways proposed. We look at how instructional content is developed and disseminated. Our analysis is grounded less in organizational structures than in the decisions in-structors and learners make during learning. (Readers interested in the theoretical background for this kind of analysis can consult general texts on instructional de-sign such as Gagné, Briggs, & Wager, 1992. Readers more interested in technology-supported instructional design could look at sources such as Clark & Mayer, 2008, and Horton, 2000.)

Primarily the utopian model oversells what instructors are able to deliver and what students are able to absorb. Through our experience at RPI we have seen pragmatic challenges for both instructors and learners:

- Learning distance technologies and keeping up with product revisions takes time.
- Managing multiple technologies during class sessions is difficult.
- Designing automated training such as computer-based training involves long development times.
- Automated training is very difficult to develop for fields such as technical communication in which student work involves designing original products such as user interfaces.
- Technical communication and user interface design are dynamic fields with rapid change in knowledge bases and practices, thereby greatly shortening the lifetime of training materials.
- Designing training materials tuned to specific job titles assumes that there is an instructional design knowledge base matched to job titles. That knowledge base may not exist.
- Designing different training materials for learners with different learning styles is complex. Designing for so many learning styles demands separate kinds of content and complex assembly of information modules (learning objects). It does not involve just a database management system to assemble objects.
- Designing applications of knowledge for learners to use is time-consuming, but otherwise learners can't tell if they understand the material.
- Evaluating learners' applications of knowledge in design work must go beyond multiple-choice exams. Instructor effort rises linearly with the number of learners. The more feedback instructors provide on student work, the larger the instructor effort per student.
- Content must be frequently updated and respond to learners' questions.

All of the activities in this list take instructors' time. That instructors need to actually read and evaluate student work limits economies of scale with large numbers of students.

Shifting from instructors' hands-on evaluations of student work to computer-based evaluations may not be the answer. F2F instruction may require about three hours of preparation for each delivered hour. Our experience at RPI suggests that distance delivery requires about three times that amount. By comparison, computer-based training requires over ten times as much preparation time as distance education per hour of delivered material (Alessi & Trollip, 2000).

One reason that distance education has not fulfilled the promise that Shank and Driscoll describe is that instructors can't manage the effort needed. Another reason may be that the effort required on the part of learners is larger than it first seems to be. It can include:

- Learning how to use the technologies to receive content.
- Juggling the technologies during learning sessions, including recovery from frozen hardware and software.

- Learning and using several distance-education platforms when learning from more than one instructor.
- Updating knowledge of distance-education platforms when learning over an extended period.
- Sustaining motivation when instructional material consists of just lecture or online page turners.
- Sustaining motivation when students have to work alone and can't interact with others.
- Taking the time to work through applications of theoretical content to concrete actions relevant to work goals.
- Applying theoretical concepts to design decisions relevant to work goals.

Again, these things also take time and effort, this time on the part of students. And neither distance technologies nor knowledge management systems help all that much. In fact, the technology can increase the load, and knowledge management may not solve problems dealing with content.

However, through more than ten years of distance instruction and research that is described later in this chapter, we have found some instructional methods that match how learners work. Before describing this work, we should briefly discuss the current state of distance-education media and what future developments are needed to reduce the problems faced by instructors and learners.

Though hardware used in distance education has progressed rapidly, it is not up to the demands of instructional utopia described by Shank (2008a), and much of the development she projects for Web 2.0 (Shank, 2008b) is just underway. For example, we do not have very high Internet bandwidth either downstream or upstream, so we do not have multiple camera angles with which to watch classrooms and have only the crudest video images moving upstream. In addition, distance software is not as sophisticated as other commercial applications such as Microsoft Office. Our experience at RPI suggests that a variety of technologies can be made to work, but all the required technical functionality needs to be cobbled together rather than being workable off the shelf in an integrated package.

Windowed systems are limited regarding how many windows can be shown at once and how detailed they can be. The computer screen has limited real estate and can show lots of detail in a small number of windows or much less detail in many windows. Instructors' or learners' resizing windows for optimal display can be problematic, as we will describe in our report of data obtained from watching learners during class sessions.

Internet bandwidth limits what even makes it to the video screen. Full-motion video of classroom activities must be compressed to wedge it downstream from instructors to students. Video compression and Internet distribution produces time delays that are inconsistent among users and at different times. Downstream audio generally is packaged with downstream video, but it is affected by the options set for compression. If video is privileged during compression, audio may be delayed past what appears in video. If audio is privileged, video may freeze while audio plays on. Such choices can make for disconcerting mismatches between the two media streams.

Compared to downstream video, the choices for upstream video are much simpler: because the bandwidth is so limited and fragile, upstream video probably should be avoided for all but the smallest groups of learners. Otherwise, the medium freezes or breaks, being more of an annoyance than an advantage. We describe our research on this topic later in this chapter.

Upstream audio doesn't demand that much bandwidth by itself, but it still can be low in fidelity because of microphone problems. We have found that upstream audio also can be fragile, especially when more than one learner microphone is open at a time.

Audio-video players such as Microsoft's Media Player are used to present moving images such as classroom video or film segments. Internet bandwidth limits, though, force instructors to reduce image detail considerably. For example, even a humble consumer-level still-photo camera that has a video option can generate a 55-megabyte file for 30 seconds of live video. Imagine how much the information produced by a 90-minute class would have to be compressed to make it manageable via streaming video for Internet distribution. The resulting video information can't be enlarged much without producing a lot of image deterioration. To get a sense of this, enlarge a You-Tube window to the full computer screen. Distance-education video tends to be lower in resolution than that.

When many different hardware technologies are used for distance education, several software programs also are required. In addition, perhaps because the development history of that software is shorter than that of commercial software such as integrated office products, the user interfaces of distance-education software is not quite as evolved.

The net effect is that instructors and students are forced to learn software driving the link to the Internet, a multiwindowed synchronous distance platform, an audio-video display program, an instant messaging program, voice over Internet protocol (VoIP) for upstream digital audio, and an asynchronous distance platform to access archived material and to pass through the system security gateway. In addition, the research we are about to describe has shown that students who take several courses may need to learn multiple software products because instructors do not use the same software.

In sum, the pragmatic challenges that siphon time and the technical challenges that add to the physical and cognitive load for both instructors and students may be the reason that, though distance education holds out the promise of anywhere-anytime training, the actual rates of usage are lower. But distance education still is workable; one just needs to be realistic about its demands.

At RPI we have been able to use many distance methods aside from having either instructors or students travel: synchronous satellite, mailing out videotapes or CDs, videoconferencing, audio-only via a phone bridge or Internet-based VoIP, video streaming, and Internet-based multiwindowed interface. Other universities have successfully delivered education via asynchronous text (e.g., bulletin boards), synchronous text (e.g., systems similar to instant messengers), and other methods. At RPI, we found that for each of these systems we used, instructors and students needed to adapt how they used media. In this chapter we concentrate on Internet-based platforms that match what is current in the marketplace.

The Internet-based platform used during the last few years at RPI involved the following:

- An asynchronous system to manage student access to other resources such as archived video and grades (WebCT/Blackboard)
- An audio-video player for synchronous images of on-campus classroom interaction (Microsoft Media Player)
- A multiwindowed interface (Elluminate or Adobe Connect)
- A window for instant messenger text
- A window for presentation slides
- A window for an electronic whiteboard
- A possible window for live video of classroom interaction
- A possible window for external software applications
- Possible windows for upstream video from learners
- Possible connections to upstream audio from learners
- Windows for programs run externally to the multiwindowed interface (e.g., links to video files stored on YouTube).

The reason that RPI uses so many varieties of hardware and software is that we have found learners prefer being actively involved in sessions to passively watching an instructor lecture at them. At the current stage of development, no single kind of hardware or software handles all the information moving downstream from instructors to learners or in the other direction.

Although RPI has been providing professional training in technical communication for more than 50 years and mediated distance education for more than 10 years, our 3 years of research still provided surprises. In particular, as we will describe, students' uses of distance technologies and learning preferences deviated from instructors' plans and perceptions. In addition, different groups of students have had different experiences and encountered different problems.

RPI's research on student perception and performance is of three types, each revealing unique, complementary, but slightly different issues: surveys, observations, and comparative user testing. The research techniques are described elsewhere in this book; here we concentrate on findings.

Findings from the Survey

For three years, samples of students in two courses filled out an extensive survey asking about their experiences and perceptions of alternate instructional techniques. The courses involved design of online support systems and software user interfaces taught by two instructors, Robert Krull and Roger Grice. Evaluative data regarding other courses and other instructors were gathered outside this study, for different purposes, and using somewhat less extensive questionnaires. Those results are not reported here.

The initial questionnaires were designed by two distance students, William Wetmore (Bell South) and Louis Ruggiero (IBM). For the first wave of data collection, Wetmore also handled hosting the questionnaire on a web server.

After the first wave of data collection, the survey was modified by David Lumer-man, Barry Young, and Robert Krull to reflect changes in the software platform used for distance learning at RPI and to streamline the number of questions asked. Michael Lynch transferred the questionnaires to another web server.

Students filled out the survey near the end of 15-week semesters. Most students in the sample were master's degree students in technical communication, though a few were doctoral students in communication, and a very few were seniors in various majors.

We were interested in students' perceptions of the overall distance learning environment and process, but our initial results directed our attention to systematic differences between the perceptions of on-campus and distance students. That we had responses regarding the courses taught by two instructors in each wave gave us an indication that instructors could differ in their approaches to the same instructional environment but could not let us project to systematic patterns among all instructors. However, student responses did raise the issue of variability in instructional techniques among all the instructors involved in the distance program at RPI.

Since the hardware and software platforms underwent continuous evolution during the study period, we are also able to compare student perceptions of the changes. Specifically, we asked questions about WebCT, Elluminate, and Adobe Connect. Additional data comparing Elluminate to Adobe Connect were gathered via comparative user testing and are described later in this chapter.

Overall, student perceptions of the distance-learning environment were positive through all three years' worth of data collection. This pattern generally matched the perceptions of instructors' involved in the distance graduate program and obtained through several forms of data collection that on-campus and distance students performed comparably in courses and were comparably happy with their experiences.

So distance learning seemed workable and produced results similar to those found with F2F instruction. This may not be an astounding finding. Shank (2008a) concludes that many studies on varieties of e-learning have found little difference in the efficacy. (Shank cites meta-analyses of studies comparing instructional modalities by Bernard et al., 2004, and by Russell, 1999, though not the latter publication of his work). However, because our survey was so detailed, we were able to detect systematic differences in students' perceptions. In particular, we found that the load on students generated by technology and the compensatory communication etiquettes necessary resulted in systematically different experiences for on-campus and distance students. We have come to call this the "parallel universe" of distance education.

Both on-campus and distance students thought the required technology was workable and, in some ways, provided advantages over traditional classrooms. But distance students were more dependent on technology for access to information and opportunities for participation. This affected both how they behaved during class sessions and how they felt about their experience.

Distance technology placed physical and psychological loads on students due to the balkiness of the technology to commence and continue working during class sessions, low fidelity of images and sound, and time delays introduced by Internet bandwidth limitations. Although the course platforms never stopped working completely, when pushed to their limits, platform components could stop working for individual students or, very occasionally, would freeze a component for several students or an instructor. Distance students in particular could have to restart their connection to the distance-learning platform. Besides the aggravation of having to do that, students also felt that periodically they would miss segments of class discussions. The more instructors and students pushed the limits of the technology, the more likely the technology was to fail. Some instructors became cautious trying platform components that were demanding of Internet bandwidth or computer resources, thereby slightly impoverishing the richness of course media.

The various software programs used over the three years were comparable in performance overall, though they differed in some performance details. There did seem to be a general trend toward less hardware and software fragility, despite an increase in the complexity of functions offered by the technology.

Another kind of technology-related load on learners involved something largely invisible to individual instructors. Students who took courses for several instructors would find themselves needing to learn more than one set of class software and more than one way of using the same software. That occurred because instructors, without suspecting it, used the distance platforms in different ways. Students found that they had to adjust for each course and instructor, adding overhead to taking courses.

On-campus students were less dependent on the distance-learning platforms but faced technical challenges nonetheless. They saw and heard some kinds of information through the same media as distance students: instant messages, application program sharing (e.g., software demos), upstream audio from distance students. When on-campus students used the same technologies as distance students, they would encounter similar challenges, such as losing their connections to the multiwindow platform. In fact, until the third year of the study, on-campus students actually had less reliable connections to the Internet during class sessions than did distance students.

One of the surprises in the first wave of data collection was that the on-campus students found the distance platform so attractive that a substantial number of them chose to attend classes electronically rather than face-to-face. In other words, because they had trouble maintaining Internet connections in the on-campus classroom, they stayed home and would connect to instructors and other students via the instant messaging chat window. One instructor found that this was becoming so problematic, due to low F2F class attendance, that he adjusted his teaching style to force on-campus students to attend in person.

On-campus students also had to adapt their communication style to the classroom technology a bit just so that distance students could hear and see them clearly. On-campus students needed to speak more loudly and distinctly to be heard. In addition, during discussion among on-campus participants, the course production staff would turn a motorized classroom camera toward an on-campus student while that person was talking. If the student spoke before the camera showed his or her image, distance students wouldn't know who spoke. If the student waited for the camera to catch up, it produced an uncomfortable pause in discussion.

During the last year of data collection, the production staff sometimes just left one classroom camera on the instructor and did not move the camera to show students who were speaking. Because of the small video window and its low resolution, this technique produced the effect for distance students of watching a postage stamp–sized face of the instructor for an entire semester. Questionnaire results indicated that distance students would have preferred to see student faces instead of just the single view of instructors.

A similar problem occurred regarding on-campus audio. If on-campus students did not use a handheld microphone or did not speak loudly enough for ceiling microphones to pick up their voices, distance students would not be able to hear them. If on-campus students did use a handheld microphone, there would be an awkward pause while a microphone has handed across the classroom to them. This kind of issue is in the domain of communication etiquette rather than being purely technical.

The questionnaires provided reinforcing feedback to instructors that told them where they needed to adjust their delivery to reduce the demands of the technology on learners. Visual information and media were particularly problematic areas.

Low-fidelity images were at times all that the distance system could distribute. That required instructors to display information such as live-motion video, presentation slides, and workshop reports with less detail than normal or larger in size than normal. For instructors to disseminate illegible visuals and to talk about them as if everyone could see them clearly was regarded as poor form. On the other hand, at times instructors were constrained by the technology and worked around it as well as they could. Learners might not realize that instructors were trying to respond to learner needs but could do only so much. For example, at one point, due to technology changes, instructors were no longer able to use a computer program that let them enlarge areas of the screen to make them more legible in low-fidelity situations. Whereas before they had been able to show small screen items in greater detail, they no longer could. Learners may not have realized the sudden constraint on instructors. Would the instructors' having mentioned the constraint been good etiquette or bad etiquette? Would learners have seen it as an acknowledgement of their needs or as the instructors' whining?

Although instructors generally were the ones generating visual materials, students periodically gave class presentations via these media. This was problematic if students tried to send information upstream during class time. The upstream Internet paths were too limited to allow high-fidelity images or sound. One solution was for students to send information to instructors ahead of class time by mailing CDs or by e-mailing attachments. Then students could call in by phone to provide live narration.

That the instructors and learners arranged this work-around was largely transparent to other students, but everyone seemed to appreciate it.

A similar set of issues with low-fidelity and time delays occurred with other media as well. When it was used several years earlier, videoconferencing produced time delays of a few seconds between one person's speaking and the audience's hearing it. If participants didn't allow for this, they would end up speaking over each other, rendering all audio unintelligible. Everyone had to learn that there would be time delays and that it was better to wait for the time periods to transpire without trying to fill in with the small comments people typically insert to acknowledge to others that they are being heard.

More recently, when videoconferencing was supplanted by Internet-based video streaming, there have been even longer time delays between events in the live classroom and learners' seeing the stream. This has produced a fundamental etiquette issue for distance students. Should they ask a question even if the topic about which they wanted information had transpired in the live classroom a minute earlier? Because learners feared that it was not acceptable to interrupt instructors, instructors had to let learners know that it in fact was acceptable.

In addition, because our research and text messages to the classroom from learners showed how serious an etiquette problem this was, we assigned teaching assistants the task of collecting student questions and explicitly interrupting instructors so that instructors could answer the questions. Students reported reacting differently if they knew a teaching assistant was monitoring the chat discussion, feeling that questions they raised would be responded to rapidly. Sometimes, though, students would let their chat discussions wander from the class agenda if they didn't think the professor was watching that discussion directly. That aspect of communication etiquette is beyond the scope of this chapter.

The electronic whiteboards used for workshops produced their own problems: The text-entry systems required by these whiteboards did not correspond to common systems on either word processors or presentation programs. This produced a lot of carnage when learners entered and edited information for such simple tasks producing a bulleted list. It would take a few class sessions for learners to accept the limited text-handling tools available and to not blame the skill and motivation of students working with them.

Similarly, the whiteboards offered only crude means of adding graphics. Though some students were ingenious in producing informative graphics with limited means, most students gave up on graphics entirely. In either case, it became acceptable for students to describe how beautiful their graphics would have been if only they had the tools to generate them. That may have become acceptable classroom etiquette, even if it was educationally impoverished.

Control over what was written on the whiteboards and who wrote on the whiteboards were two other etiquette problems. Not everyone could add information to the whiteboards simultaneously, and, because of the whiteboards' limited editing tools, it was difficult to compile separately generated bits of information. Learners gradually evolved means of assigning control over the whiteboard and of action on the workshop participants' text-based comments made via instant messenger. That these became visible etiquette issues at all was due to the crankiness of the technology. Generally, students chose one representative to work on the whiteboard and restricted others to making comments via instant messenger.

One distance platform offered students the possibility of having their own cursors on whiteboards. Each learner's cursor appeared on the screen with the name of learner attached. Instead of being an advantage, this actually made learners feel attacked by "cursor bees" as all the cursors zoomed around the whiteboard. Learners found that they had to drop back to their prior etiquette of limiting who could act on the whiteboard.

Some of the findings we have just described came exclusively from the surveys we sent out in our three waves of data collection. Other findings, such as the one about cursor bees, were reinforced by our qualitative observations of classrooms and our comparative user testing.

Findings from Qualitative Observations

To examine usability features of the distance-learning platforms in greater detail we performed several kinds of qualitative observations. We observed F2F classes and distance classes, and some observations were performed in person and some via distance technologies. We recorded events that were related to hardware and software problems, such as establishing and sustaining media links, compensating for low fidelity and time delays, and negotiating control over information dissemination.

Observations at a distance were performed through the channels used by distance participants: instant messenger; telephone and Internet-based VoIP; electronic slide presentations by learners, sometimes accompanied by audio narration, and occasional upstream video. By observing classes both live and via distance technologies, we were able to compare our impressions of how classes operated from the standpoint of on-campus and distance participants.

We also had a handful of on-campus students work alone in a separate classroom to simulate the learning environment of distance students. We watched each of these students for approximately half a class period (60 to 90 minutes), noting what they did and said during the sessions.

Finally, we also analyzed how the distance technologies supported our research group (consisting of Robert Krull, David Lumerman, Michael Madaio, and Dustin Kirk). Our research group met electronically about once every two weeks during the academic year for more than one calendar year. We explicitly observed our own group processes for about the first half-semester of the project. During that time we tried text-based communication, live audio, and live video. We were even able to use the Adobe Connect course platform prior to its general release to the campus community. We were fortunate to receive help from Adobe in setting up working sessions and accessing Adobe's training materials. We also received several hours of training from Adobe staff and are very grateful for their support.

Because our research group used these technologies so frequently, we were able to obtain data that foretold likely problems. We then were able to triangulate what we saw in our working sessions through our observations of actual classes, and we were able to set up our comparative user testing to further explore our hypotheses about how instructors and students would use the course platforms. Interestingly, actual classes were able to adapt to the platforms more quickly and with fewer problems than we expected.

Overall, the results of our observations were in accord with the results of the surveys. Although technological hurdles place a load on instructors and students, distance education is workable for both instructors and students and provides enough advantages for distance students to compensate for its challenges. However, we also found that the distance environment can be demanding, especially when setting up new hardware and software and when orienting new participants. Fortunately, these demands lessen as participants gain experience.

We also observed the limits of a downstream-oriented instructional model focused on a master presenter. It seems that learners seek to balance that model with one that is multidirectional and collaborative. Learners were motivated to take an active part in learning, making themselves felt during class sessions and contributing to discussion and problem solving. They were not pleased when technology problems forced them to be passive.

Looking at participant actions in more detail, we saw how much time distance students needed to get hardware and software rolling before classes started. After getting their computers and web browsers running, they would need to go to the Learning Management System (WebCT), get past the security gate, start the multiwindow platform (either Elluminate or Adobe Connect), sign into the class session (and a secondary breakout room, if that was necessary), start the audio-visual player to access the compressed video stream, and get their headsets and microphones operating if they intended to use VoIP. If they intended to use a web browser to run secondary video (for example, for a specialty site such as YouTube), they would need to start that as well. To get all these connections made successfully could take a half-hour and, when things went badly, several passes at launching software.

Once class sessions started, on-campus and distance students had somewhat different experiences. Our questionnaire results showed that the two groups of students interacted differently with instructors and other students. That these two groups of students have somewhat different experiences may be inevitable, but it is likely to be worthwhile for instructors to try to integrate the two subcommunities. For example, having students compare their work experiences should enable them to identify novel solutions when they face analogous problems. Students have said that reports from other students about their work projects have been among the most valuable parts of courses.

One thing that makes the two student universes different is how they related to the instructors and to each other. F2F classes tend to be dominated by communication directed to an instructor or via an instructor to other students. Ten years ago, for example, one of our doctoral students (Johel Brown-Grant) cataloged the source of F2F comments in a group of distance courses in science, management, and engineering. Brown-Grant found that, for a typical 90-minute class, only 11 minutes' worth of F2F comments were made by students. The rest were made by instructors. Even a casual glance at the number of instant messenger comments made by distance students shows that distance students volunteer more comments.

One factor suppressing student comments in face-to-face classes is the social etiquette that suggests that only one person should speak at a time. If more than one person speaks at once, the person supposedly holding the floor at the time cannot be heard. Typically, instructors are holding the floor, and it would not be possible to hear them if others spoke simultaneously.

This constraint does not hold for distance classes due to both technology and etiquette. The technical reason is that so much "speaking" in distance classes is done via instant messenger text. Many students can be typing text simultaneously without interrupting each other or the instructor. The messaging system compiles comments as they arrive. Students can examine messages by scrolling through them.

Of course, when there are too many text messages it is difficult for students to read them all or for instructors to respond to them. The net effect can also be dispiriting for learners. They try to add information and contribute to workshops, but there is little response to their input. At RPI teaching assistants were delegated the task of responding to student input that should receive instructor attention. For small classes, instructors themselves were responsible for reading instant messages. Courses needed to enact an etiquette that it was worthwhile for instructors to take time from other class activities to scan instant messaging text for important material and to act on it. The resulting pattern of classroom discussion might not be typical of F2F classes, but it links F2F to distance students in a meaningful way.

The more general etiquette issue is that, since the instructors were not interrupted by students' instant messages, the distance students were able to carry on spirited discussions in parallel with the instructors' lecturing. Sometimes these parallel discussions wandered considerably from the central theme of lectures, but often these discussions enabled students to deal with annoying but significant pragmatic issues (e.g., From what presentation file is the instructor lecturing now?), administrative issues (e.g., Has the instructor announced the date of the midterm exam yet?), and thematic issues (e.g., What did the instructor mean by "visual flow"?). In prior years, when course video was distributed by satellite or videoconferencing, distance students co-located in distant classrooms would have such discussions face to face. As more and more students migrated to solitary Internet-based participation, the discussion moved online.

For both on-campus and distance students these discussions could have major instructional benefits. As students became more adept at exploiting these side discussions, more and more students built working relationships with one another. For instance, once the WiFi connections in the teaching classroom became reliable, more on-campus students used their laptops to be involved in the instant messaging discussions. In some courses about half the on-campus students participated in or monitored these discussions. This use of the learning platform is not one anticipated by the educational literature that touts the virtues of face-to-face classrooms.

Distance-learning technology is evolving rapidly, but it still is not as robust as other computer software such as word processors and spreadsheets. Both our classroom observations and comparative user tests revealed frequent program freezes, Internet service interruptions, and unpredictable bandwidth-induced delays in information transfer. Downstream video was most subject to time delays but was more predictable in terms of all-out failure: moving video either worked or didn't. Typically, video of the live classroom worked most of the time. When run through course software platforms, video similar to YouTube video did not work most of the time, and participants had to use their web browsers to reach a site that would run such video correctly. With practice, instructors were able to get more kinds of video to run on the course platforms, particularly on Adobe Connect.

Upstream video from student cameras was very brittle. When more than one or two students tried to have their cameras active at once, the course platforms lost connection with one or all the students. Courses generally avoided using almost any video of this type.

Downstream audio worked most of the time; upstream audio via VoIP broke down frequently. Even when VoIP did not break down, multiple learners' having microphones open simultaneously produced unwanted echoes and feedback. The problem could be reduced, though, if learners used microphone-equipped headsets. Also it seemed that Internet audio problems diminished over time as instructors and learners gained experience with ways to minimize hardware problems.

One work-around was to use some other medium for audio than the course support platform. We used telephone and Skype with some success, though, again, this worked best when participants used headsets rather than speakers that produced feedback loops.

Distance education often involves breaking large classes into smaller workshop groups. The Elluminate platform was designed with that process in mind, while the initial design of Adobe Connect was built around a more centralized communication structure. That meant that, when using Connect, instructors needed a work-around to produce breakout groups. One work-around was to set up entirely separate Connect sessions for the workshop groups, treating each workshop session as a separate course. When workshops were called for, students would sign onto a separate course and would do their work there. They would then return to the main classroom to hear about other students' workshop results.

For instructors this could mean taking time to set up breakout sessions when workshops were launched. At RPI teaching assistants generally did this. It also meant that material from multiple workshops would need to be reintegrated at the end of workshops. This required instructors to collect information electronically and paste it into the main session or to have students wander from one online course session to another. Though this dance would be managed without utter failure, it seems like an unnecessary one.

In summary, observations of student performance in classes concurred with what we found through three waves of surveys: Distance education is workable but produces a physical and psychological load on learners. The observations of learner performance provided additional details about specific technology-induced problems and about the effectiveness of communication etiquette in mitigating those problems. As mentioned before, based on our research team's experiences with these technologies, we had expected even more problems than we actually saw in classrooms. We were a little surprised by how flexible instructors and learners were in adapting to new hardware and software.

Our observations also showed how important collaboration was during class sessions. We have already mentioned that workshops were one way that learners could collaborate and that the technology to support workshops posed challenges to learners. We set up comparative user testing to explore this means of collaboration.

Findings from Comparative User Testing

We had students work in pairs so that it was easier to catalog their activities. Students worked at separate locations and were connected by either the Elluminate or Adobe Connect. We did not use web camera video links because such cameras generally would not be available during classes, and video links turned out to be very fragile in our research group testing. But test subjects did have the opportunity to use live audio, something that turned out to be greatly preferred to instant messaging via text.

The students in our comparative user tests had had prior experience with the Elluminate platform via classes; at the time of testing, they had almost no experience with Adobe Connect. This meant that the students' ability to complete with Adobe Connect would indicate that the product was at least as usable as Elluminate for the task we posed for the tests: compiling bulleted lists of positive and negative features of distance education.

As we have mentioned, all of the test subjects preferred live audio to text messaging and immediately shifted to it for exchanging verbal information. In addition, the test subjects' effusive comments during posttest debriefing showed how much they liked the audio. This was the most dramatic, novel finding from the comparative user tests. Since survey results had not brought out a preference for live audio, it may be that learners can struggle through with text messaging as long as live audio is not available.

Unfortunately, live audio proved to be typically brittle in the two-person test sessions as well, failing at some point in nearly every session. So live audio is appealing but unreliable when run through the course platforms we tried. Running live audio through a telephone bridge or an external software system such as Skype is more expensive or awkward.

The electronic whiteboards proved to be nearly as problematic in the two-person workshops as in real classes. Requiring nonstandard means of entering text makes it difficult for students to produce workshop reports without devoting a lot of attention to the normally trivial task of making up bulleted lists.

One of the whiteboards did offer a simple-to-use but problematic option. It showed an eraser object as the first one on a toolbar. Instead of erasing the last action or initiating a dialogue allowing users to specify what to erase, the eraser wiped out everything on the whiteboard without asking for confirmation or providing the option to undo. Neither the participants in our tests nor students in actual classes liked this feature much.

Students in the comparative user tests, like students in actual classes, did not like that Adobe Connect would not allow them to adjust the sizes of windows on their own screens without, at the same time, adjusting the sizes of windows of other users' screens. That the windows worked this way was a function the product's design philosophy: people running meetings should have control over information dissemination, including over windows containing the information. For students to be able to act on the contents of the whiteboard, they needed to be given a user status that also allowed them to adjust the window containing the whiteboard. If they were given control over that window, they were at the same time given control over all other windows and over all windows appearing on all users' screens. That last link to all users' windows produced accidental alterations during our laboratory test sessions.

When test subjects could not use live audio, they were forced to use instant messaging in their discussions. Instant messaging worked as well in the comparative user tests as in live classes. Lab testing did reveal a problem, however. When students used the messenger during workshops, they would need to look back and forth between two places on the screen—the whiteboard and the messenger window. Since the messages would scroll out of sight as new text was entered, students would have to scroll the messenger window to see if they had read all comments.

One could ameliorate this problem by enlarging the messenger window and moving it as close as possible to the whiteboard window; but students' being unable to do this to their own taste eliminated this possibility. One reason students liked live audio so much was that it did not require them to alternate their attention between two windows in this way.

Implications for Professional Training

Professional associations have several means of communicating with their members: scholarly and applied journals, international and regional conferences, and training seminars. But professional associations also provide value to their members through less formal communication such as conversations that take place outside of conference sessions. Can distance-education techniques be adapted as substitutes for all these media? Perhaps, but our research suggests that there will be technical and etiquette challenges for such adaptations to work effectively.

The research reported here has shown that prior to and during learning sessions there is considerable load on participants to get technology to run and to keep it running. The larger the number of participants and the more types of media used during sessions, the more the load and the more likely technology is to break. Demands for support for new technology are unlikely to slow down in the future, especially for support of handheld devices. One of the coauthors of this chapter has already participated in conferences and seminars that have supported learners' using the iPhone as hardware and Twitter for software. During the fall 2008 university semester, coauthor Robert Krull already was using YouTube in nearly every class session of a course on mass media. That kind of use demanded a high-bandwidth Internet connection. Will professional associations try to support technological change at this rate?

For semester-long courses, particularly ones that are supported by a technical support staff, this load seems manageable. For training programs involving just a few sessions or for one-shot seminars with little technical support, the load may be overwhelming. As distance technologies evolve, they will become less brittle and will require less support. Most media technologies have followed that trend. Until then, it may be easier to limit one's ambitions by using simple technologies and few media.

Because upstream technologies are less robust than downstream technologies, instructors have experienced fewer failures than have learners, particularly learners who try to originate messages. That may be problematic for training sessions emphasizing collaborative learning. Learners may be willing to lose a few minutes during a semester-long course, but they may not be willing to lose the same amount of material from a short seminar. Learners will be even more irritated if they are unable to supply comments during workshops or if they are thwarted in using live audio. Again, it may be wise not to push the technology envelope.

Our research has shown that, while instructor presentation skill is important, it is equally important that instructors encourage peer-to-peer learning. Instructors may be particularly effective when they can encourage learners to articulate their goals, describe their professional contexts and work processes, and apply seminar content to their own needs. Enabling learners to do that by electronic means requires instructors to gain experience in marrying their knowledge of technical subjects to their knowledge of instructional design, their interpersonal skills and their capacity to bend media to their needs.

We discovered that RPI's instructors varied in the selection of technology and in its use, thereby putting a load on students who take courses from more than one instructor. Professional associations may face a similar problem if many instructors offer courses and do so on their own terms, but learners may not find it worthwhile to spend more time preparing for seminars than they actually spend in the seminars. That is likely to mean that professional associations will need to specify to instructors the technology and teaching processes they may use. Since communication technologies change rapidly, it also means that professional associations will need to balance standardization with the speed of adoption of new media and processes. It may also mean some involvement in training instructors and learners about the distance environment.

For example, a coauthor of this chapter (Robert Krull) once had to answer 40 to 60 e-mails a day about technology for just one distance course when the distance-learning platform changed at RPI. He was expecting that amount of churn, but people with less experience may become overwhelmed.

Novice learners may face comparable challenges. They may not be sure that they have the right technology, may not be sure how to use the technology, and may not know who can help them. If they contact a professional association or a seminar instructor, how long should they expect to wait for an answer, and how much support should they expect to be offered? A related issue is learners' needing contact with instructors outside of formal instruction times. For example, learners may want suggestions about work projects to which they are applying seminar concepts and do not want to bring up publicly during seminars. Should professional associations schedule network connections to run slightly longer than the formal seminar time to allow instructors and learners to communicate informally on such topics?

If users don't feel supported and find that their problems snowball, they are likely to drop out. High dropout rates can threaten the fiscal viability of distance training. Professional associations may, then, be faced with the burden of supporting instructors and learners. Standardizing the distance platform can reduce the amount of support it is necessary to provide. Professional associations also could require instructors to develop some technology-related skills on their own and could set prerequisites for learners planning to take professional training. Perhaps, though, providing some low-level training such as a website for potential instructors and learners may be more efficient than providing a catastrophe recovery effort on a continuing basis.

Distance-learning platforms seem to require their own communication etiquette to overcome the shortcomings of technology. Novice instructors and learners may need to adjust their expectations and behavior to minimize their own annoyance and maximize their learning.

Time delays, low-fidelity images and sound, and brittle upstream technologies can make the distance experience less than ideal. We have described some work-arounds that we used at RPI. Some of the work-arounds, unfortunately, involve adding yet more technology. That may not be a route that a professional association wants to pursue.

Other work-arounds involve the way participants would need to adapt their communication styles to the environment. The examples we have given included participants' waiting through Internet-induced time delays and instructors' monitoring instant messengers to detect questions from learners that must be answered quickly. Professional training seminars may need to build a similar repertory of etiquette and will need to make participants aware of them prior to training sessions. It would not be workable to spend a substantial portion of training sessions dealing with etiquette rather than covering course content. Until participants become familiar with the etiquette used for a specific professional training series, it may be necessary to add a module about etiquette to the low-level preparatory training mentioned in the preceding section.

We began this chapter by describing unrealistic expectations about what distance platforms can deliver. We have also described how technology can affect human communication problems such as learners' feeling isolated from the instructor and from each other. Unrealistic expectations, perhaps ones produced by overly optimistic advertising, can affect participants' perceptions of others' goals, feelings, and communication. For example, why is the instructor ignoring my tech problem and not replying to my text message about it? In this instance, a learner can misattribute a technical limitation to a communication etiquette issue. Clarifying what expectations learners should have about likely technology problems, pragmatic communication process issues, and communication etiquette can mitigate such misunderstandings. Whether a professional association should solve this kind of problem through low-level online training, a support staff, or both is an open question.

We have described some fundamental communication etiquette issues that are likely to affect professional training as well: delays in the cycles of electronic "conversations," when it is appropriate to interrupt instructors, and when an assistant should be assigned to handle technical or course content issues rather than expecting instructors to deal with them. Since these issues have choices regarding solutions that are comparable to the ones we just discussed, we won't discuss such issues further here.

We began this chapter with the overpromised utopias of distance education and the tepid responses of learners. We hope that by describing the results of our research on learner perceptions of distance education and their behavior during classes at RPI we have been able to outline the ways in which participants have been able to make distance education work and the ways in which professional associations can adapt academic distance-education methods to training for working professionals.

Summary of Relevant Principles

1. Design for Diverse Users	Different instructors tend to use the components of web-based learning platforms differently, requiring students to adjust to new configurations with each course.
2. Design for Usability	Students using web-based learning platforms encounter problems using electronic whiteboards, which did not follow standard conventions for text entry and graphics manipulation.
3. Test the Backbone	Internet bandwidth is still a major backbone problem for students working at a distance, leading to software disruptions, low fidelity of images and sound, and time delays in interactions.
4. Extend a Welcome	Students can take up to 30 minutes readying the technologies needed to participate in class from a distance—not much of a welcome!
5. Set the Context	Dealing with technological limitations requires changes in communication etiquette, a change in the context for which students need preparation.
7. Share Control	Students prefer an interface that allows them to control the sizing and arrangement of their windows; some technologies give all of this control to the instructor.
8. Support Interaction Among Users	Students prize interactions with other students, using text messaging to create a discussion parallel to the instructor-student interaction. When given the option for smaller working groups, they were eager to move this interaction to live audio.

An Interactive Image

Audrey Bennett, RENSSELAER POLYTECHNIC INSTITUTE
Sarah Diodato, TIMES UNION
Angelo Gaetano, CLINTON HIGH SCHOOL

In *The Future of Technical Communication*, Giammona (2004) argues that the next generation of technical communicators will need a new skill set that includes (but is not limited to) an ability to collaborate with diverse users, design visual information, and use current media tools. Today's revolutionary media tool is Web 2.0, which is internationalizing the discipline of technical communication at a breakneck pace. Web 2.0 as a concept describes the facilitation of user control of content development and distribution via the World Wide Web. More importantly, Web 2.0 encompasses global reach and collaboration with users. The question then is: In what kind of global collaborations are technical communicators in academia and business engaged or expect to engage in our current Web 2.0 age?

Within academia, Web 2.0 has enabled technical communication classes to interact and collaborate with classes situated remotely in other parts of the world to complete internationally relevant coursework (St. Amant, 2005; Herrington & Tretyakov, 2005; Cook & Grant-Davie, 2005). Even within the workplace, due to current economic challenges, technical communicators are outsourcing to cheaper labor—that is, culturally diverse workers in other parts of the world (Giammona, 2004). However, with Web 2.0, professional technical communicators can expect to engage in new types of global collaborations that share control of content development and distribution with users globally. This case study explores the usability of another type of global collaboration—the Web 2.0–mediated codesign and distribution of images. Benkler (2006) calls this "the manipulation of symbols" and lists it as a key activity in the networked information economy that has emerged.

Present-day web-mediated collaborations with global users of different cultures create a confounding communication problem—with global reach comes the challenge of cross-cultural communication, both verbally and visually, but primarily the latter because of the World Wide Web, which enables global interaction and depends heavily on image-based information to communicate effectively. Whereas enabling users to toggle between translations of a web interface's verbal data might facilitate cross-cultural verbal communication with greater ease, communicating with culturally diverse users visually requires another skill set: cross-cultural visual literacy—that is, an ability to communicate with images across cultures. Culture affects the way we interpret images in that it problematically hinders the clear transmittance of meaning to culturally diverse users (Horton, 2005; Lipton, 2002; Coe, 1996; Hager, 2000; Forslund, 1996; Pettersson, 1982). Thus, this case study aimed at solving this communication problem through the use of interactive aesthetics (Bennett, 2002a, 2002b)—that is, the use of images that enable users to localize visual elements (e.g., text, color, images, positioning) to render a more culturally appropriate aesthetic; images that visually reveal meaning if users interact with them; or an image-based infrastructure that engages remotely situated design team members in the design process.

Background

As shown in Figure 15.1, a multidisciplinary team of educators and graduate students tested the usability of three iterations of a poster—a culturally specific image designed for cross-cultural communication. The original design of the image was a print poster to promote awareness of HIV/AIDS and safe sex among Kenyans and potentially

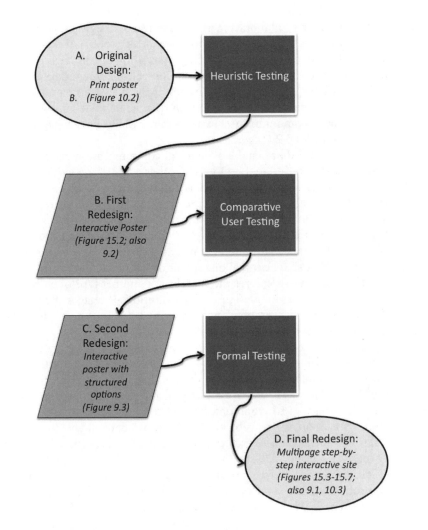

Figure 15.1 Project flow for the interactive image project.

other cultures around the world. It was designed in summer 2003 in a transnational, participatory workshop comprised of laypeople situated in Kenya and educators situated in the United States. The workshop was facilitated by a virtual design studio constructed of existing instructional and communication technologies for synchronous and asynchronous dialogue and interaction. Bennett et al. (2006) describe this workshop and research methodology as participatory in that it allowed Kenyans to control the visual and verbal development and design of the poster. After undergoing a round of heuristic testing with Jakob Nielsen's heuristics (1995) and garnering feedback from a multicultural group of users, we transformed the print poster into the first redesign, a web-based interactive poster to allow users of various cultures to customize and distribute it to others. Comparative user testing helped us to refine this design further into the second redesign, an interactive poster with structured options. And finally, following formal testing, we produced a multipage step-by-step interactive website.

Evaluating the Original Design

As noted earlier, a small group of Kenyan laypeople participated in a U.S.-sponsored participatory workshop to design the print poster shown in Figure 10.2. The intent of the workshop was to raise awareness of the HIV/AIDS epidemic among Kenyans and encourage them to take action and change unsafe sexual behaviors.

The participatory design workshop was conducted in a community resource center in Kenya with a U.S. graduate student—a native Kenyan studying abroad in the United States. Educators situated in the United States participated in the workshop by way of a virtual design studio constructed of existing instructional and communication technologies for synchronous and asynchronous dialogue and interaction. The outcome of the workshop was Figure 10.2, a culturally specific image—a print poster on HIV/AIDS awareness and prevention.

We conducted heuristic testing of this print poster with a user group comprised of:

- One African American, face to face
- One African (Nigerian), face to face
- One Malaysian undergraduate external to the seminar, via SurveyMonkey
- Three Asian undergraduates external to the seminar, via SurveyMonkey
- Many White graduate students—face to face and at a distance via Elluminate with some telephone support.

Designed specifically for the evaluation of website interfaces, we adapted Nielsen's heuristics to evaluate the printed poster's interface. Our reason for doing this is based on the premise that users can interact with a poster the same way that they do with a web page. In particular, our team asked evaluators to answer the following questions:

- If you saw this poster on a wall, would you go over to it to read it?
- Tell me what this poster communicates to you.
- Describe what you see.
- What does the red ribbon mean to you?

- What does the image of Kenya mean to you?
- What does the image of the woman mean to you?
- What emotions do you feel as you look at this? Which parts of the poster make you feel that way?
- Can you read the words?
- If you were working in a health office and this image was given to you, what would you do?
- Who would you tell about this poster?
- Could this poster influence your behavior?
- Could this poster influence the behavior of others?

The reaction to the poster during this first phase of heuristic testing was mostly negative. While evaluators understood the message was about HIV/AIDS in Africa, few had a very strong emotional response to the poster. Most of the evaluators said that they would not go over and read the poster. The strongest emotions seemed to be about the overall message of poster—HIV/AIDS. Evaluators seemed to notice and feel most strongly about the image of the woman, followed by the red ribbon, and then the map of Kenya.

The woman's face being blurred was a big issue among evaluators. Testers did not understand it or misconstrued its purpose. Some thought it represented shame or social stigma about being HIV-positive. Other testers felt that having the woman talk first goes along with the verbal message: "Let's talk about it," though one tester did not know what the woman would talk about. Ironically, some evaluators thought it contradicted the message of "Let's talk about it." One tester felt the woman's hand gesture made a strong emotional impact. Most of the testers got some meaning from the red ribbon: It stands for HIV/AIDS awareness. Others did not necessarily think the ribbon looked like an AIDS ribbon. One of the most memorable responses came from a Nigerian graduate student studying in the United States, who did not know that the red ribbon represented HIV/AIDS. He interpreted it as serving to wrap up Kenya like a gift.

It is important to remember that this example was created by Kenyan laypeople who felt it would be effective among their peers. While our team attempted to choose evaluators from diverse backgrounds for the heuristic testing, most lived in the United States and did not have a connection to Africa. Therefore, in most cases, the map of Kenya did not mean very much to them. Most evaluators felt that they could not relate to the map of Kenya because they did not have knowledge of Kenya, and they felt that others like them would recognize the shape on the map to be the Kenya. A few evaluators, however, made the connection from the map that Kenya has an HIV/AIDS problem, though some were confused by the purpose of the cities on the map. In addition, the text was small and difficult to read. While some testers liked the colors used, others felt that they were too heavy, especially the dark blue used with the map of Kenya. One tester questioned whether these colors would be difficult to see by someone who was colorblind.

Overall, evaluators did not understand how they were supposed to "act now" and what they were supposed to talk about. The call to action seems to need more detail and clarification. Without more information, it is hard to act. In the context of the health office, evaluators said that they would show more interest in it and possibly hang it up and share with others. Some of the evaluators said that they would tell others, although some felt there was not enough information to pass along. One African American evaluator said she would talk to family members about it. Others were either not sure if they would tell anyone or they would if there were more information. Almost all of the evaluators said this poster would not influence their behavior. However, interestingly, most evaluators felt that it would somehow influence the behavior of others.

The testing team also offered the following feedback about the poster. For instance, they recommended or commented:

- "Find a more gripping image. People's gaze is automatically drawn to faces, so blurring the face is a mistake."
- "Add a call to action. People need to know what the first step is in taking action. If you're saying that the first step is to talk about it, then say who to talk to. Or if the first step is to get tested or start a community program or something, then make it clear exactly how to do that."
- "Try beginning with one person's experience in a way that's very emotional (but fast), and then introduce the statistics afterwards. This is emotionally compelling, but then introduces the scope of the statistics with each one of those infections feeling real and compelling."
- "One way to ensure that people will read the emotional story first is to make it in a larger and more eye-catching font."
- "Another useful trick is to use some second-person language. Say something along the lines of 'every time you have unprotected sex, there's a 10% chance you're getting HIV'—where the word *you* is the differentiator."
- "The white background, the quality of the image of Kenya and of the ribbon, and something about the font all make it look amateurish. You need the confidence and trust of your audience. Find some way to make the image look more professional."

The heuristic evaluation revealed that the original design violated the following three Nielsen heuristics:

- "The system should speak the users' language, with words, phrases and concepts familiar to the user, rather than system-oriented terms; and, follow real-world conventions, making information appear in a natural and logical order" (Nielsen, 1995). Some testers had questions or were confused about some elements of the poster (the woman's face being blurred, the shape and style of the ribbon). This may have been due to cultural differences between Kenyans and the evaluators. Since the poster was created by native Kenyans, the visual and verbal content more accurately reflect their experience.
- "Dialogues should not contain information which is irrelevant or rarely needed. Every extra unit of information in a dialogue competes with the relevant units of information and diminishes their relative visibility" (Nielsen, 1995). This heuristic brings into question the relevance of the cities on the map of Kenya. There is no

additional information about these cities in relation to the message of the poster. Also, there are no statistics specifically associated with the cities, and no additional relevant information about the cities is offered. Finally, in the summer 2003 participatory design workshop that generated the original poster, the Kenyans noted no special reason why the names of some cities appear in larger type than others.

- "Even though it is better if the system can be used without documentation, it may be necessary to provide help and documentation. Any such information should be easy to search, focused on the user's task, list concrete steps to be carried out, and not be too large" (Nielsen, 1995). We can interpret from this heuristic that, ideally, the poster should be able to get its message across on its own without verbal support. HIV/AIDS awareness is a large issue, and, although an image can capture a user's attention and begin to create awareness, there is no way to fit everything the user needs to know about the subject on one poster. This poster gives no reference to where a user could find supplemental information (a website or even a phone number to call). It gives specific commands to the user—act now and talk about it—but does not provide any information on how the user can do that.

While Nielsen's heuristics were helpful in pointing to some of the issues with the print poster, they were insufficient in evaluating *all* of them. For instance, our poster could have guided evaluators through a more interactive communication process that explained the context, function, and form of what they saw. Then evaluators may have been able to answer the following questions with greater ease:

- What is the poster about?
- Who is the poster from?
- Who is the poster for?
- Why is the poster designed this way?
- What can you do with the poster?
- Explain how you can change or modify what you see?
- Which image would you [prefer to] use?

Our original design could have given the user more control over what they took away from the interpretation experience, thereby making the process of extracting meaning more participatory. For instance, had we provided multisensory interaction tools and guidelines for effective design, evaluators could have modified the poster to their culturally-based preferences. Then, with a more participatory dissemination process as well, evaluators could have distributed the final poster to anyone in a variety of ways, such as via cell phone or e-mail.

After completion of the heuristic testing, the Usable Content Seminar met to discuss the derivation of new principles for engaging web-based communication. The following is a summary of the new set of principles applicable to our image example and their implications for its first redesign:

Extend a Welcome	Evaluators did not understand who created the poster or for whom it was intended. Thus, they did not feel compelled to go over, read it, or

explore it further. Our goal in the first redesign was to provide an introduction to the project describing its origin and instructions for what the user can do with it.

Set the Context

It was necessary to explain the context of the poster to the evaluators, because nothing on the poster did this. When the evaluators were presented with the health office scenario, they said they would go over and read it and maybe even share it with others. Our goal in the first redesign was to provide an introduction to the project describing its origin and instructions for what the user can do with it.

Make a Connection

Most of the evaluators could not connect to the poster because they did not have knowledge of Kenya. They also had trouble making a connection with the woman in the image because they were distracted by her blurred face. Our goal in the first redesign was to provide images of people from various ethnic groups to allow users to choose images they can relate to. Also, it would be useful to provide different maps and other geographical images.

Design for Diverse Users

The poster was designed initially with only one audience in mind—Kenyans. Therefore, the evaluators did not feel a connection to the poster because they could not relate to it. For some, there was little to no emotional attachment because they did not know a lot about Kenya. Thus, our goal in the redesign phase was to target a multicultural audience and include an option of images that evaluators could choose.

Design for Usability

Although this version of the example was not electronic, and there was no way for users to make errors, some visual problems became apparent during testing. The yellow text for the cities was difficult to read. Also, some evaluators mentioned that they did not understand the purpose of the cities on the map and why some were in larger type than others. Our goal, then, in the first redesign was to allow users to create their own posters where they can decide on the size and color of text.

Share Control

The evaluators did not have any control over their interaction with this example, except for their own internal response to it. Some provided recommendations as to how they would change it, but there was no way for them to implement those changes. Our goal in the first redesign was to have an online, interactive poster applet that would allow users to modify the poster or create their own poster.

Create a Sense of Place   No navigation was required for this example, because it was a one-page, two-dimensional image. Our redesign goal was to design a website where tools are easy to recognize and use, intuitively, without needing additional instructions. We also planned to provide easy-to-access help documentation for the website.

Support Interaction Among Users   The initial example does not provide a way to interact with other users. Most evaluators were not sure how to "act now" and would have liked further instruction, such as a link to visit a website or information on attending a program about the subject. Our goal in the first redesign was to provide links to sources where users can find more information, including statistics that they can add to the posters. We also aimed to allow users access to a blog where they can discuss their designs. Finally, we wanted to provide functionality for users to save and share their posters.

Plan to Continue the Engagement   The example does not offer a way for the user to continue to interact with it. Some evaluators said they may make copies of the poster or talk to others about it, but that is all that can be done. As mentioned above, the poster says, "Act Now," and "Let's talk about it," but it does not help the user to reach that next level. Our goal in the first redesign was to provide links to sources where users can find more information, including statistics that they can add to the posters. The poster should also allow users access to a blog where they can discuss their designs.

The First Redesign

Heuristic testing revealed that the overall emotional experience in a communication transaction was directly related to the degree of cultural resonance of the image with users. Users have a stronger response to colors and images that have meaning from their cultural perspective as well as photos that depict people who are of the same ethnicity and gender. Therefore, we decided to create an interactive poster that would allow visitors to modify the poster or create a new one and then distribute it to their peers. Users of the interactive poster could choose from a variety of images and styles to create their own message about HIV/AIDS awareness in a way they would want to tell it. An interactive poster was a good choice for the

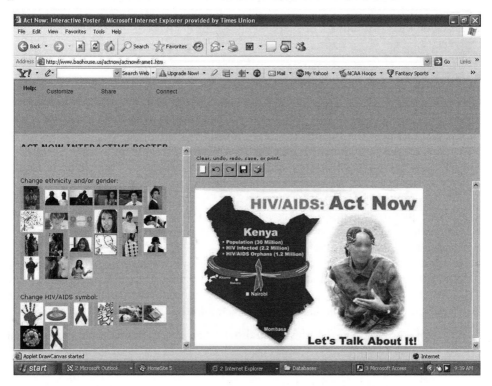

Figure 15.2 First redesign as an interactive poster.

next phase of this project, because its users are not meant to be formally trained or professional communication designers. Therefore, it presents the challenge of giving users more control without compromising the tenets of effective design. It allows us an opportunity to assess what instructional tools can be provided to lay-people to help them design powerful, effective messages without requiring formal design skills or additional training.

Based on the results of the initial heuristic evaluation, our team developed an interactive poster (Figure 15.2). In summary, our goals in this iteration, based on the aforementioned discussion of heuristics for tech-mediated communication, were as follows:

- Design an interactive poster that allows users to modify it or create their own.
- Target a multicultural audience.
- Provide an introduction to the project describing its origin and instructions for what the user can do with it.
- Provide images of people from various ethnic groups to allow users to choose images, including maps and other geographical images, that they can relate to.
- Provide links to sources where users can find more information, including statistics that they can add to the posters.

- Provide tools that are easy for the user to recognize and use, intuitively, without needing additional instructions.
- Provide easy-to-access help documentation.
- Allow users access to a blog where they can discuss their designs.
- Provide users with a way to share what they have created with others.

Evaluating the First Redesign

During comparative user testing, our team conducted tests on both the original print poster and the new, interactive poster. The purpose of testing in this way was to compare results between the two designs using a similar testing protocol. There are some limitations in the comparison in that the new, online example allowed the evaluator to perform observable tasks. However, this was not possible with the poster example. The protocol for the online example was as follows:

- The evaluators were asked to sign a consent form and complete a pretest survey.
- Evaluators were presented with the example, which opened to the interactive poster in a Firefox browser.
- Evaluators were then asked to take two or three minutes to look over the example and to explore it using the tools. During this portion of the test, evaluators were asked the following questions to explore their initial reaction to the poster and their sense of being welcomed and connected to the site's purpose:
  - o This site is designed with several different audiences in mind. Do you feel that you are an appropriate user?
  - o What are your first feelings about this site? Does it seem welcoming or not? What makes it feel that way?
- After the evaluators had a chance to explore the site on their own, they were presented with a specific task. For this example, the evaluators were asked to create a poster using the images and tools available. As evaluators chose images or colors, the example team member asked them why they made those choices.
- After the evaluators created the poster, they were asked how they would share it. Because the example was still a prototype, the functionality did not exist to save the evaluators' creations as PDF files or allow them to e-mail the posters. Therefore, instead of observing this task, the evaluators were asked to describe how they would like to share it, and who, if anyone, they would share it with. The evaluators were asked if there is any other action they would take now that they are familiar with the example. They were also encouraged at this point to make any additional comments.
- After the test was concluded, evaluators were asked to complete a posttest survey.

The protocol for the print example was similar, but, as stated earlier, it could not mirror exactly the protocol used with the online example, because exploration of this example is not necessarily an observable task. Instead, actions that can be taken included noticing, reacting, determining meaning, and so on. The only way to "observe" these actions was through conversation with the evaluator, similar to the way testing was conducted during heuristic testing.

To compensate for this, this portion of the protocol was altered so that when evaluators were asked to explore the poster, they would describe the images and colors and how the different elements of the poster affected them. This was accomplished by using similar questions from heuristic testing. One exception is that we did not include the question from heuristic testing concerning the scenario of someone working in a health office. We did not feel that this scenario was appropriate for the goals of the first redesign, which is meant to target a universal audience.

During comparative user testing, 10 evaluators were separated into two groups. Six participants used the interactive poster, and four observed the original printed poster. The evaluators ranged in age from 17 to 55 and were divided equally among gender. There were five ethnic groups represented:

- Four Whites
- One Indian
- One Latin American
- One Bosnian
- Two African Americans.

All of the participants indicated they had no physical disabilities, used the Internet every day, and had a minimum of six years' experience using the Internet. Five users indicated they were somewhat proficient with technology, and four considered themselves very proficient. Over half of the users belonged to online communities, and four belonged to RSS/news feeds. Eight of the ten users indicated they had shopped online, and six users said they belonged to an online community.

Regarding the original design, the feedback closely resembled the feedback from heuristic testing:

- *Welcome.* Most evaluators claimed they would not go over to the poster and read it if they saw it hanging on the wall. They did seem to understand the meaning of the poster—it was about HIV/AIDS—but they did not understand the context of the poster or its target audience. One evaluator felt it was not really meant to solve the problem but to get people talking about it.
- *Exploration and Connectedness.* Evaluators noticed the image of the woman before anything else. What they were most interested in was the fact that her face was blurred. There were different interpretations as to what this meant. Three evaluators did not understand what she had to do with HIV/AIDS. One evaluator said he thought it would be more effective if she were talking with someone. All evaluators understood the meaning of the red ribbon as an AIDS ribbon. However, most were confused by the map of Kenya, especially the cities on the map. They did not understand why those cities were included, and why they were represented with different type sizes. One evaluator said the cities were distracting, and another asked why the map was only of Kenya. Some evaluators said they did feel sad or concerned for people with AIDS, but most said that they did not have a strong emotional response to the poster. Some evaluators were college students who felt they already had some knowledge on the subject. The poster did nothing to increase their awareness, and, because they were inundated with other, more effective messages on a daily basis, this particular poster would not influence them. All evaluators thought this poster could influence others, if it were used in

the right context. In addition, as in phase one of testing, evaluators felt that they needed more detail in the call to action, other than just "Act Now."

- *Sharing.* Two evaluators said they would share the poster, and had some unique ideas for doing that (e.g., post on websites, change language, post in buses and cabs). Two evaluators did not think they would be interested in sharing the poster.

The testing results of the first redesign as an interactive poster are as follows:

- *Welcome.* College students and those associated with a college setting thought that they would be appropriate users. In a few cases, they mentioned a scenario of using the example for a class project or for promoting a campus HIV/AIDS awareness event. This is a scenario that should be considered during future design iterations of the example. Other evaluators said they felt they were appropriate users because they could use images that represented someone from their ethnic background. Despite this, most evaluators still felt they could use more explanation of the site's purpose.

- *Exploration and Connectedness.* All the evaluators liked the concept of an interactive poster. They could see the benefit of having tools and images available to them to create a message without having to hunt for these items in different places on the Internet. Some usability problems with the tools detracted from the total experience for most users. In particular, the evaluators were frustrated that they could not edit or remove images and text after they had been placed on the poster without either starting over or using the erase tool. Some evaluators were more interested than others in creating the poster during the test. The college students were more interested in the design capabilities that were available, and they focused on playing with the tools. Others, especially those who identified with the example as representing their ethnic background, focused more on creating a specific message about HIV/AIDS. Some evaluators said they would have liked to have seen examples of what others had done.

- *Sharing.* As with the original example, sharing was an action that was discussed more than observed, due to the fact that the redesign was still a prototype and did not have this functionality available. However, some evaluators were creative, copying the image and saving it in Paint. Others said they would print it or e-mail it. One evaluator said she might post it online on her Myspace page.

While there had been improvement since the original design, most evaluators felt there needed to be more of a welcome and an explanation of the context of the example. The structure and functionality of the site also needed to be improved so images loaded faster. More exploration needed to be done to find ways to build a community among users. Finally, functionality needed to be created to allow users to more easily share their posters with others.

We determined that the second redesign should incorporate the following considerations:

- There should be a welcome or description so that users immediately understand the site's purpose and what they are supposed to do with it.

- The design should be intuitive so that non-graphics experts can easily create a poster that looks professional and can send a powerful message.
- More options for images and graphics should be available that appeal to people from all ethnic backgrounds.
- Functionality for sharing the poster should be created so users can easily e-mail the poster or save it and print it out.
- A blog or other online user forum should be created to allow users to share and comment on each other's posters and to collaborate on topics related to HIV/AIDS.

Using these recommendations, we designed the second redesign of the interactive poster (see Figure 9.3). Due to an abundance of positive responses from evaluators regarding the interactive capability of the image, we decided that the second redesign should remain interactive. However, due to the poor design image outcomes generated by evaluators during the previous testing process, we decided that evaluators should be given less control over the final aesthetic makeup of the image.

Whereas the previous version facilitated open creativity in the interpretation process, the second redesign—in the form of another partially working prototype—facilitated closed creativity with limited control over the final design of the image. Evaluators were presented with a two-column, web-based, flash-enabled image. After reading the title in the upper left-hand corner, in working form, they would be able to change the language of the text on the screen. Then, they could read the image visually followed by the verbal background information below it. The second column on the right contained step-by-step instructions for modifying the image to evaluators' cultural preference. As with the first redesign, evaluators could change the country, the cultural identity, text of the image, and even the design of the red ribbon. However, in the second redesign, they could not add anything new to the image or erase it and start from scratch. They also would not be able to change the colors. Finally, evaluators would be guided on how to share their images and connect with others who are affected by the HIV/AIDS pandemic.

In formal testing of the second redesign, we wanted to measure emotional reactions to the site. Were students intrigued and engaged? Did they find the site meaningful? Would they return or tell others about the site? We set a goal of finding the level of interest students had in the site. Following the common protocol, five participants, all members of minority groups, were given a brief introduction to the site, told they would fill out questionnaires after the testing, and then were allowed to explore the site. We observed the students to see what they did, but we offered no help. A follow-up survey was given approximately two weeks later. Results of this formal testing suggest that people generally understood how to use the exemplar and were comfortable navigating through the features. They seemed more connected to others with the second redesign than they had been with the earlier designs, but the connection was not as strong as we hoped. And people wanted stronger interaction, more interactive features.

The final redesign of the interactive poster is shown in Figures 15.3 through 15.7. Page one (Figure 15.3) welcomes the viewer and offers background information. Page two (Figure 15.4) provides instructions for using the poster. The next page (Figure 15.5) is the interactive poster for intuitive interaction. Figure 15.6 provides an

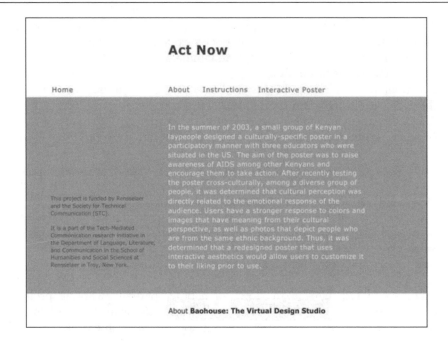

Figure 15.3 Final Redesign: Page One welcomes the viewer and offers background information.

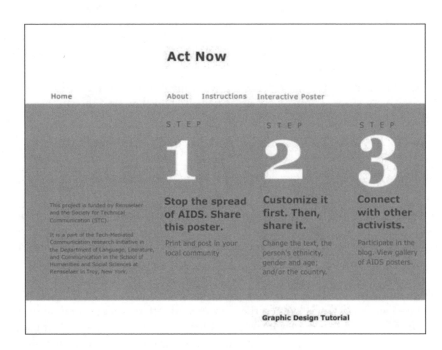

Figure 15.4 Final Redesign: Page Two provides instructions for using the poster.

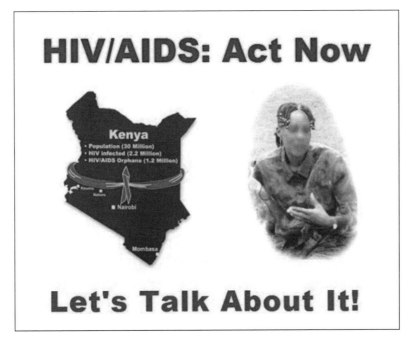

Figure 15.5 Final Redesign: Interactive poster for intuitive interaction.

Figure 15.6 Final Redesign: An example of how the poster could be modified verbally and visually.

Figure 15.7 Final Redesign: Page showing how the poster can printed to pdf for email or to a local or network printer for posting on a community board.

example of how the poster could be modified verbally and visually. Figure 15.7 shows that the poster can be printed to PDF for e-mail or sent to a local or network printer for posting on a community board. The final redesign also included links to continue the engagement via online social networking venues (see Figure 10.4). To see the most recent version of the interactive poster, visit http://www.aninteractiveposter.info.

Conclusion

Kiwanuka-Tondo and Snyder (2002) confirm the effectiveness of informational and promotional document design as tools for HIV prevention and awareness in Africa, and this case study suggests how a culturally specific HIV/AIDS prevention poster could be designed to appeal to an international, multicultural audience. Whereas a universal aesthetic tends to be unattainable by way of traditional, high design methods, this research project discloses how technology can elicit input from the audience and give them more control over the interpretation of culturally specific images. We redesigned the Kenyan print poster with interactive cultural aesthetics (i.e., customizable visual language such as type and images to attain cross-cultural resonance) and online accessibility (see www.aninteractiveposter.info) to allow users to share control of the poster, customizing it to their liking, and to support interactions among users by printing and posting it in their communities. Through the use of interactive cultural aesthetics and online accessibility, the interactive poster epitomizes effective cross-cultural graphics in four ways.

1. Effective cross-cultural graphics are designed for diverse users. The interactive poster includes multicultural graphics.
2. Effective cross-cultural graphics give users some control over the design process. At first glance, the interactive poster may appear to be just a static graphic—a digitized, two-dimensional poster. However, upon further interaction, users soon discover opportunities to change the images and text of the poster to their cultural preference.
3. Effective cross-cultural graphics set a clear context for discovery and interaction. The interactive poster exists at a URL online that is accessible via search engines. Users searching for online resources on "HIV," "AIDS," and other relevant topics may navigate to the interactive poster.
4. Effective cross-cultural graphics create a sense of place. The interactive poster provides clear navigation through an introductory section, a brief tutorial, the interactive poster, and beyond.[1]

Summary of Relevant Principles

1. Design for Diverse Users	The redesigns of the interactive poster offer users customization options, enabling it to be of interest to diverse users.
2. Design for Usability	Irrelevant information about Kenyan cities in the original design distracted and confused users, creating usability problems.
4. Extend a Welcome	The first redesign added an introduction to the project, helping users to understand its origin and purpose. Without this kind of welcome, users were confused.
5. Set the Context	The call to "act now" in the original design made little sense to users because it was without context. Users suggested that if it had been placed in the context of a health office, the call to act now would have made more sense.
6. Make a Connection	Reactions to the original design of the poster suggested that users could not make a connection when content was specific to a culture other than their own. Connection improved when users could make choices about the design of the poster.
7. Share Control	The first redesign gave users too much control over design choices, leading to poorly designed posters. The second redesign shared control with users, offering users a menu of choices that improved the final design content.
8. Support Interaction Among Users	Allowing users to share their posters with others via e-mail and social media gave a sense of purpose to their design work.

(Continued)

9. Create a Sense of Place	The multistep process of the final redesign created a sense of place for users, clarifying the process and users' location in it.
10. Plan to Continue the Engagement	The call to "act now" on the original design left users confused about how to continue the engagement. The redesigns offered better support for continuing the engagement, providing users with the opportunity to distribute the poster to others.

Note

1. Some of this material was originally published as Audrey Bennett et al, "The Heuristic Evaluation of a Culturally-Specific Graphic for Cross-Cultural Communication." *IASDR Conference Proceedings, Emerging Trends in Design Research, 12-November, 2007.* © 2007, School of Design, The Hong Kong Polytechnic University.

Beyond Engagement

Bill Hart-Davidson
Michigan State University

The valuable contributions the chapters in this volume make to both our understanding of usability as a concept and to the collection of professional practices that constitute user-centered design share a focus on engaging users as partners in the success of a new product or service. Signaled in the title by the word *engagement,* the authors here offer a perspective on usability that shifts the focus of being user centered from a front-loaded process of good design practice to an extended relationship, one that should exist as long as people are actively using a product or service. An engagement, after all, is merely the way relationships begin.

My focus in this afterword keeps this discussion going by suggesting what lies beyond successful initial engagements with users. I will begin by pointing to the ways that the design principles discussed here—especially setting context, sharing control, and supporting interaction among users—work to build relationships by invoking shared values. Building and maintaining relationships between users and developers, even creating user and/or developer communities, are primary goals when information systems are engineered to be persistent and ever-improving services rather than products. Whether these services are sponsored by for-profit enterprises or nonprofit cultural institutions, building meaningful relationships with clients and customers means continually ensuring that successful engagements take place. And this, in turn, may mean major shifts in the ways organizations and companies think about their core missions.

My aim here is to raise questions about whether techniques that foster engagement in a meaningful way can also become durable techniques for building and maintaining relationships among service providers and stakeholder groups. I'll draw upon several specific examples—situations discussed in this volume and others that foreground the ways relationships among service providers and users are changing. Let me begin with a case of a well-known and popular web-based service whose sponsor recently announced that the service would be discontinued or maybe not: del.icio.us.

Yahoo! and Del.icio.us

Chances are that if you are interested in this book, you know about del.icio.us. Begun in 2003 by Joshua Schacter, del.icio.us is a social bookmarking service that allows users to store and share lists of links to resources on the web. For individual users, the service offers the benefit of permitting access to bookmarks from any device and/or software rather than storing them in the preferences of a particular browser on a particular machine. But perhaps what has made del.icio.us transformative as a service is the way users assign descriptive tags to bookmarks, creating a "folksonomy" or bottom-up system of categorization.

If we think about del.icio.us's affordances in terms of the principles showcased in the chapters on Principles 7 and 8—sharing control and supporting interactions among users—we can see that the design of del.icio.us constitutes an elegant and low-friction way to build community by allowing people who share similar interests to find one another and share resources. It works something like this: I add a bookmark to my del.icio.us repository and tag it with the term "user engagement." The tag becomes a link. I click the link and get a list of other resources tagged with the same term. Each of these resources has a user ID associated with it, and I quickly identify two or three users who obviously share an interest in user engagement as a research topic based on the resources they have shared and tagged.

The element of shared control here could in some instances be seen as a weakness: the ability for users to arbitrarily assign descriptive terms rather than adhering to a controlled vocabulary. But if a goal of del.icio.us is to permit groups of users to self-assemble and share resources in a way valuable to the group members, then the ability to create tags that are highly esoteric, even deliberately so, is a strength rather than a weakness. Shared control and support for user interaction, in other words, allow groups to build additional value within the service, value that does not erode the primary sources of value provided to individual users such as anytime, anywhere access to bookmarks.

In 2005, del.icio.us was acquired by the Internet company Yahoo! In late 2010, technology news sites such as TechCrunch published a PowerPoint slide reportedly leaked from an internal Yahoo! presentation that showed the del.icio.us service as one of several on a list of services scheduled for sunset (Is Yahoo shutting down del.icio.us? [update: del.icio.us responds, 2010]). Rumor and panic began to spread. Would Yahoo! really be discontinuing the service? What would happen to users' data? To the group affiliations users had built? And if Yahoo! could shut down del.icio.us, what about other Yahoo! properties like Flickr, where users had arguably even more valuable and/or personal data than bookmarks (photographs and video)?

Twenty-four hours later, Yahoo! had responded to the rumors and speculation with a post to the del.icio.us blog (What's next for del.icio.us? (2010)) designed to clarify the situation and calm users' fears. The response noted that the service would not be shut down and that Yahoo! would continue to maintain it while considering what to do with the service going forward. In the response, the authors of the post allude to a future home for del.icio.us "outside the company," a statement that many in the tech community have interpreted as a desire to sell the service. The response also reminds users of and provides a link to a utility in the service that allows users to export their data out of del.icio.us.

So what has happened with del.icio.us? As of February 1, 2011, nothing had changed about the way the service works in strictly technical terms. But what undeniably changed is the nature of the relationship between Yahoo! and its users. All of the work done at the level of user experience design to create a satisfying user experience, to grow the number of users, and to make it as easy as possible for users to create value for themselves and others (the ability to bundle bookmarks and share bundles, for instance)—all of that work to engage users and keep them engaged was significantly damaged with a single PowerPoint slide. What the slide made explicit—or seemed to—was a sentiment quite the opposite of that which all of the other engagement work suggested: we value our relationship with you, our users. That slide said, in effect, "yeah, not so much."

When User Experience Is All There Is: Services, Sunrise, Sunset

One of the most important lessons to learn from the Yahoo! del.icio.us situation is that when you are in the business of providing a service to users, and when you have successfully built into that service the capacity for users to share responsibility for maintaining its value, there is virtually no distinction between the user experience and the bottom line. It seems clear that Yahoo! has struggled to monetize the value its users have built in and around del.icio.us. But it is also clear that discontinuing one service may hurt others such as Flickr that have been more profitable. Violating users' trust is the risky proposition here. Suddenly ending a relationship or signaling that users' information may not be secure may well make financial sense when del.icio.us is considered as a stand-alone product that is not generating much revenue. But del.icio.us is more than that to the millions of users who have contributed to it. It is a set of relationships: between the users and the sponsor, Yahoo!, but also between users and other users as well. Damaging all of these relationships is risky for a company that is already in financial difficulty and depends on other, similar services to succeed in order to thrive. Moreover, these are risks that were likely never considered early in the design of del.icio.us or Flickr.

In the introduction, Geisler and Grice draw on the work of Joshua Porter (2008) to explain how design for user engagement has expanded the scope of design teams' efforts to include key moments such as users' first contact with a product or service, moving users from a trial period to signing up, and encouraging users to become regular or even passionate users. Both regular and passionate users of a service like del.icio.us build the value of the service by adding links and tags and sharing these with others who may then sign up, add more links and tags, share these with others, and so on. In his book *Designing for the Social Web*, Porter calls this sequence of key steps "the usage lifecycle." And it is a wonderful tool for encouraging all the members of a design team, but especially user-experience professionals, to consider how best to engage users, allowing them to recognize the usability and usefulness of a new service. New and important aspects of the user experience are revealed as important challenges represented in Porter's diagram (http://bokardo.com/archives/designing-for-the-social-web-the-usage-lifecycle/) by hurdles.

Under each hurdle, we have a name for a new goal and a new measurable objective by which to evaluate our efforts at creating a successful user experience. Indeed, I would venture that anybody designing a new web service today is obligated to address in his or her pitch for support how users will move along this lifecycle. This is especially true where services depend on the activity of users to build and maintain value, as we see not only with del.icio.us and Flickr but also with multiplayer online games and many other types of services. But what the del.icio.us story makes clear is that, as valuable as this extended view is, we still are not seeing the whole life cycle. Indeed, the straight line might more accurately be depicted as an arc, reminded as we were that a service may rise and set like the sun. If we imagine the arc of a web service as a day, Porter's stages do not include the late afternoon, the evening, or the sunset.

Key Questions: Extending the Usage Life Cycle

1. What do "regular" and "passionate" use look like in detail? Do these stages of use have their own critical moments of engagement upon which continued user-sponsor relationships depend?
2. What should happen as user enthusiasm and activity level drop and a service begins to wind down? Are best practices emerging for the conduct of amicable separations? Is it even feasible to plan for these moments?
3. On a pragmatic level, what should happen to user data and other sources of user-generated value (e.g., group affiliations) when a service is scuttled or sold off?

Designing Sustainable Relationships

When we consider systems as enduring services rather than stand-alone products, we can begin to cast the longer arc of the usage lifecycle as a holistic design problem. One way to approach this problem is to ask if the design principles presented in this volume might be used to not only foster initial engagement but sustain meaningful relationships with users over time. We've seen that the success of del.icio.us is attributable to the principles of sharing control and supporting interaction among users. If we consider these principles in terms of building and maintaining relationships, we can identify important values invoked by these principles that are foundational for strong relationships and are exemplified in the case studies. In Case Study 1, Zappen's elaboration of the strategy of shared control as employed in the Connected Kids Galleries reveals that both the design team and the stakeholder groups shared an interest in ensuring that users' efforts to contribute content were reciprocated and that young users in particular felt that their contributions were acknowledged and valued. The challenges encountered by the design team to fostering regular or passionate use as revealed in tests were, moreover, related to areas of conflicting value: safety and privacy versus autonomy and creativity.

Calling explicit attention to the values a given design approach invokes is, in itself, an important step toward fostering relationships among stakeholders if we consider the basis of strong relationships to be shared values. Friedman (2008) proposes a framework for systematic consideration of shared values as part of the design process. Borrowing Friedman's general approach, we can infer a range of values from the principles of user engagement discussed in this book, many of which are mentioned by Friedman. Table 16.1 lists those values that might be drawn from the strategies and cases discussed by Krull, Zappen, and Fernheimer.

As the examples in the table demonstrate, design activity focused on building relationships is inherently value laden. Design teams might do well, then, to foreground

Table 16.1 Relationship values of the 10 basic principles with their design challenges.

Principles of User Engagement	Relationship Values	Design Challenges Revealed in Case Studies
Principle 7 and Case Study 1: Sharing Control	• Reciprocity • Egalitarianism • Safety • Autonomy • Creativity	The Connected Kids Galleries were designed as spaces where user-created content could be shared, but also as safe spaces where parents and others could be assured that information would not be used without consent.
		At the level of technical implementation, value conflicts can develop as designers must balance support for creativity and safety, autonomy and reciprocity. Without balance, users may never get to the stage of regular use or may, over time, lose interest in the service and stop contributing.
Principle 8 and Case Study 4: Fostering Interaction Among Users	• Trust • Identity • Accountability • Courtesy	Krull and his colleagues highlight values that teachers and students may take for granted in traditional face-to-face learning environments but that surface in concrete ways in e-learning and distance-education settings. Implicit in many of the examples of challenges faced by students are issues of trust, identity, and accountability: How can students communicate to teachers that their work and level of participation are adequate and authentic?
		More immediate and persistent challenges arose when technological constraints such as low bandwidth or modes of access that reinforced the authority of the teacher required explicit attention to classroom etiquette: When can a student break in to ask a question? When and how can students address one another?
Principle 5 and Case Study 2: Set the Context	• Universal accessibility • Ownership • Happiness/ Enjoyment	Fernheimer's group learned that the design of wiki spaces to facilitate collaborative authoring could only proceed so far without live tests in the context of use: real classrooms. The reason? Values that were explicitly shared by both the team and users could not be reduced to the presence or absence of technical features such as group editing of a shared document.
		Group dynamics, especially the power dynamics associated with the social context of the classroom, played a part in whether and how these features were used by individuals. Tests in settings absent these power dynamics could not, then, predict outcomes of more realistic use situations.

the shared values to which users and sponsors of a given service adhere. They might also consider several kinds of activities as a routine part of design work that address the goal of creating lasting relationships with users:

1. Strategize ways that the features of the service can explicitly evoke shared values that are foundational to the user-sponsor relationship.
2. Identify potential value conflicts and how these manifest in concrete ways for users.
3. Create features, use policies, or provide options to address value conflicts in a proactive way rather than waiting for significant problems to arise.

Sites that rely on user-contributed content to build the long-term value of a service, for instance, must consider and balance the needs for this content to be shared and reused by others and for individual users' contributions to be recognized and valued appropriately. Photo-sharing services like Flickr and Picasa offer users a range of Creative Commons licensing options that they can assign to images, and then offer advanced search options that include specific aspects of these licenses as filtering options. This permits users to see in explicit ways how a service balances the potential value conflict between personal property and shareability. The values are expressed as technical functions, but also visible and available as options in ways that all stakeholders can reference as they discuss the terms of their relationship and how to continue or strengthen it.

Key Questions: Values That Support Strong Relationships With Users

1. What other relationship values should we add to the list in column two of Table 16.1?
2. What types of values correlate strongly and/or unambiguously with specific technical functions, and which ones are more difficult or rely more on contextual dynamics to surface?

Building Relationship Skills: Developing Strategies for Listening

We don't need the user-experience version of Dr. Phil to tell us that the most deceptively simple requirement of good relationships is simply for the parties to learn to listen to one another. Since the field of technical communication began to evaluate and advocate usability evaluation methods in the late 1980s in relation to print documentation (e.g., see Sullivan, 1989), a primary concern has been to find ways to listen to and learn from those most directly affected by the products we make. As our focus shifts from products to services, we find once again that learning to listen is our first priority. With web-based services that are meant to be persistent and available 24/7, this means finding ways not just to stage interactions and solicit opinion but also to monitor channels of communication internal and external to the service that users may be using to provide feedback directly or indirectly.

In December 2009, I visited a telecommunications company on a consulting visit to speak with a global marketing group promoting communication systems designed for municipal and emergency services. The purpose of the visit was to discuss ways the telecom might use social media as part of its marketing efforts. The company was especially interested in Twitter. Another division of the company had just launched a high-profile consumer product with a huge branding effort, major media advertising campaigns, a website, and a Facebook page. But Twitter had them stumped. How were they supposed to use it to get their message out?

"You're not," I told them. "Twitter is for listening, not for talking." Telling marketers that a hot new social media channel is off limits for sending messages yields a lot of wrinkled brows and crossed arms. But gradually I was able to explain, and to demonstrate, how the Twitter service could show them how and when to talk to both current and potential customers if they first took the time to listen carefully. We plugged in some hashtags that corresponded with the consumer division's product launch, and, as you might expect, a stream of feedback—all of it in real time—appeared on the projector screen. I stopped talking. They stopped scowling. And we just listened—or watched, actually—what people were saying about their product.

Marketers have started to get the message about social media. Today, it is not uncommon to mention a brand or product name with a hashtag in a service like Twitter and be contacted soon after by a customer service representative with an offer to solve a problem or thank you for your business. If marketers can learn to listen before they speak, so can user experience designers.

One way to do this to take advantage of the service account-based architecture to track users' progress and use experience and to anticipate important engagement points based on the usage life cycle. To do this, it is necessary to zoom in tighter on specific user roles and work flows as they correspond to the high level indicators of use represented by the hurdles in Porter's life-cycle diagram. For instance, during the beta release of a peer-review coordination service designed for teachers and students that I and others have developed,[1] we tracked when users reached significant milestones that we might learn from: when teachers create their first review, when students complete their first review assignment, when a teacher receives revised papers following a successful review session. We also tracked when specific kinds of activities in the system occur that could indicate a problem: when the due date passes on an assignment with less than two-thirds of the class responding, when a teacher creates and begins to customize a review but stops before it is complete.

During our beta period, we wanted to develop a relationship with these users that let them know that we appreciate their willingness to pilot our service and that we valued their feedback as a way to make it better. But we also know they are busy people. If they were not, they would not need our service! For this reason, we rely on activity tracking to let the users know that we are there, that we are listening, and that we are ready to help. In the cases where users reach a new engagement milestone, we may send users a quick note via Twitter to acknowledge it, such as "Hope your first review went great!" If not, we might reach out with an offer of help. After the first completed review, we send teachers an invitation to complete a questionnaire asking how we could improve the user experience. We also listen via the same channels, and note when someone has mentioned the service, experienced a problem, asked a question, or recommended us to a colleague. We try to follow up quickly in each of those instances with an appropriate response. And by "we" I mean the user experience team. Each interaction gives us new ideas about how to improve the overall user experience, whether it is adding a new tutorial, changing the label or adding microcopy to the user interface or adding a new feature. This kind of contact is no longer the exclusive domain of technical support or customer service. Or maybe it is more accurate to say that our entire development effort, but especially the user experience team, is focused on customer service now. And each cycle of effort begins and ends with listening.

Note

1. The service is called Eli. It was developed at Michigan State University and has been made commercially available in partnership with Bedford St. Martin's. More information about Eli is available at http://bedfordstmartins.com/Catalog/other/Eli.

References

Alessi, S. M., & Trollip, S. R. (2000). *Multimedia for learning: Methods and development.* New York: Allyn & Bacon.

Apple Computer. (2005). *iMac G5 user's guide.* Cupertino, CA: Apple. Retrieved from http://manuals.info.apple.com/en/iMac_G5_2005_Users_Manual.pdf

Barber, W., & Badre, A. (1998). Culturability: The merging of culture and usability. *Proceedings of the 4th Conference on Human Factors and the Web.* Basking Ridge, New Jersey: AT&T Labs. Retrieved from http://zing.ncsl.nist.gov/hfweb/att4/proceedings/barber/.

Barthes, R. (1977). The death of the author. In S. Heath (Trans.). *Image—Music—Text* (pp. 142–148). New York: Hill & Wang.

Benkler, Y. (2006). *The wealth of networks: How social production transforms markets and freedom.* New Haven, CT: Yale University Press.

Bennett, A. (2002a). Dynamic interactive aesthetics. *Journal of Design Research, 2*(2).

Bennett, A. (2002b). Interactive aesthetics. *Design Issues, 18*(3), 62–69.

Bennett, A. (2012). *Engendering interaction with images.* Bristol, UK: Intellect.

Bennett, A., Eglash, R., Krishnamoorthy, M., & Rerieya, M. (2006). Audience as co-designer: Participatory design of HIV/AIDS awareness and prevention. In A. Bennett (Ed.), *Design studies: Theory and research in graphic design* (pp. 179–197). New York: Princeton Architectural Press.

Bernard, R. M., Abrami, P. C., Lou, Y., Borokhovski, E., Wade, A., Wozney, L., Wallet, P. A., Fiset, M., & Huang, B. (2004). How does distance education compare with classroom instruction? A meta-analysis of the empirical literature. *Review of Educational Research, 74*(3), 379–439.

Bleacher Report. (2010a). *Bleacher Report raises the bar for citizen sports journalists with new editorial guidelines.* Retrieved from http://bleacherreport.com/pages/editorial-standards-announcement

Bleacher Report. (2010b). *Question: What is Bleacher Report?* Retrieved from http://forum.bleacherreport.com/2010/01/19/question-what-is-bleacher-report/

Bleacher report. (n.d.). *Wikipedia.* Retrieved from http://en.wikipedia.org/wiki/Bleacher_Report

Bolter, J. D., & Gromala, D. (2003). *Windows and mirrors: Interaction design, digital art, and the myth of transparency.* Cambridge, MA: MIT Press.

Bolter, J., & Grusin, R. (1999). *Remediation: Understanding new media.* Cambridge, MA: MIT Press.

Brinck, T., Gergle, D., & Wood, S. D. (2002). *Usability for the web: Designing web sites that work.* Morgan Kaufmann Series in Interactive Technologies. San Francisco: Morgan Kaufmann, Academic Press.

Bruns, A. (2008). *Blogs, Wikipedia, Second Life, and beyond: From production to produsage.* Vol. 45. Digital Formations. New York: Peter Lang.

Burdeau, G. (1990). *Pueblo peoples: First encounter*. Lincoln, NE: VisionMaker Video.

Butler, K.A. (1996). Usability engineering turns 10. *Interactions, 3*, 59–75.

Caltrans. (2012). *Caltrans announces QuickMap—an online service for real-time travel and traffic information* (California Department of Transportation press release). Retrieved from http://www.dot.ca.gov/hq/paffairs/news/pressrel/12pr103.htm

Carliner, S. (2008). A holistic framework of instructional design for e-learning. In S. Carliner & P. Shank (Eds.), *The e-learning handbook: Past promises, present challenges* (pp. 15–26). San Francisco: Pfeiffer.

Carr, T., Morrison, A., Cox, G., & Deacon, A. (2007). Weathering wikis: Net-based learning meets political science in South African University. *Computers and Composition, 24*(3), 266–284.

Chen, H.L., Cannon, D., Gabrio, J., Leifer, L., Toye, G., & Bailey, T. (2005, June). *Using wikis and weblogs to support reflective learning in an introductory engineering design course*. Paper presented at the American Society for Engineering Education Annual Conference and Exposition, Portland, OR.

Children's online privacy protection act of 1998. Retrieved from http://www.ftc.gov/ogc/coppa1.htm

Christensen, C. (1997). *The innovator's dilemma: When new technologies cause great firms to fail*. Cambridge, MA: Harvard Business Press.

Clark, R.C., & Mayer, R.E. (2008). *E-learning and the science of instruction* (2nd ed.). San Francisco: Pfeiffer.

Clarke, J. (2005). Cross-cultural design for children in a cyber setting. In N. Aykin (Ed.), *Usability and internationalization of information technology* (pp. 253–276). Human Factors and Ergonomics. Mahwah, NJ: Lawrence Erlbaum.

Coe, M. (1996). *Human factors for technical communicators*. New York: John Wiley.

Comparison of wiki software. (n.d.). *Wikipedia*. Retrieved from http://en.wikipedia.org/wiki/Comparison_of_wiki_software

Cook, K.C., & Grant-Davie, K. (2005). *Online education: Global questions, local answers*. Amityville, NY: Baywood.

Coover, R. (2001). Worldmaking, metaphors and montage in the representation of cultures: Cross-cultural filmmaking and the poetics of Robert Gardner's *Forest of Bliss*. *Visual Anthropology, 14*(4), 415–433.

Crossmedia. (n.d.). *Wikipedia*. Retrieved from http://en.wikipedia.org/wiki/Crossmedia

Csikszentmihalyi, M. (1991). Design and order in everyday life. *Design Issues, 8*(1), 26–34.

Danchak, M.M., & Huguet, M.P. (2004). Designing for the changing role of the instructor in blended learning. *IEEE Transactions on Professional Communication, 47*(3), 200–210.

Driscoll, M. (2008). Hype versus reality in the boardroom. In S. Carliner & P. Shank (Eds.), *The e-learning handbook: Past promises, present challenges* (pp. 23–54). San Francisco: Pfeiffer.

Druin, A. (1996). The activity of innovation. In A. Druin & C. Solomon (Eds.), *Designing multimedia environments for children* (pp. 192–219). New York: John Wiley.

Druin, A., Bederson, B., Boltman, A., Miura, A., Knotts-Callahan, D., & Platt, M. (1999). Children as our technology design partners. In A. Druin (Ed.), *The design of children's technology* (pp. 51–72). San Francisco: Morgan Kaufmann.

Dumas, J. (2007). The great leap forward: The birth of the usability profession. *Journal of Usability Studies, 2*, 54–60.

Dumas, J.S., & Redish, J.C. (1993). *A practical guide to usability testing*. Exeter, UK: Intellect Books.

Edelson, D. (1993). Socrates, Aesops and the computer: Questioning and storytelling with multimedia. *Journal of Educational Multimedia and Hypermedia, 2*(4), 393–404.

Felker, D., Pickering, F., Charrow, V.R., Holland, M., & Redish, J. (1981). *Guidelines for document designers*. Washington, DC: American Institute for Research.

Fernheimer, J.W., Nieusma, D., Chi, L., Montoya, L., Kujala, T., & Padula, A.L. (2009). Collaborative convergences in research and pedagogy: An interdisciplinary approach to teaching writing with wikis. *Computers and Composition Online*. Retrieved from http://www.bgsu.edu/departments/english/cconline/Fernheimer.pdf

Forslund, C.J. (1996). Analyzing pictorial messages across cultures. In D.C. Andrews (Ed.), *International dimensions of technical communication* (pp. 45–58). Arlington, VA: Society for Technical Communication.

Friedlander, L. (2008). Narrative strategies in a digital age: Authorship and authority. In K. Lundby (Ed.), *Digital storytelling, mediatized stories: Self-representations in new media* (pp. 177–194). Vol 52. Digital Formations. New York: Peter Lang.

Friedman, B. (2008). Value sensitive design. In D. Schular (Ed.), *Liberating voices: A pattern language for communication revolution* (pp. 366–368). Cambridge, MA: MIT Press.

Gagné, R.M., Briggs, L.J., & Wager, W.W. (1992). *Principles of instructional design* (4th ed.). Orlando, FL: Harcourt Brace Jovanovich.

Garza, S.L., & Hern, T. (2006). Using wikis as collaborative writing tools: Something wiki this way comes—or not! Retrieved from http://critical.tamucc.edu/wiki/WikiArticle/Home

Gazda, R., & Flemister, M. (1999). Design and production of video for instructional multimedia: Psychological implications and proposed guidelines. *Journal of Visual Literacy*, 19(1), 85–98.

Giammona, B. (2004). The future of technical communication: How innovation, technology, information management, and other forces are shaping the future of the profession. *Technical Communication*, 51(3), 349–366.

Gilutz, S., & Nielsen, J. (n.d.). *Usability of websites for children: 70 design guidelines*. Fremont, CA: Nielsen Norman Group.

Gough, D., & Phillips, H. (2009). *Remote online usability testing: Why, how and when to use it*. Retrieved from http://www.boxesandarrows.com/view/remote_online_usability_testing_why_how_and_when_to_use_it

Gould, J., & Lewis, C. (1985). Designing for usability: Key principles and what designers think. *Communications of the ACM, 28*, 300–311.

Gurak, L. (2001). *Cyberliteracy: Navigating the internet with awareness*. New Haven, CT: Yale University Press.

Hager, P.J. (2000). Global graphics: Effectively managing visual rhetoric for international audiences. In P.J. Hager & H.J. Scheiber (Eds.), *Managing global communication in science and technology* (pp. 21–43). New York: John Wiley.

Hall, E.T. (1959/1973). *The silent language*. Garden City, NY: Anchor Books.

Hamilton, T. (2000). Chemistry and writing: A collaborative writing project. *College Teaching, 48*(4), 136–138.

Harrison, T.M., Zappen, J.P., & Adali, S. (2005). Building community information systems: The Connected Kids case. *Computer, 38 (12)*, 62–69.

Herrington, T., & Tretyakov, Y. (2005). The global classroom project: Troublemaking and troubleshooting. In K.C. Cook & K. Grant-Davie (Eds.), *Online education: Global questions, local answers* (pp. 267–283). Amityville, NY: Baywood.

Hofstede, G. (1980). *Culture's consequences: International differences in work-related values*. Beverly Hills, CA: Sage.

Horton, W. (2000). *Designing web-based training*. New York: John Wiley.

Horton, W. (2005). Graphics: The not quite universal language. In N. Aykin (Ed.), *Usability and internationalization of information technology* (pp. 157–187). Mahwah, NJ: Lawrence Erlbaum.

Horton, W., & Horton, K. (2003). E-learning tools and technologies. New York: John Wiley.

Hoschka, P. (1998a). CSCW research at GMD-FIT: from basic groupware to the social Web. *ACM SIGGROUP Bulletin, 19 (2)*, 5–9.

Hoschka, P. (1998b). *The Social web research program. Linking people through virtual environments.* GMD German National Research Center for Information Technology, Sankt Augustin, Germany. Retrieved from http://mitarbeiter.fit.fraunhofer.de/-hoschka/Social%20Web

Is Yahoo shutting down del.icio.us? [update: del.icio.us responds]. (2010). Retrieved from http://techcrunch.com/2010/12/16/is-yahoo-shutting-down-del-icio-us/

Jenkins, H. (2006). *Convergence culture: Where old and new media collide.* New York: New York University Press.

Jenkins, H. (n.d.). *Game design as narrative architecture.* Retrieved from http://web.mit.edu/cms/People/henry3/games&narrative.html

Johnson, R.R. (1998). *User-centered technology: A rhetorical theory for computers and other mundane artifacts.* Studies in Scientific and Technical Communication. Albany: State University of New York Press.

Kellner, D. (2002). Critical perspectives on visual imagery in media and cyberculture. *Journal of Visual Literacy, 22,* 81–90.

Kirkpatrick, M. (2010). How the Old Spice videos are being made. *ReadWriteWeb.* Retrieved from http://www.readwriteweb.com/archives/how_old_spice_won_the_internet.php

Kirsch, N. (2005, June 29). Apple's iMac G5's gain popularity, but offer lackluster memory options. *Legit Memory Review.* Retrieved from http://www.legitreviews.com/article/215/1/

Kiwanuka-Tondo, J., & Snyder, L. (2002). The influence of organizational characteristics and campaign design elements on communication campaign quality: Evidence from 91 Ugandan AIDS campaigns. *Journal of Health Communication, 7*(1), 59–77.

Kolb, D.A. (1984). *Experiential learning.* Englewood Cliffs, NJ: Prentice Hall.

Komlodi, A., Hou, W., Preece, J., Druin, A., Golub, E., Alburo, J., . . . Resnik, P. (2007). Evaluating a cross-cultural children's online book community: Lessons learned for sociability, usability, and cultural exchange. *Interacting with Computers, 19*(4), 494–511.

Kostelnick, C. (1995). Cultural adaptation and information design: Two contrasting views. *IEEE Transactions on Professional Communication, 38*(4), 182–196.

Kress, G. (2004). Reading images: Multimodality, representation and new media. *Information Design Journal, 12*(2), 110–119.

Krug, S. (2005). *Don't make me think! A common sense approach to web usability* (2nd ed.). Berkeley, CA: New Riders.

Kussmaul, C., Howe, S., & Priest, S. (2006). Using wikis to foster team communication, cohesion, and collaboration. *Journal of Computing Sciences in Colleges, 21*(6), 66–68.

Laporte, M., padme, tochinet, & btiffin. (n.d.). *Why wiki syntax is important.* Retrieved from http://tiki.org/Why%20Wiki%20Syntax%20Is%20Important

Lessig, L. (2006). *Code: Version 2.0.* New York: Perseus Books Group, Basic Books.

Lessig, L. (2008). *Remix: Making art and commerce thrive in the hybrid economy.* New York: Penguin Press.

Leuthold, S. (1998). *Indigenous aesthetics.* Austin: University of Texas Press.

Lipton, R. (2002). *Designing across cultures: How to create effective graphics for diverse ethnic groups.* Cincinnati, OH: How Design Books.

Lowry, P.B., Nunamaker, J.F., Booker, Q.E., Curtis, A., & Lowry, M.R. (2004). Creating hybrid distributed learning environments by implementing distributed collaborative writing in traditional educational settings. *IEEE Transactions on Professional Communication, 47*(3), 171–189.

Marcus, A. (2005). User interface design and culture. In N. Aykin (Ed.), *Usability and internationalization of information technology* (pp. 51–78). Mahwah, NJ: Lawrence Erlbaum.

Masayesva Jr., V. (1984). *Itam Hakim, Hopiit.* Watertown, MA: Documentary Educational Resources.

Miller, C.H. (2008). *Digital storytelling: A creator's guide to interactive entertainment* (2nd ed.). Amsterdam: Elsevier, Focal Press.

Mirel, B. (2003). *Interaction design for complex problem solving: Developing useful and usable software*. San Francisco: Morgan Kaufmann.

Molich, R., & Nielsen, J. (1990). Improving a human-computer dialogue. *Communications of the ACM, 33*(3), 338–348.

Moxley, J., & Meehan, R. T. (2007). Collaboration and teaching: Using social networking tools to engage the wisdom of teachers. Retrieved from http://teachingwiki.org/default.aspx/TeachingWiki/CollaborationLiteracyAuthorship.html

Neill, S. (2008). Assessment of the NEOTHEMI virtual museum project: An on-line survey. *Computers & Education, 50*(1), 410–420.

Nielsen, J. (1993). *Usability engineering*. San Diego: Morgan Kaufmann, Academic Press.

Nielsen, J. (1994a). Enhancing the explanatory power of usability heuristics. *Proceedings of the ACM CHI'94 Conference* (pp. 152–158). New York: ACM.

Nielsen, J. (1994b). Heuristic evaluation. In J. Nielsen & R. L. Mack (Eds.), *Usability inspection methods* (pp. 25–62). New York: John Wiley.

Nielsen, J. (1995). 10 usability heuristics for user interface design. *Alertbox Newsletter*. Nielsen Norman Group. Retrieved from http://www.nngroup.com/articles/ten-usability-heuristics/

Nielsen, J. (2000). *Designing web usability: The practice of simplicity*. Indianapolis: New Riders.

Nielsen, J., & Loranger, H. (2006). *Prioritizing web usability*. Berkeley, CA: New Riders.

Nielsen, J., & Molich, R. (1990). Heuristic evaluation of user interfaces, *Proceedings of the ACM CHI'90 Conference* (pp. 249–256). New York: ACM.

Nielsen, J., & Pernice, K. (2009). *Eyetracking web usability*. Berkeley, CA: New Riders.

Niezen, R. (2005). Digital identity: The construction of virtual selfhood in the indigenous people's movement. *Comparative Studies in Society and History, 47*(3), 532–551.

Nightingale, V. (2007). New media worlds? Challenges for convergence. In V. Nightingale & T. Dwyer (Eds.), *New media worlds: Challenges for convergence* (pp. 19–36). Melbourne: Oxford University Press.

Norman, D. A. (1988). *The design of everyday things*. New York: Doubleday, Currency.

Norman, D. A. (2004). *Emotional design: Why we love (or hate) everyday things*. New York: Perseus Books Group, Basic Books.

Norman, D. A. (2007). *The design of future things*. New York: Perseus Books Group, Basic Books.

Norman, D. A. (2010). *Living with complexity*. Cambridge, MA: MIT Press.

Ozawa, R. K. (2005). *Moblog, the mobile log of Ryan Kawailani Ozawa*. Retrieved from http://www.lightfantastic.org/imr/extras/moblog/archives/003056.html

Pettersson, R. (1982). Cultural differences in the perception of image and color in pictures. *Educational Communication and Technology Journal, 30*(1), 43–53.

Porter, J. (2008). *Designing for the social web*. Berkeley, CA: New Riders.

Potts, L. (2009). Using actor network theory to trace and improve multimodal communication design. *Technical Communication Quarterly, 18*, 281–301.

Potts, L., & Jones, D. (2011). Contextualizing experiences: Tracing the relationships between people and technologies in the social web. *Journal of Business and Technical Communication, 25*, 338–358.

Potts, L., Seitzinger, J., Jones, D., & Harrison, A. (2011). Tweeting disaster: Hashtag constructions and collisions. *SIGDOC '11: Proceedings of the 29th ACM international conference on Design of Communication* (pp. 235–240). New York: ACM.

Privacy Rights Clearinghouse. (n.d.). *Children's online privacy: A resource guide for parents*. Retrieved from http://www.privacyrights.org/fs/fs21-children.htm

Raymond, E. S. (2001). *The cathedral and the bazaar: Musings on Linux and open source by an accidental revolutionary* (Rev. ed.). Sebastopol, CA: O'Reilly Media.

Rheingold, H. (2003). *Smart mobs: The next social revolution*. New York: Basic Books.

Rice, D.J., Davidson, B.D., Dannenhoffer, J.F., & Gay, G.K. (2007). Improving the effectiveness of virtual teams by adapting team processes. *Computer Supported Cooperative Work, 16*(6), 567–594.

Rogers, E.M. (1995). *Diffusion of innovations* (4th ed.). New York: Free Press.

Rush, M. (1999). *New media in late 20th-century art.* London: Thames & Hudson.

Russell, T.L. (1999). *The no significant difference phenomenon as reported in 355 research reports, summaries and papers.* Raleigh: University of North Carolina Press.

Schneider, S. (2005). Usable pedagogies: Usability, rhetoric, and sociocultural pedagogy in the technical writing classroom. *Technical Communication Quarterly, 14*(4), 447–467.

Schriver, K. (1997). *Dynamics in document design: Creating texts for readers.* New York: Wiley Computer.

Search, P. (2002). Hyperglyphs: New multiliteracy models for interactive computing. In R. Griffin, J. Lee, & V. Williams (Eds.), *Visual literacy in message design* (pp. 171–177). Loretto, PA: International Visual Literacy Association.

Search, P. (2007). Digital storytelling for cross-cultural communication in global networking. In R. Griffin, M. Avgerinou, & J. Giesen (Eds.), *History, community, and culture: Celebrating tradition and transforming our future* (pp. 1–6). Loretto, PA: International Visual Literacy Association.

Shank, P. (2008a). Thinking critically to move e-learning forward. In S. Carliner & P. Shank (Eds.), *The e-learning handbook: Past promises, present challenges* (pp. 15–26). San Francisco: Pfeiffer.

Shank, P. (2008b). Web 2.0 and beyond: The changing needs of learners, new tools, and ways to learn. In S. Carliner & P. Shank (Eds.), *The e-learning handbook: Past promises, present challenges* (pp. 241–278). San Francisco: Pfeiffer.

Shedroff, N. (2001). *Experience design 1.* Indianapolis: New Riders.

Sless, D. (2004). Designing public documents. *Information Design Journal, 12*(1), 24–35.

Society for Technical Communication. (2005). Letter of intent instructions: STC research grants. Retrieved from http://www.stc.org/PDF_Files/RFP2005.pdf

Sorensen, C. (2012). Behavioural tracking: You're being stalked across the web. *Macleans.ca.* Retrieved from http://www2.macleans.ca/2012/08/07/behavioural-tracking-youre-being-stalked-across-the-web/

Spinuzzi, C. (2003). *Tracing genres through organizations: A sociocultural approach to information design.* Acting with Technology. Cambridge, MA: MIT Press.

St. Amant, K. (2005). Distance education in a global age: A perspective for internationalizing online learning communities. *ACM SIGGROUP Bulletin, 25*(1), 12–19.

Steele, E., & Angwin, J. (2010, August 3). The web's cutting edge, anonymity in name only. *Wall Street Journal.* Retrieved from http://online.wsj.com/article/SB10001424052748703294904575385532109190198.html?mod=googlenews_wsj

Sullivan, P. (1989). Beyond a narrow conception of usability testing. *IEEE Transactions on Professional Communication, 32*(4), 256–264.

Sun, H. (2001). Building a culturally-competent corporate web site: An exploratory study of cultural markers in multilingual web design. *SIGDOC '01: Proceedings of the 19th Annual International Conference of Computer Documentation, Communicating in the New Millennium* (pp. 95–102). New York: ACM.

Sundararajan, B. (2009). Impact of communication patterns, network positions and social dynamics factors on learning among students in a CSCL environment. *Electronic Journal of e-Learning, 7*(1), 71–84.

Tapscott, D., & Williams, A.D. (2006). *Wikinomics: How mass collaboration changes everything.* New York: Penguin Group, Portfolio.

Terenzini, P.T., & Pascarella, E.T. (1994). Living with myths: Undergraduate education in America. *Change, 26*(1), 28–32.

Tidwell, J. (2006). *Designing interfaces*. Sebastopol, CA: O'Reilly Media.

U.S. Department of Health and Human Services. (n.d.). Heuristic evaluations. Retrieved from http://usability.gov/methods/test_refine/heuristic.html

Vancouver International Digital Festival. (2006). *2006 id award winners*. Retrieved from http://2006.vidfest.com/index.php?id=71

Vdrio-Baron, S., Townsend, A., & Shelley, M. (2009). Toward a proposed methodology to assess e-government websites usability in the context of cultural dimensions. *Proceedings of the 10th Annual International Conference on Digital Government Research* (pp. 332–333). Los Angeles: Digital Government Society of North America.

Warnick, B. (2005). Looking to the future: Electronic texts and the deepening interface. *Technical Communication Quarterly, 14*, 327–333.

Warnick, B. (2007). *Rhetoric online: Persuasion and politics on the World Wide Web. Vol. 12.* Frontiers in Political Communication. New York: Peter Lang.

Warren, Robert, W., Airoldi, E., & Bank, D. (2008). Network analysis of Wikipedia. In W. Jank & G. Shmueli (Eds.), *Statistical methods in e-commerce research* (pp. 90–91). Hoboken, NJ: John Wiley.

Watters, A. (2012). Udacity's CS101: A (partial) course evaluation. *Hack [Higher] Education* [Web log at *Inside Higher Ed*]. Retrieved from http://www.insidehighered.com/blogs/hack-higher-education/udacitys-cs101-partial-course-evaluation

Weiss, E. (1991). *How to write usable user documentation*. Westport, CT: Greenwood.

What's next for del.icio.us? (2010). Delicious blog. Retrieved from http://blog.delicious.com/blog/2010/12/whats-next-for-delicious.html

Williams, R., & Tollet, J. (2000). *The non-designer's web book*. Berkeley, CA: Peachpit Press.

Winn, M. (2002). *The plug-in drug: Television, computers and family life* (25th anniversary ed.). New York: Penguin.

Worth, S., & Adair, J. (1972). *Through Navajo eyes*. Bloomington: Indiana University Press.

Zappen, J. P., Adali, S., & Harrison, T. M. (2006). Developing a youth-services information system for city and county government: Experiments in user-designer collaboration. *Proceedings of the 7th Annual International Conference on Digital Government Research* (pp. 259–264). Los Angeles: Digital Government Society of North America.

Zappos.com. (n.d). *Wikipedia*. Retrieved from http://en.wikipedia.org/wiki/Zappos.com

Appendices

Appendix 1

Heuristic Evaluation

Greeting and Preparing Participants

- Give a tour of the equipment. Be sure to mention that you're recording the session (if you are).
- Build rapport.
    - o "Testing today should be straightforward. We just want to observe you doing some tasks with this [exemplar]. Let's get you set up and comfortable.
    - o Can you tell me a little bit about yourself before we start with the testing?"
- Mention that "this isn't my [program/design/whatever]. Don't worry about offending or bothering me."
- Mention that "we're testing the game, not you. We need to find any problems with it, and we don't really care about how successful you are with each task."
- Explain think-aloud protocol; "Feel free to speak aloud of anything that comes across your mind."

Task Session

- "OK, any questions before we get started?" (If so, answer. If not, then begin.)
- Explain the background of the exemplar.
- If participants ask questions, ask them what they'd do with the exemplar as if they were on their computer at home (or another real situation, as applicable to the exemplar). Remind them that you wouldn't be able to help them in such a situation.
- If participants fail a task, don't tell them how to do it. Instead, after they've had some time, direct them to move on to the next task.

During this time, note usability problems. If possible, categorize them under Nielsen's heuristics. This can be done later, but be sure your notes are clear.

If there's any indication of trouble or conflict, use probes to find out what's going on. Use active listening to clarify problems. Remember that, in the end, the goal is specific and concrete design feedback.

If at any time participants stop speaking aloud, remind them to "speak aloud, talk aloud, and tell me what you're thinking."

Probes

- It looks like something's going on. What's happening there?
- How does that part of the game make you feel?
- What are you looking at?
- What are you thinking?
- Tell me what you're trying to do.
- What do you expect to happen?
- Are you reading anything?
- Why did you choose that?
- Is this what you expected to see?
- What are you looking for?
- You look confused—can you tell me why?
- What do you think about the layout of this screen?
- Tell me what you think a [X] is. How is it different from a [Y]?

Debriefing

- We appreciate your time today. You've been a great help. Thanks very much! Thanks for being here.

Appendix 2

Comparative User Testing

Protocol

Setup and Welcome

1. Make sure the exemplar is working correctly, then close web browser (user will start from desktop).
2. Make sure you have something to keep time with.
3. Prepare consent form, pretest survey, posttest survey, and pen.
4. Smile and greet participants, confirming their names.
5. Build rapport with the participants. Establish casual atmosphere, comfortable give and take. Spend a few minutes getting to know the participants and letting them know that you are a nice, trustworthy person.
6. Explain the consent form, and ask participants to fill out the pretest survey. (Leave the room; get them a glass of water or something, so they do not feel pressured for time).
7. Introduce participants to the computer; make sure they are comfortable with the controls.
8. Explain that the purpose of testing is to improve the site and learn about the experiences people have when they are using different kinds of websites and programs. Mention that nothing they say will offend or bother you. Emphasize that the test is not about how well they do at anything, since it is a test of the website, not the participant.
9. Ask participants to think out loud as they are exploring the site, and tell them you may prompt them from time to time to tell you what they are thinking or why they are doing something.
10. Make sure participants are comfortable and ready and have no questions before beginning the test.

Conducting the Test

1. Ask the users to open a web browser and visit the exemplar site. Time how long it takes users to get to the site (enter on data sheet).
2. If participants ask questions, ask them what they'd do with the exemplar as if they were on their computer at home (or an alternate real situation, as applicable to the exemplar). Remind them that you wouldn't be able to help them in such a situation.

3. Allow the participant to spend two or three minutes familiarizing themselves with the site, looking around, and exploring a little. Then ask questions about welcome, appropriateness, and connectedness:

   a. This site is designed with several different audiences in mind. Do you feel that you are an appropriate user?
   b. What are your first feelings about this site? Does it seem welcoming or not? What makes it feel that way?

4. Instruct participants to perform an *exploration* task (determined by exemplar team). Remind participants to think out loud and to tell you what they're doing. For this part, especially ask probing questions about the kinds of emotions, likes/dislikes, things that attract their attention, and so on. Be aware, however, of when a participant needs to experience something without distraction.

   a. EXAMPLE PROBE: You just spent some time [watching/doing X]. What made you do that instead of moving to something new?

   Allow enough time that participants seem to have really experienced what the site has to offer, but not so much that they feel they have nothing more to do. If a participant doesn't know where to go or what to do, *gentle* nudges are okay, such as, "you haven't looked at X, does it seem like something you'd want to find out more about?"

5. Pay attention for moments when you can ask about *connectedness*.

   a. EXAMPLE PROBE: Do you feel you have anything in common with the people pictured here? What?
   b. EXAMPLE PROBE: When you read these comments, do they help you make a connection with that person?

6. Instruct participants to complete the *retrieval* task (determined by exemplar team). Remind participants that you cannot help them but that you are testing the site, not their performance. See #2 above.

   a. Measure the time it takes to complete the task (or time until giving up).
   b. Count the number of mouse clicks required to complete the task.
   c. Record whether the user is successful at the task.

7. Ask participants about what they might do now that they have spent some time with the exemplar.

   a. What about this website would you want to share with someone?
   b. How would you share it? Who would you share it with?
   c. Are there any other actions you might take now that you have seen this exemplar?

Concluding the Test

1. Thank the participants for their time, and inform them you have just a few more questions on a short survey that you'd like their help with. Give participants the

posttest survey and a pen. Tell them you'll wait outside and that they should take as long as they need to fill out the survey. (Children will probably need a parent's help.)
2. Wait just outside the door for the participants to complete the survey. Thank participants again after they've given you the form, and make sure they are comfortable finding their way out of the building. If possible, escort them to the exit.

USABLE CONTENT SEMINAR II

PHASE III DATA

You should have one copy of this form for each participant tested on each exemplar.
Exemplar: WIKI GALLERY GRAPHICS INDIGENOUS EDUCATION
Time for Setup/Loading Site: _____
Welcome Questions

    a. This site is designed with several different audiences in mind. Do you feel that you are an appropriate user?
    b. What are your first feelings about this site? Does it seem welcoming or not? What makes it feel that way?

Exploration and Connectedness Observations

Retrieval Task

    Time to Complete/Give up Task _____
    Number of Mouse Clicks for Task _____
    User Successful?   YES   NO
Sharing Questions

    a. What, if anything, about this website would you want to share with someone?
    b. How would you share it? Who would you share it with?
    c. Are there any other actions you might take now that you have seen this exemplar?

Additional Tester Comments:

Phase III Pretest Questionnaire

Please answer each question briefly as best as you can.

1. How old are you? (Check one.)

    ☐ Under 12
    ☐ 12–17
    ☐ 18–25
    ☐ 26–40
    ☐ 41–55
    ☐ Over 55

2. Do you identify with any ethnic or cultural group? If so, what?

3. How long have you been using the Internet, if at all?

4. How would you rate your proficiency with technology? (Check one.)

   ☐ Not very proficient
   ☐ Somewhat proficient
   ☐ Very proficient

5. Do you have any physical characteristics or impairments that would affect your ability to use a commercial website? (Please list all that apply.)

6. How often do you use the World Wide Web to find specific information (not including e-mail)?

   ☐ Daily
   ☐ A few times a week
   ☐ A few times a month
   ☐ Almost never
   ☐ Never

7. How often do you use the World Wide Web for entertainment (not including e-mail)?

   ☐ Daily
   ☐ A few times a week
   ☐ A few times a month
   ☐ Almost never
   ☐ Never

8. Do you belong to any online communities? If yes, which ones?

9. Do you subscribe to any online news alerts or RSS feeds? If yes, how many?

10. Have you ever purchased anything using the Internet? If yes, about how often do you use the Internet for shopping of any kind?

Phase III Posttest Survey

Please circle the number that most closely matches your feeling about each question.

1. At first glance, how interested were you in exploring the site?

| 1 | 2 | 3 | 4 | 5 | 6 | 7 |

Not very interested   Very interested

2. How much did you enjoy exploring this site?

| 1 | 2 | 3 | 4 | 5 | 6 | 7 |

Did not enjoy at all   Enjoyed very much

3. How likely are you to visit this site or a similar site in the next three months?

| 1 | 2 | 3 | 4 | 5 | 6 | 7 |

Very unlikely   Very likely

4. How much did your interest in this subject change?

| 1 | 2 | 3 | 4 | 5 | 6 | 7 |

Much less interested   Much more interested

5. How much knowledge do you feel you gained from your visit to this site?

| 1 | 2 | 3 | 4 | 5 | 6 | 7 |

None   A lot

6. How likely are you to suggest this site to one or more friends?

| 1 | 2 | 3 | 4 | 5 | 6 | 7 |

Very unlikely   Very likely

7. This site helped you to make a connection with other people.

| 1 | 2 | 3 | 4 | 5 | 6 | 7 |

Strongly disagree   Strongly agree

8. The overall site experience was engaging.

| 1 | 2 | 3 | 4 | 5 | 6 | 7 |

Strongly disagree   Strongly agree

9. How difficult was it to navigate the site?

| 1 | 2 | 3 | 4 | 5 | 6 | 7 |

Very easy   Very difficult

10. It was easy to see what to do next when exploring the site.

| 1 | 2 | 3 | 4 | 5 | 6 | 7 |

Strongly disagree   Strongly agree

11. The home page was easy to understand.

| 1 | 2 | 3 | 4 | 5 | 6 | 7 |

Strongly disagree   Strongly agree

12. How well do you think you could relate to other potential users of this site?

| 1 | 2 | 3 | 4 | 5 | 6 | 7 |

Very poorly   Very well

13. What was most difficult to understand or do on this site?

14. What was the easiest to understand or do on this site?

PLEASE RETURN THIS SURVEY TO THE TESTER BEFORE LEAVING.
THANK YOU VERY MUCH FOR YOUR TIME!

Formal Evaluation

Preliminary Heuristic Evaluation

1. Design for Diverse Users

   - Labeling uses simplest possible language.
   - Action buttons and other fields are easily differentiated from surrounding page elements.
   - Equivalent alternatives to auditory and visual content are provided.
   - There is no reliance on color for comprehensibility.
   - Color contrast is differentiable to the colorblind.
   - User has control of time-sensitive content changes.
   - Design is independent of device or platform.

Observations

2. Design for Usability

   Task completion
   Number of tasks attempted
   Number of tasks completed
   Percentage of tasks completed

   Number of features or commands used
   Time to complete a task
   First time
   Second time
   Ratio of second time to first time

   Time spent on errors
   Error time
   Total time
   Percentage of time on errors

Use of documentation
Number of times help or documentation accessed
Time spent using help or documentation
Percentage of time spent using help or documentation

User frustration
Number of times user expresses frustration or anger

3. Test the Backbone

Missing components
Number of missing hardware and software components that are required
Number of missing hardware and software components that are optional and desirable

Time spent on setup
Time spent downloading software components
Time spent connecting hardware components
Time spent troubleshooting setup of hardware or software

User frustration with setup
Number of times help is accessed during setup of hardware or software
Number of times user expresses frustration or anger during setup

4. Extend a Welcome

Orientation time
Time spent on initial page before navigating
Time spent on initial page before using site features

6. Make a Connection

Relationship
Number of times user visits site
Number of personalization features use
Number of times user discloses personal information

Engagement
Total number of links followed
Approximate number of links followed within a topic or cluster before switching to something new

8. Support Interactions Among Users
In this section, interactivity is defined as any site component that allows for user input or modification to the site that could not be accomplished through changing standard browser preferences. For example, uploading a photograph is interactive, adding a

comment to a blog is interactive, and moving shapes on the screen to compose a drawing is interactive. Changing the background color or font size to make reading easier is a browser preference and not interactive in the sense meant here.

Willingness to interact
Total number of interactive features visited
Total time spent with interactive features

Degree of interactions
Number of times user shares something of his or her own creation
Number of people with whom user shares his or her own creation

Quality of interactions
Number of context-inappropriate contributions or attempted contributions to interactive features

9. Ensure a Sense of Place

Disorientedness
Total number of times user gets lost
Number of times user expresses surprise, confusion, or dismay at visual location of site element

10. Facilitate Movement

Ability to complete task
User was able to complete the task.
Time required to complete task
Number of distinct pages visited during task completion
Number of times user backtracked during task completion

Search Feature (only if user chooses to use it)
User found desired result using search feature
Number of search results
Number of searches user performed

11. Plan to Continue the Engagement

Repeatability of experience
User returned to site after initial visit.
Time elapsed between first and second visits
Number of times user returned
Frequency of return visits (i.e., per day, week, or month)
Average number of contributions to interactive features made during repeat visits only

User told other people about the interaction.
User completed other actions or interactions inspired by this site or interactions on this site.

Posttest Questionnaires

To be completed by the test subject after initial experience

1. Were there any parts of the site that were difficult or impossible for you to access? If so, what?

2. How clear was the language used on the site?

   Very clear   Somewhat clear   Neither clear nor unclear
   Some what unclear   Very unclear

3. How useful was the site to you?

   Very useful   Somewhat useful   Neither useful nor useless
   Somewhat useless   Very useless

4. How satisfied were you with the experience of using this site?

   Very satisfied   Somewhat satisfied   Neither satisfied nor dissatisfied
   Somewhat dissatisfied   Very dissatisfied

5. How professional did the design of this site seem to you?

   Very professional   Somewhat professional   Neither professional nor
   unprofessional   Somewhat unprofessional   Very unprofessional

6. How frustrated or pleased were you with the amount of effort needed to get the site running properly?

   Very fru\strated   Somewhat frustrated   Neither frustrated nor pleased
   Somewhat pleased   Very pleased

7. Do you feel the amount of effort needed to get the site running properly was worth it?

   Very worth it   Somewhat worth it   Indifferent   Somewhat not worth it
   Not worth it at all

8. How welcoming was the site?

   Very welcoming   Somewhat welcoming   Neither welcoming nor unwelcoming
   Somewhat unwelcoming   Very unwelcoming

9. How much did you like the visual experience of the site (if applicable)?

   Strongly liked   Somewhat liked   Neither liked nor disliked
   Somewhat disliked   Strongly disliked

10. Please list a few words that describe your overall experience using this site:

11. Please list a few words that describe your reaction to the visual experience of this site (if applicable):

12. How easy was it for you to navigate this site?

    Very easy   Somewhat easy   Neither easy nor difficult   Somewhat difficult
    Very difficult

13. How comfortable did you feel that you understood the organization of the site?

    Very comfortable   Somewhat comfortable   Neither comfortable
    nor uncomfortable   Somewhat uncomfortable   Very uncomfortable

14. How valuable was this site to you?

    Very valuable   Somewhat valuable   Neither valuable nor unvaluable
    Somewhat unvaluable   Very unvaluable

15. Did you feel you could use the site efficiently?

    Very efficiently   Somewhat efficiently   Neither efficiently nor unefficiently
    Somewhat unefficiently   Very unefficiently

16. How connected did you feel to other people when using this site?

    Very connected   Somewhat connected   Neither connected nor disconnected
    Somewhat disconnected   Very disconnected

17. How strongly did you relate to other people who might use this site?

    Very strongly   Somewhat strongly   Neither strongly nor weakly
    Somewhat weakly   Very weakly

18. Did you spend more or less time than you expected to spend on this site?

    Much more   Somewhat more   About what I expected   Somewhat less
    Much less

19. How responsive was the site to your need for personalization?

    Very responsive   Somewhat responsive   Neither responsive nor unresponsive
    Somewhat unresponsive   Very unresponsive

20. Did you wish for more or less control over aspects of site design or navigation?

Wished for much more   Wished for a little more   Did not wish for more or less
Wished for a little less   Wished for much less

21. How pleased or frustrated were you with the site's responses to your actions?

Very pleased   Somewhat pleased   Neither pleased nor frustrated
Somewhat frustrated   Very frustrated

22. Did you wish the site had more or fewer interactive features?

Wished for a lot more   Wished for a few more   Was content with interactivity
Wished for a few less   Wished for a lot less

23. Did you ever feel lost while exploring this site? When?

24. Overall, was your experience with this site positive or negative?

Very positive   Somewhat positive   Neutral—neither positive nor negative
Somewhat   negative Very negative

To be completed by the test subject at future date

1. How strongly do you remember the site?

Very strongly   Somewhat strongly   Neither strongly nor weakly
Somewhat weakly   Very weakly

2. How many times did you revisit the site after your initial experience with it?

3. If you revisited the site more than once, about how often did you revisit the site?

4. Did you revisit this site more or less often than you expected to?

Much more   Somewhat more   About what I   expected Somewhat less
Much less

5. Did you tell anyone else about your experience with this site? If so, whom?

6. Did you take any other actions based on your experience of visiting this site? If so, what?

Index